The Collect
Book of Novelty Pans

Jeanne Gibbs

4880 Lower Valley Road, Atglen, PA 19310 USA

Items and products in this book may be covered by various copyrights, trademarks, and logotypes. Their use herein is for identification purposes only. All rights are reserved by their respective owners.

The text and products pictured in this book are from the collection of the author of this book, its publisher, or various private collectors. This book is not sponsored, endorsed or otherwise affiliated with any of the companies whose products are represented herein. Trademark owners include Alien Productions; American Greetings Corp.; Big Idea Productions; Bobbs-Merrill Co., Inc.; Brentwood Television Funnies, Inc.; Cartoon Network; DC Comics; Disney; Gullane (Thomas) Limited; Hallmark Cards, Inc.; Hanna-Barbera; Hasbro Inc.; HIT/K Chapman; Jim Henson Productions, Inc.; KI; King Features Syndicate, Inc.; LFL; Lyons Partnership, L.P.; Marvel Characters, Inc.; Mattel, Inc.; Mirage Studio, USA; Nest Productions Inc.; Nintendo; Original Appalachian Artworks, Inc.; Peyo; Playboy Enterprises, Inc.; Precious Moments; R. L. May Trust; Ragdoll Productions (UK) Limited; Sabar; Sesame Workshop; Shari Lewis Enterprises, Inc.; The Itsy Bitsy Entertainment Company; The Pillsbury Company; Those Characters From Cleveland, Inc.; Titan Sports, Inc.; Twentieth Century Fox Film Corporation; United Artists; United Feature Syndicate, Inc.; Universal Press Syndicate; Viacom International Inc.; and Warner Bros. Copyrights and/or trademarks are also held by Wilton Industries, Inc.; Amscan, Inc.; Nordic-Ware, Inc.; Wear-Ever, Inc.; Mirro, Inc.; and other pan companies identified in picture captions. This book is derived from the author's independent research.

Dedication

I dedicate this book to the memory of my father, Roy Flipp, who collected pigs; and to my mother, Jean Smith Flipp, who collects frogs; and to my husband, Coy Replogle, who collects pink depression glass and who never once complained about the stacks, hills, and mountains of pans that turned our house into an obstacle course for the duration of this project.

It is great to be in a family where "because it is fun" is a sufficient reason to spend time, effort, and money to acquire all manner of odd or ordinary items.

Happy collecting!

Designed by Joseph M. Riggio Jr.
Type set in Zapf Humanist Dm BT/Humanist 521 BT

ISBN: 0-7643-1857-8
Printed in China
1 2 3 4

Published by Schiffer Publishing Ltd.
4880 Lower Valley Road
Atglen, PA 19310
Phone: (610) 593-1777; Fax: (610) 593-2002
E-mail: Info@schifferbooks.com
Please visit our web site catalog at **www.schifferbooks.com**
We are always looking for people to write books on new and related subjects. If you have an idea for a book, please contact us at the above address.

This book may be purchased from the publisher.
Include $3.95 for shipping.
Please try your bookstore first.
You may write for a free catalog.

In Europe, Schiffer books are distributed by
Bushwood Books
6 Marksbury Avenue
Kew Gardens
Surrey TW9 4JF England
Phone: 44 (0) 20 8392 8585
Fax: 44 (0) 20 8392 9876
E-mail: Bushwd@aol.com
Free postage in the UK. Europe: air mail at cost.

Acknowledgments

If you were looking for a collector's handbook on novelty cake pans, what would you hope to see in it? That is the question four pan collectors helped me answer over the months this book was in progress. Vicki Horton of Pardeeville, Wisconsin; Denise Mayoff of Richardson, Texas; Nila Pudwill of Bismarck, North Dakota; and Cheryl Thompson of Des Moines, Iowa, all provided opinions and insights on everything from "what is a novelty pan?" to "does this small pan look better pictured on the left or on the right of this large pan?" In addition, they generously loaned me pans to make this book as comprehensive as possible. I valued their input and enjoyed their enthusiasm for their collections and for this project. I also thank Jean Penn of Comanche, Oklahoma, for her input and the loan of a few of her particularly good finds.

Double-checking the detail that appears in the picture captions in this book was an important but tedious job, cheerfully and competently undertaken by Minnesotans Tara Gibbs, Mary Jodeit, and Elizabeth Larson. Mary also agilely threaded her way through piles and stacks and mounds of cake pans, selecting what I needed and helping me arrange them during the photography sessions. I am grateful to Diane Collins, who loaned me photographic equipment and instructed and coached me on its use. Without her help I'd still be taking unusable practice shots of out-of-focus and unevenly lit pans.

Producing a book is always a team effort, not only on the author's end, but on the publisher's side as well. I thank Donna Baker, the editor who guided me through the book building process, for her patience and encouragement, and I also appreciate the hard work and specialized skills of the many people at Schiffer Publishing who played critical roles in the production of this book. It has been a pleasure to be part of this process.

Contents

Part I: Introduction 4

Chapter 1. Novelty Pan Collecting 101 4

What is a novelty cake pan? 4
What kinds of novelty pans does this book include? 4
What does the book leave out? 5
What is anodized aluminum? 6
What are coppertone and goldtone aluminum? 7
Who makes novelty pans? 7
What is a stand-up novelty pan? 7
What is a licensed novelty pan? 9
What sizes do novelty pans come in? 10
What paper items come with pans? Are they collectible? 10
What are lay-ons? What are they worth? 12
Are pan names consistent and meaningful? 12
Are stock numbers useful to collectors? 13
Where can novelty pans be purchased? 13
What flaws or problems are possible? How do they affect the desirability of a pan? 13
How should the pans be cleaned? 16
Do novelty pans get retired? How long do they stay in circulation? 16
Who collects novelty pans? 16
How do collectors display and store their collections? 17

What kind of information appears on the pans themselves? 17
How is this book organized? 19
What information appears in the picture captions? 20
What do novelty pans cost? 20

Part II: The Pans 21

Chapter 2. Animals: Domestic, Wild, and Imaginary 21
Chapter 3. People: Guys, Gals, and Dolls; Where they Live and How They Get Around 42
Chapter 4. Celebrations: Fun and Games, Food, Festivities 58
Chapter 5. Holidays and Seasons 75
Chapter 6. Licensed Images 100
Chapter 7. Simple Shapes, Plain and Fancy 130

Part III: Road Map 145

Index of Pans by Names and Keywords 145
Index of Pans by Stock Numbers 151
Index of Licensed Pans by Image Owner 155
Index of Pans by Manufacturer (Excluding Wilton Pans) 156
Index of Stand-up Pans by Mold Type 156
Index of Pans by Earliest Date 157
Index of Pans by Size (Excluding Full-Size Pans) 159
Bibliography 160

Part I

Introduction

Chapter 1
Novelty Pan Collecting 101

Devil's food. Spice cake with penuche icing. Pound cake. Yellow cake with raspberry filling. Poppy seed lemon cake. These items satisfy the sweet tooth. They also conjure up pleasant associations with balloons and confetti and candles and presents and happy times. In the United States, a decorated cake is so closely linked with birthday celebrations that a cake-and-candles silhouette is immediately recognized as a birthday icon. A tiered decorated cake is often used as a symbol for weddings. Other festive events, such as grand openings, anniversaries, christenings, and graduations often include cakes as well. A decorated cake, be it whimsical or elegant, small or gigantic, simple or elaborate, is a source of pleasure beyond its food value.

And yet, however attractive and imbued with nostalgia cakes may be, they are not collectible! Some people have embraced collecting novelty cake pans as a way to "have their cake and eat it, too." Like metal lunch boxes and porcelain egg cups, cake pans are functional items made to be used. They do not come with certificates of authenticity, they do not get "retired," and they are not individually numbered or signed. A large part of the charm of such a collection is the fact that these very items, or ones just like them, were used—and continue to be usable—to produce celebration cakes.

What is a novelty cake pan?

Here "novelty" is being used to mean something unusual and out of the ordinary. If most of our cakes were triangular, then a round cake would qualify as novel, and rounds would be novelty pans. But as it is, most cakes are round or rectangular, and so other shapes are considered novelty pans.

Many novelty pans produce a cake shaped like a person or an animal. These are sometimes called figural pans, and their shapes include astronauts, gingerbread folks, old-fashioned rag dolls, owls, butterflies, cows, and dragons, to name just a few. There are also pans shaped like inanimate objects, such as slot machines, umbrellas, horseshoes, or guitars. The majority of pans in this book represent a recognizable object, person, or animal. A special category of such representational pans is that of Licensed Character pans, discussed on pages 100-129.

There are also wonderful novelty pans that are interesting for their shapes, such as those with scallops, fluted edges, rippled surfaces, swirls, dips, and dots.

Novelty pans can be made from a variety of materials. It is not the material that makes them novel, but their shape.

What kinds of novelty pans does this book include?

The full range of novelty pans available today is too large for a single book. This book covers a segment very popular with collectors and with home bakers. It focuses on novelty cake pans made of formed aluminum.

In the interest of space, some types of pans were not included in the book. This heavy-duty foil pan is by Wilton; the box is dated 1979. *Courtesy of Denise Mayoff.*

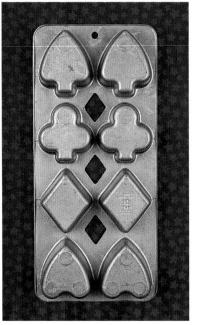

This multi-cavity cast-aluminum pan was called the *Parti-Fours Pan* in the 1961 *The Good Housekeeping Book of Cake Decorating*. It was called the *Bridge Party Pan* in a Nordic Ware booklet from the early 1970s.

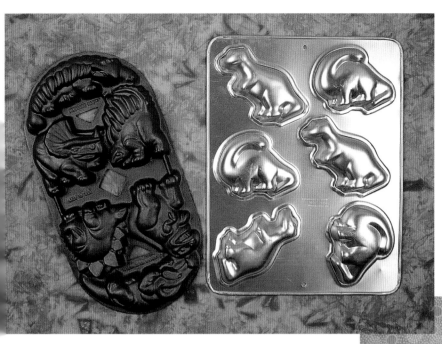

The dinosaurs on this cast iron pan by John Wright Co. are wonderfully detailed. The formed aluminum pan next to it is described on page 39 in the chapter on Animals.

What does the book leave out?

There are delightful novelty pans made of cast iron, cast aluminum, heavy aluminum foil, tinned steel, copper, and even ovenproof plastic. These are interesting and collectible objects in their own right. They are omitted only because a single volume could not do justice to every kind of material.

These cat pans were both made in Portugal. The one on the left is tinned steel; the one on the right is formed aluminum.

This full-sized goose pan by Pantastic is oven-safe plastic.

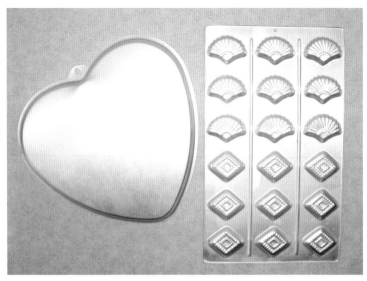

Cookie pans may make small cookies or huge cookies, but they are generally too shallow to use for cake batter.

This coppertone mold is suitable for gelatin or candy, but is too shallow to be considered a cake pan. The deeper mold next to it is part of a Wilton set (shown on page 143), and is considered an individual serving size cake pan.

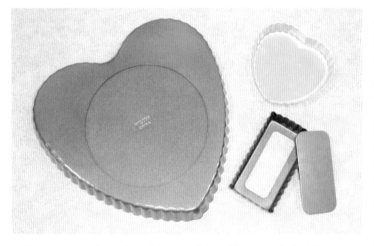

Tart pans come in a variety of shapes and sizes. They are typically shallow and have a removable bottom.

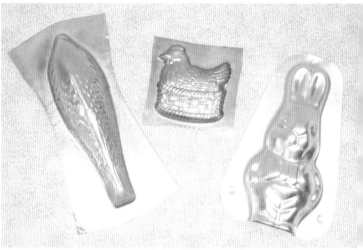

The fish and hen molds in this picture are not aluminum. The bunny mold is. All are chocolate molds. The bunny was also marketed by Wilton as a cake mold and is included in the Animals chapter on page 25.

As noted, this book is devoted to cake pans. Tart pans, cookie molds, pans for flans, and molds for candy need not apply. These distinctions, however, sometimes involve a judgment call. I have included a few chocolate molds because they were sold in early Wilton Yearbooks and are therefore of interest to collectors of Wilton pans—and because some of them may also be used for baking and were marketed that way. But in general chocolate molds are a distinct collectible worthy of their own book. Most full-size gelatin molds and many smaller gelatin molds are suitable for baking cake batter, and some were marketed with that dual purpose clearly featured. I have included many examples of such molds. Other molds marketed primarily for gelatin are very shallow and are not very suitable for baking. I have left those out.

What is anodized aluminum?

Aluminum is an extremely popular material for baking pans and other cookware. It is a plentiful natural resource (which helps keep the cost reasonable), it conducts heat well, it is light (and therefore easily handled in a home kitchen), and it readily lends itself to manufacturing either by casting or forming from rolled sheets.

Aluminum does not rust in the way that iron products will, but it is subject to oxidation. To control this oxidation, most aluminum used in cookware and in many other applications is put through a process called anodizing. Aluminum is submerged in an electrolyte bath and an electrical current is passed through the solution. This causes the aluminum to produce a porous surface film that is extremely hard. Note that this film is not a coating applied externally, but an integral part of the aluminum itself.

Anodizing aluminum not only improves its corrosion-resistance, but also helps the metal resist abrasion. The anodized film is very durable, but it is possible to gouge or scratch the surface, removing the film in that spot.

The anodizing process also introduces opportunity for esthetic treatment. The degree of matte or shine to the finish can be controlled during the pre-treatment step. After the porous film is produced on the aluminum, the pores can be filled with organic dyes or metallic salts can be deposited at their base, allowing this naturally silver-white metal to take on a rainbow of colors. The final step in the process closes the pores, usually by causing them to swell in a hot water bath.

Almost all of the pans in this book are made of anodized aluminum. There are also examples of aluminum coated with colored enamel or a non-stick material.

What are coppertone and goldtone aluminum?

One of the most popular colors for aluminum kitchenware has been a pink/orange tone similar to the color of polished copper. This is often called coppertone, to avoid confusion with items made of copper. The color is achieved during the anodizing process. The coppertone aluminum items in this book range from a very faint pink to a bright and deep burnt orange.

Another popular color for novelty pans, especially those from the early 1970s, is a golden hue often referred to as goldtone. Examples of this finish can be seen on two Winnie the Pooh™ pans licensed by Disney, shown in the Licensed Images chapter, page 103.

Other colors were popular for other kinds of kitchenware, such as aluminum tumblers, mugs, and salad bowls, but the most common colors for novelty pans (after the natural color of aluminum) are the coppertone and goldtone. A delightful exception is the set of individual snowflake molds of several different colors, shown in the Holidays and Seasons chapter, page 89.

Who makes novelty pans?

The most prolific producer of novelty pans is *Wilton Industries, Inc.*, located in Woodridge, Illinois. This privately owned company has been training professional bakers and cake-decorating hobbyists since 1929. Over the years they have sold a very large range of products related to both cake decorating and cookie and candy making by mail order and through retail stores. Some of the products have been manufactured in their own facilities, but their novelty pans are made in Asia. In the 1960s and 1970s, pans were made in Japan and Korea; then China and Indonesia became the most frequent manufacturing sites. The novelty pans offered in Wilton publications of the 1960s were probably not made exclusively for Wilton, but by the early 1970s Wilton offered pans of their own design. Some collectors limit themselves to pans by Wilton.

The bulk of the novelty pans offered by Wilton are documented in its annual Yearbook. The catalog section of this publication includes all the pans that a consumer can order directly from Wilton or find in many retail stores. Wilton also offers novelty pans not included in the Yearbooks. Often these are somewhat simpler versions of the mainline pans, and they are sold in stores that don't typically carry a large range of Wilton items. Some (but not all) of these pans are labeled "1-2-3."

Nordic Ware, founded in 1946 and headquartered in Minneapolis, Minnesota, is a family-owned, American manufacturer of kitchenware products. In the realm of baking products they are best known for their trademarked Bundt® pans. They have also offered a number of novelty pans and molds over the years, and still sell holiday molds through their website and in retail stores.

Another American company that has marketed novelty pans made for them in Asia is *Amscan, Inc.*, now of Elmsford, New York, a manufacturer and distributor of party goods. Their pans are quite popular with many collectors.

You will also find a few pans in this book by *Wear-Ever, Mirro,* and *West Bend* as well as by some less familiar names. There is a pan from Sweden, two from Italy, and several from Portugal. And let us not overlook one of the busiest producers of vintage goods of all kinds, *Unknown.* Actually, *Unknown* is alive and well and still producing novelty pans. I recently ordered new pans from a cake-decorating supply source and they came with no identifiers other than a paper sticker "Made in Portugal," so they are listed as maker unknown.

What is a stand-up novelty pan?

Pans that produce cakes of an upright figure are called stand-up pans, or sometimes 3-D pans. Pans marketed primarily for molding gelatin and similar food may produce tall "standing" cakes, but are usually referred to as tall molds or tall ring molds rather than "stand-up" molds. Tall molds may have very elaborate designs, but are not usually figural. A stand-up cake pan may produce a snowman; a tall mold may produce a multi-tiered cake with the lowest tier fluted, the next tier plain, the next tier with a pleated look, etc.

The fish on the left is made of copper and lined with tin. The pan next to it (also shown on page 36) is coppertone aluminum.

The simplest kind of stand-up pan is a one-piece mold with sloped sides. This enables the cake or molded food to slip out when the pan is inverted. This is called an open mold. All tall molds and tall ring molds fall into this category, and a few stand-up cake pans do as well.

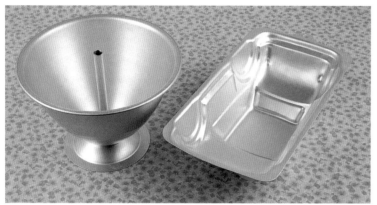

These open molds only need to be inverted to remove the molded cake.

Pan designers have come up with several ways to produce a cake that has nips, tucks, and other detail that would otherwise prevent the cake from slipping easily out of an open mold. There are two basic solutions for producing figural stand-up cakes. The first is to provide one or more pans used to make the cake in separate sections, which are then joined together before frosting and decorating. The second is to provide the pan in two (or more) pieces, which are joined together before filling with batter and disassembled to remove the one-piece cake.

The sets that make two cakes that are joined after baking can also be used to make flat cakes rather than stand-up cakes. For example, each half of the Sports Ball pan by Wilton will produce a semi-spherical cake that can be placed directly on a serving tray or on another cake. Sometimes a single pan is provided, which may be used alone to make a flat cake or used twice to make two cakes that are then joined together to make a stand-up cake.

To make a ball cake in this pan set, each half is baked separately and the two halves are joined together with frosting. Some stand-up pans need a stand, as this one does, and others have stands built into the design.

Multi-part pans that are assembled before being filled with batter come in two basic styles. In one case, the bottom section of the pan (which will usually become the front of the figure) is filled to the brim with batter and the top section is snapped on top of it. The rising batter fills the top half (the back of the completed figure), producing a three-dimensional cake. In this style pan set, the top piece usually has one or more holes for steam to escape. While these pans are called "snap-together" molds, it is often difficult to fit them together tightly, especially with one half filled with batter! Many bakers tie a string around the assembled pan, to prevent the rising batter from dislodging the top pan piece.

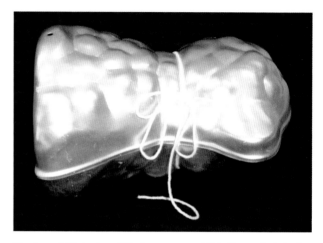

The face of this lamb mold is shown on page 27 in *Chapter 2, Animals*. Here it is shown as it would go into the oven.

The other way of assembling a pan before filling it with batter is to clamp the halves together with spring clips or hinged clamps. Round spring clips come with these pans but many bakers find them difficult to use. Some bakers simply discard the original clips and use hinged clamps instead. The round spring clips are interchangeable among the pans. For many bakers and collectors, their absence or presence with a vintage pan has minimal or no impact on the desirability of the pan.

These second type of pans are open at the top, for filling and for steam to escape. Some have built-in supports to keep them upright in the oven; others have a separate stand. A support can often be jerry-rigged, for example by placing the pan in a loaf pan, but the original stand is desirable both for bakers and for collectors.

The round clips on the right come with clamp-together molds, but many bakers prefer the hinged clamps shown on the left. This mold has a built-in stand.

Because the batter in these pans can be quite deep, the pans often come with a metal core which is inserted into the batter to conduct oven heat to the center. When needed, heating cores are included as part of the stand-up pan set. Sometimes they are also available to purchase separately. Cores from different sets are not identical, but they often can be interchanged successfully. They do not typically have a stock number stamped on them and they are not pictured in Yearbooks or catalogs, making it difficult to determine what pan a specific core matches. Bakers need at least one core that fits the clamp-together pans they have. Collectors can decide whether the heating cores are an essential part of their collections.

The pan on the left is a clamp-together mold with a separate stand. It is shown with a heating core. The other pan is a clamp-together mold with a built-in stand. It doesn't need a core.

Notice that the standing heating cores are of two different heights. The one on its side displays a broken tab. Many tabs get broken off after repeated use. The cores are still usable, but they are less convenient without the tab.

Another way to produce stand-up cake presentations is with the use of accessories. In these cases, the cake itself is flat and a novelty stand gives it dimension. Probably the most well-known pan set in this category is the Wilton Piano set, sold from the mid-1960s through 1990. It consists of grand-piano-shaped pans in two sizes, along with plastic pieces including a stand with legs that the cake sits on, a bench, a piano top with a leg to hold it in an open position on the cake, a keyboard, and even two little candelabras. Two versions of this pan set are shown in the Celebrations chapter, page 66.

Below is a summary of the stand-up pan categories and their characteristics. A listing of the stand-up pans by mold type is provided in Part III.

Pan Type	Cake Units	Main Mold Pieces	Other Parts
Open mold	One	One	Stand, heating core
Join-after-baking	Two	One or two	Stand
Snap-together	One	Two	None
Clamp-together	One	Two	Stand, heating core, clips or clamps
Accessorize or Stack	Two or more	Multiple	Accessories to use for cake presentation

What is a licensed novelty pan?

A license is permission to do something, such as get married or hunt deer or fish. Many license arrangements involve a fee, and include restrictions. For example, even after you pay for a deer-hunting license, you must abide by restrictions regarding where you may hunt and how many you may bag.

In the world of novelty pans, permission is granted by an owner of a popular image for a cake pan company to make a pan representing that image. The pan company pays for this permission, and abides by the requirements and restrictions specified by the owner of the image. These licensed pans are generally sold for home use only, and are not intended for commercial use, for example by a bakery or a home-based cake business.

Wilton Industries has been celebrating America's delight in make-believe celebrities for more than three decades. They have been licensed by copyright and trademark holders to create more than one hundred character pans, ranging from Alf™ to Ziggy™, with more added each year.

The identifying stamp on most licensed pans shows the owner of the image as well as the maker of the pan. The year on such pans may reflect a copyright or trademark date, rather than the year the pan was issued. Two Wilton licensed pans from 1985 have a "for home use" notation stamped them, and beginning in 1995 another thirty pans have such a notation.

There are a few surprises among Wilton licensed pans. The Troll, though he may look very familiar and famous, is just a generic, everyday troll, and is not a licensed pan. The Flower Power™ pan, on the other hand, may seem like a pretty generic daisy pattern, but is in fact a licensed pan.

Sometimes sellers refer to non-licensed pans by using trademarked names. The Frog pan is called Kermit, the Van pan is called Scooby's Mystery Bus, the Storybook Doll is called Raggedy Ann, etc. Note that these names were never used by Wilton, and Wilton never shows them decorated as licensed characters or objects. Collectors know that Wilton made a Frog pan, not a pan of a trademarked frog character. To some sellers, all frogs look alike, and they are all named Kermit! If in doubt, look for (or ask about) the name of the image owner stamped on the pan.

What sizes do novelty pans come in?

Because of their irregular shape it is often difficult to measure novelty pans consistently. Different results will also be obtained depending on whether the measurements are taken inside the pan or outside, and whether they include the extended rim or flange. If exact size is critical to you, find out exactly where the measurements were made, or measure the pan yourself. Exact dimensions are seldom a major consideration for novelty pans. Instead, the relative size of the cake they would produce is usually the size-related factor of interest.

Pans that are sold with the primary focus on using them for gelatins, pâté, etc., are often described by the liquid volume they will hold, measured to the brim. A 4-cup mold will hold a quart of water, for example. (By the way, such pans are often, but not always, referred to as molds.)

For baking cakes, pans are not filled to the brim with batter and pans sold primarily as cake pans are not usually referred to by the full volume of liquid they would hold. Instead, they may be described by the amount of batter that should be used in them (for example, 1-1/2 cups) or how they compare to the volume produced by a typical "standard" cake mix.

In this book, pan sizes are given as follows:

Double

Holds two cake mixes or approximately 9 to 11 cups of batter. Filled to the brim (for example, with gelatin), holds approximately 18 cups of liquid.

Full

Holds one cake mix or approximately 4-1/2 to 6 cups of batter. Filled to the brim, holds about 9 cups of liquid.

A full-size novelty pan holds the equivalent of a 9" x 13" x 1.75" rectangular pan. The dimensions can vary considerably, but the volume is fairly consistent among full-size novelty pans.

Pans sold in sets to make cakes that are intended to be stacked as layers are considered full-size if the pans together hold one cake mix (or the equivalent.)

Cakes made in these pans are estimated as providing 12 servings.

Small

Holds less than a cake mix but more than an individual serving. Typically holds 1 to 3 cups of cake batter. There isn't as much standardization among these pans as for full-size pans.

Individual

Makes one serving. Typically takes 1/4 to 3/4 cups of batter.

Multi-Cavity

Has cavities for making several single-serving cakes. A muffin pan is an example in this category.

Mixed Set

A set consisting of different sized pans that together take more than a standard cake mix.

There are many pictures throughout the book with pans of more than one size, to help provide a sense of scale.

What paper items come with pans? Are they collectible?

Some novelty pans, especially older ones, were packaged originally in boxes, often with a picture of a finished cake and some or all of the instructions for making it.

Most pan boxes are colorful and attractive, but not sturdy.

The more usual practice now, at least for flat pans, is to sell the pans hanging from pegboards or stacked on a shelf, with no box or bag. Stand-up pans are still often sold in boxes.

Pans may be sold with paperwork ranging from very simple single-color labels to very detailed full-color die cuts the size and shape of the pan. Flat pans by Amscan and Wilton usually include a die-cut full-color insert when originally sold. These may be on glossy paper or cardstock, and sometimes are double size, folded to fit the pan. One common format is for the front to include a picture of the finished cake and the back to include instructions, but there are many variations. Sometimes pictures of several finished cakes are supplied, to show alternate uses of the pan. Recipes for cakes or frostings may also be included. Wilton is currently including its instructions in more than one language on many inserts, but get out your magnifying glass—that text is necessarily small to fit on a piece of paper that will fit inside the pan! Stand-up pans typically do not include inserts. Multi-cavity pans may be wrapped in cardstock that serves as a partial box and takes the place of an insert.

Here you can see both the front and back of two Wilton pan inserts.

The inserts for Wilton's line of individual serving size pans called Singles!™ are folded. Not many full size pans have foldout inserts; this Barbie™ pan does.

The backs of the inserts vary in content.

Here is an assortment of inserts and wrappers printed on poster board.

In addition to or instead of the instructions that are printed on the box or insert, many pans come with instruction sheets or booklets, which may cover general cake decorating techniques as well as specific baking and decorating directions for one or more cakes that can be made with the pan.

Some pans come with only a label. Some include booklets.

Many Wilton pans include a booklet formed from a single sheet. The format and sheet size varies from pan to pan.

While even very grungy pans usually clean up very well, the same cannot be said for paper goods. Since these items are often consulted by the baker when making a cake, they are often stained with cake batter or frosting. They may be creased, wrinkled, folded or torn. The inserts and boxes almost always have one or more price stickers or boldly marked prices. The instruction sheets may have handwritten notes. Even inserts from brand-new pans on the dealer's shelves will be wrinkled to fit the contours of the pan. Paper goods that have been stored in less-than-archival conditions may have a musty odor or water damage. The paper goods associated with novelty pans are of-

ten irregularly shaped and odd sizes. Filing, storing, or displaying them takes some ingenuity.

Functionally, the paper goods are not typically necessary for using the pans. General instructions are widely available, decorating ideas for most Wilton pans are available in Wilton Yearbooks, and enthusiastic pan users often exchange pan instructions on websites devoted to cake decorating. Wilton's Yearbook website, for example, contains instructions for current pans in a downloadable, printable format that is, in my opinion, more practical than the odd-sized folded sheets and easier to read than the minuscule print of multi-language inserts. And if you get cake batter on it, you can just print a clean copy for next time!

Attitudes of novelty pan collectors range from "I never buy a pan without all of its original paperwork" to "an insert or the instruction sheet is a nice bonus, and I'd pay a little extra to get those with a pan" to "I collect metal, not paper, and I'm not interested in the packaging at all." It is your collection. You decide what you want to collect!

What are lay-ons? What are they worth?

Some pans are originally sold with a plastic item intended to be placed on the finished cake. A computer may have a plastic keyboard, a loving cup may have plastic handles, and a licensed character pan may have a plastic face or torso. These pieces are commonly called lay-ons. Among people who buy pans to bake in, attitudes range from "I love the added touch of the lay-ons and I just don't buy pans that don't have their original lay-ons," to "I wouldn't put one of those tacky plastic pieces on a custom cake I make if I had to serve store-bought cookies instead!" Among pan collectors, the lay-ons are generally considered desirable, if not essential. I would expect to see pans with lay-ons selling for more than those same pans without them, but I have seen so many exceptions that I hesitate to call it a pattern. Decide whether the lay-ons are important to you, and if they are, expect to pay more or wait longer to find those pans—at least in some cases.

Pans are pictured in this book with their lay-ons next to them if the pan itself has detail where the lay-on goes, and with their lay-ons on the pan, if the area under the lay-on is plain.

Are pan names consistent and meaningful?

Discussions of novelty pans remind me a little of discussions at family reunions where there are several sets of cousins with similar or identical names, and the same person may be referred to by different names by different people. It is sometimes hard to follow the conversation!

For novelty pans, the name on the label or in a catalog may change from time to time, and the same name may be used for more than one pan. A case in point is a doll-shaped pan originally called *Raggedy Doll* in the 1972 Wilton Yearbook, changed to *Rag Doll*, and then finally called *Storybook Doll* from 1976 until the pan was discontinued after the 1984 Yearbook. Wilton apparently liked that name so well that they gave it to an entirely different doll pan in 2001!

In this book, I have tried to follow the spelling and punctuation used by Wilton. However, these were not always consistent from one pan to the next, or even from one Yearbook to another for the same pan. The use of "mini" with or without a hyphen, and before or after the pan name has been particularly varied. The most recent Yearbooks list pans in the index under "mini" and do not use a hyphen. For example, "Mini Shell" and "Mini Star." This is the convention I have adopted for this book.

In the captions, you will see that I list the most common or latest name for a pan in the caption header, and also list within the caption other names for the pan that I have encountered. For pans not given a name for marketing or whose name I have been unable to find, I supply a simple descriptive name, such as "Butterfly" or "Acorn on Round."

Wilton's practice of (sometimes) giving pans distinctive names helps identify which of several similar pans is meant. It has a drawback, though, if you don't happen to know the name. Would you think of looking under "H" in an index if you were searching for witch? Probably not, so I have indexed pans using both their "official" names (when known) and also one or more generic theme words. As a result, you can find the *High Flying Witch* pan under "H" or under "W."

Are stock numbers useful to collectors?

It is helpful to remember that companies assign stock numbers to their products for their own internal purposes. A code that helps them track inventories or fill orders may or may not be useful to collectors of those products.

Most Wilton pans have a stock number stamped on them, in the format of 3 or 4 digits, a dash, and 3 or 4 digits. Here are four examples:

502-683
501-6074
2105-646
2105-0778

Some pans are stamped with different stock numbers from different production runs. For example, you may come across a full size horseshoe pan with the stock number 2105-3254 and another one with the number 502-3258.

The catalog section of Wilton yearbooks also contains a stock number for each item. This is often one of the stock numbers stamped on the pan, with a letter code for the issue inserted after the dash. For example, the *Rocking Horse* pan in the 2002 Wilton Yearbook has stock number 2105-J-2388. In the 1999 issue, the stock number is listed as 2105-F-2388. The pan has stock number 2105-2388. There are also examples of stock numbers stamped on pan that have no relation to the stock number(s) used in the Yearbook. For example, the Frog pan is listed in Yearbooks with stock number 2105-x-2452; my Frog pan has 502-1816 stamped on it.

Some pan inserts have stock numbers. These appear to usually match the stock number on the pan. (It would not surprise me to see exceptions.) Some instruction booklets have stock numbers. The digits after the dash appear to usually match the corresponding part of the stock number on the pan.

Wilton uses the stock numbers for its own internal purposes. There is not a one-stock-number-per-item rule.

Pans by Wear-Ever and Mirro often have a stock number stamped on them. Amscan pans usually do not.

I have cross-referenced all the stock numbers I have come across with their pan names. I hope that this will be useful for looking up the name of a pan you are interested in, as well as for distinguishing among similar pans, such as the plethora of teddy bears. This is not intended for authentication purposes. If your pan has a different stock number than the ones I list, it doesn't mean the pan isn't genuine, just that I haven't come across that particular stock number.

In the picture captions and the index I have substituted an "x" in place of the letter that represents the yearbook issue in stock numbers from yearbooks. Thus a pan that appeared in seven yearbooks will have only one yearbook stock number listed if the only element that changed from year to year is the issue identifier. For example, rather than list 2105-J-1234 and 2105-K-1234 (and perhaps dozens of other variations), the caption will just list 2105-x-1234.

Where can novelty pans be purchased?

New novelty pans are sold in hobby and craft stores, some hardware stores with substantial kitchenware departments, specialty stores for food crafting supplies, some party goods stores, and some discount chains. A party goods store may carry a few novelty cake pans, and a craft store may offer a couple dozen. Since 1995 there have been more than one hundred current Wilton pans on the market, with new issues and discontinuations each year. Few stores stock that many designs at all times, but a specialty store will have a substantial number and also may be willing to get any current Wilton pan for you by special order. Specialty stores may also carry other brands.

Current pans are also sold by mail-order and Internet specialty retailers.

Older pans may be found at garage sales, thrift shops, and flea markets, often at very low prices. The modern electronic garage sale, the Internet auction, is a continuous source of nearly any collectible you can think of, and novelty pans are there among the lunch boxes and baseball cards and candlesticks. On any given day there are approximately one thousand novelty cake pans up for auction on eBay, with two to three thousand selling each month. Selling prices are typically higher than your neighborhood yard sale and you do pay shipping, but there are constantly more choices available than you are apt to encounter in many months worth of scouring garage sales.

A few online retailers of cake supplies also offer some discontinued pans, as do some antique dealers specializing in vintage kitchenware. These tend to be priced higher than the other sources I've named. After all, those dealers have done the searching for you.

What flaws or problems are possible? How do they affect the desirability of a pan?

Although they are lightweight, pans of anodized aluminum are remarkably strong and durable. The pans do not break, wear out, rust, or disintegrate. Aside from those that got retired to sandboxes or hauled out to landfills, the novelty cake pans of the last four decades are still in circulation. Novelty pans are functional items designed to be used, and most vintage pans will show some signs of wear. Even pans that have never been used, whether they are thirty years old or issued last month, may have storage wear. Here are some of the bumps and bruises you may find on novelty pans:

Sticker residue

If this topic is not number one on every pan collector's gripe list, I am sure it is very near the top. Whether you buy an occasional pan to bake in or collect hundreds of them, you have encountered the dreaded Sticker Goo Problem. I am sure that NASA could have saved a lot of tax dollars when they researched adhesives that would withstand outer space conditions by just consulting cake pan companies. The adhesives used on pan stickers withstand anything. This problem is not limited to particular manufacturers and seems to apply no matter how the pans are packaged. I once bought a boxed set of individual-serving pans, and I was gleefully expecting that at least they wouldn't have stickers to remove. Ha! Each little pan had at least two pieces of tape holding it to the cardboard sheet inside the box. Tape residue is just as tenacious as sticker goo. The only way to collect novelty pans without dealing with the adhesive problem is to buy pans whose previous owners have dealt with it. Sometimes sellers proudly describe a pan as "never been used." If I had a choice between a pan that had never been used and one that had been carefully used a few times, I'd choose the used pan, and get the benefit of someone else having removed the stickers.

Since sticker goo is a fact of life for novelty pan collectors, I've discussed its removal in the answer on how to clean pans, page 16.

Scuffing

Pans that have been used may show some wear marks from being slid in and out of ovens or moved around on storage shelves. Even new pans, especially the ones that don't come in boxes, typically show some minor scuffing. Scuffing is external and has no effect at all on the usability of the pan. Minor scuffing is "normal" for this item, and does not detract from the desirability of a pan. Scuffing so severe that it detracts from the pattern or jumps out at the viewer does reduce the desirability of a pan.

Scratches

Anodized aluminum does not scratch during normal use, but it can be gouged or scratched with a sharp implement. Since most foods made in novelty pans are turned out onto a platter before they are served, you will seldom see scratches from cutting food with a knife inside the pan. Sometimes you will see scratches along the top inside edge, where someone used a metal utensil to loosen the cake or gelatin before turning it out. Minor scratches do not affect the functionality of the pan, but do make it less desirable as a collector's item. Gouges and deep scratches can remove the anodized layer and the pan will be susceptible to oxidation at that point, making it less desirable to bakers and collectors alike.

Dirt, grime, grease, etc.

Given a choice between a sparkling clean pan and a dirty one, I'd personally pay a premium to get the clean one. Since that is seldom the choice we face, it is nice to know that these pans clean up very well with a little elbow grease, a few soft brushes, and common cleaning products. (See the discussion on how to clean them, page 16.) Often novelty pans are displayed in kitchens. This is a logical and attractive choice, but not a very practical one for keeping the pans clean. Even in kitchens with exhaust fans and fastidious housekeepers, airborne grease is a fact of life. Often molds are described by sellers as "only used for decorative purposes." I translate that to mean, "Twenty-seven years of cooking grease is embedded in every contour of this mold." Yuck. I'd rather have a pan that was used every Thanksgiving for the cranberry mold than one that wasn't used at all. At least the former presumably got washed once a year and won't have a grease build-up more than a year deep. But, like most collectors, I buy what is available and resign myself to cleanup chores.

Dents

Given that aluminum is relatively soft, I'd expect more dents and dings than I've actually seen on novelty pans. Bends in the flange around a pan are probably the most common example of denting, and have no effect on the usability of the pan. Such dents may have a slight effect on the desirability (and therefore price) of a pan, all other things being equal. A dent on the pan itself is not necessarily fatal to its desirability. If you need an eagle pan to make a cake for your brother next month, you may happily settle for one with a dent. (Frosting covers all such flaws.) If you want an eagle pan to display as part of your collection and you have no deadline, you may prefer to wait until you find one in better condition. Even minor dents on a pan affect its desirability and therefore its price—again, all other things being equal.

A major dent that actually creases the metal and puts a break in the anodized film is generally a show-stopper.

This pan has a dent both on the outer and inner edges. Such dents will usually detract from the value of the pan.

Scorching

I have seen a few examples of pans discolored apparently by scorching. It is hard to imagine a scenario that causes a pan to scorch on its outside. Since this is definitely not part of the normal wear and tear of usage it severely reduces the pan's desirability. Such a pan is still usable, so someone who wants that particular pan to make a cake may be willing to take it, and a collector may use it as a "place holder" until a replacement is found, but neither would typically be willing to pay much for a scorched pan.

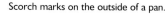

Scorch marks on the outside of a pan.

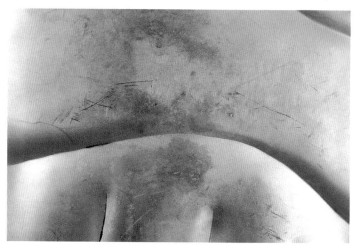

The pan on the right has the uneven chalky look that is often produced when anodized aluminum is cleaned in a dishwasher.

Close-up of the discoloration caused by a dishwasher.

Discoloration

If you come across an anodized aluminum pan with what appears to be an uneven chalky white film, chances are very good that you have found a pan that has been through the dishwasher. The discoloration is permanent, and the "film" will not wash off. If you find a pan with one area darker than the rest, with a distinct and fairly straight line between the two parts, it is likely that the pan was soaked in water, and the part that was submerged darkened. Neither of these discolorations affects the usability of the pans. A cake will bake just fine in such a pan. But from a collector's perspective, these are blemishes outside the range of normal wear and tear and they detract from the pan's desirability and value.

Drilled holes

Is there a hole in your pan? Do you want it there? Many novelty pans come with one or more holes for hanging, often in an enlargement of the flange to accommodate the hole. Some have small wire hangers. Other pans have no holes or other means of hanging, and many people drill their own holes in order to hang them. Some collectors consider this an adulteration and avoid home-drilled pans. Others consider it a handy convenience, saving them from doing it themselves. A poorly drilled hole with rough edges detracts from the desirability of a pan. The jury is out on whether a clean-edged hole drilled in the flange has an impact on desirability. Bakers probably don't care. Collectors may.

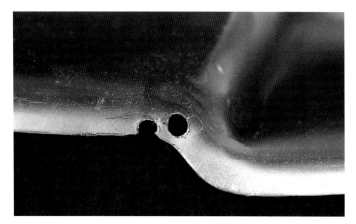

The driller missed the mark the first time!

Permanent marker

Sometimes an owner will write on a pan with a permanent marker. This has no effect on the usability of the pan. Depending on its placement and how you wish to display the pan, it may or may not be a major and distracting blemish that adversely affects its desirability as a collector's item.

Permanent marker on the exterior of the pan's side.

Erosion

It is not common to see anodized aluminum with erosion or oxidation holes unless the metal has been gouged or creased. The pan depicted here was stored in an attic for many years. The area pictured had a sticky substance over the area shown when it was unpacked, and removing the substance revealed this badly eroded metal. Some of the eaten-away spots go all the way through the pan. Unless that attic had metal-eating moths I do not know what caused these holes. I suggest that if any part of a pan is covered with something that prevents inspecting the pan that the pan be cleaned well enough to get a clear look at its condition before a sale takes place.

The result of a metal-eating mutant moth?

How should the pans be cleaned?

Hot soapy water is the best cleaning solution for aluminum pans. If necessary, a plastic scrubber or stiff pastry brush can be used on them, and wooden toothpicks are useful for cleaning crevices. For stickers, remove as much of the paper as you can by hand, and then apply a product made for the purpose (such as Goo Gone®) to the remaining adhesive. It may take several applications and a lot of rubbing in between to completely remove a particularly tenacious sticker. Resist the urge to speed things along with a metal implement.

Do not clean anodized aluminum pans in a dishwasher! Some pans are labeled "dishwasher safe" but none of them should be washed that way. It is "safe" to do so in the sense that they won't rust and they will still be usable. What they might *not* still be is pretty. The combination of minerals in the water, chemicals in the detergent, and high heat is very likely to permanently discolor the pan, turning it an uneven, chalky white. You may be lucky and not have this happen, but the risk is high.

Even hand washing the pans in hot water can cause some discoloration, depending on the mineral and alkali content of your water, especially if the pans are allowed to soak. Some pans seem far more susceptible to this than others, perhaps depending on the finishing process applied to the pan. To be safe, avoid soaking.

Do not use an abrasive cleaner. A paste of dampened baking soda can be rubbed on a stubborn dirty spot with a soft cloth.

Metal cleaners should not be used on anodized aluminum. The film on this metal is controlled oxidation, and metal cleaners are formulated to attack oxidation. Soapy water and elbow grease are your best bet.

Do novelty pans get retired? How long do they stay in circulation?

Pan manufacturers produce a functional item intended to be used. They are not in the collectibles business. They typically sell a given design as long as they judge there to be a profitable demand level for it. When they stop making it they do not "retire" it—that is, there is no promise to never sell that design again. They simply discontinue making that pan, either forever or until such time as they think it might sell well again.

About a third of the novelty pans that have appeared in Wilton Yearbooks have been in only one or two issues. Nearly ten percent have appeared in a dozen issues or more. On average, a Wilton novelty pan appears in five or six Yearbook issues.

Who collects novelty pans?

No doubt there are some people who have never baked a cake in their lives and who are attracted to novelty pans for nostalgic or esthetic reasons. A far more common pattern is for someone who bakes and decorates cakes to acquire a pan or two for use and somehow, without willing it or noticing it happen, is transformed into a collector of novelty pans. I clearly remember sitting in a beginner's cake decorating class, studying the novelty pans hung as decorations, and thinking, "Why buy a cat pan? You can put a cat or a horse or a flower garden on a square cake. A novelty shape seems so limited." Then I bought a novelty pan on sale, for a specific purpose. And that was so much fun I bought another. What can I say? A square pan may be more versatile, but novelty pans have won my heart!

In addition to being collectible in themselves, novelty pans lend themselves as embellishments to other collections. For example, a collector of Superman™ items may seek out the two licensed Superman pans produced by Wilton, and a Cabbage Patch™ Doll fan will want the Cabbage Patch licensed pans. (Pans that become part of such a collection may never see cake batter again, but are serving to give pleasure in another way.) A baker with a family member who collects owl figurines may be on the lookout for pans or molds of owls. It is these collectors-once-removed who often drive prices up in an auction. After all, if you plan to eventually own several hundred pans, you may be willing to bide your time and not pay a great deal for any one of them. The search for a bargain is part of the fun. But if all you want is an elephant pan or two, and your elephant-loving sister's birthday is next month, you may throw frugality to the winds, find a pan, pay whatever it takes to get it, and have it over with.

How do collectors display and store their collections?

This is a question I'd like more information on myself! Here are the answers I have gathered so far:

Hung on nails on the wall, using the holes that pans come with and drilling holes in the ones that don't have them. Hallways, stairways, utility rooms, guest rooms, hobby rooms, and, of course, kitchens have all been used by some collectors for these exhibits. A way to avoid drilling holes is to fasten a binder clip onto the side of the pan, and hook the handle over the nail. Office supply stores carry binder clips in several sizes and sometimes have them available in a silver color, which is less noticeable on the pan than the traditional black binders.

Stacked on a shelf of coated wire or hung from a coated wire rod that runs the length of the shelf. (These utility shelves are sold for closets and garages.) For this system, use a double hook, threading one end through the pan hole and hooking the other on the rod. For pans that don't have holes, attach an office binder clamp and put the hook through that. The shelf can be used for pans that have boxes, or for stand-up pans.

Displayed on ceiling-to-floor pegboard partitions on tracks. Hang the pans with pegboard hooks. The partitions can be slid out, one at a time, to access the pans. This method allows the pegboards to be fairly close together. Or the partitions can be mounted without the sliding tracks and spaced further apart, to allow walking between them.

Temporararily exhibited on a wall, with the remainder in large plastic storage bins. This makes use of limited wall space to showcase a small number of pans with a related theme—the display being changed seasonally or whenever the whim strikes. For the containers that hold the bulk of the collection, select units that can be stacked and that fit into the space you have available for them. Novelty pans are fairly light and you will probably be able to lift even large boxes full of pans, but when selecting boxes do

consider where they will be and how likely it is that you will need to move them often. To minimize scuffing, wrap the pans in tissue paper or place thin sheets of foam between them. To facilitate finding specific pans when wanted, make a list of all pans in each container in large letters and place a copy on the top or side of the container (or both), depending on how the containers are stacked or stored.

I look forward to learning other ways that collectors have found to display this attractive yet bulky collectible. I will share what I learn in the next edition.

What kind of information appears on the pans themselves?

Some novelty pans have absolutely no information stamped on the pan itself. When a manufacturer's mark is stamped on the pan it usually contains some of the following:

Year (of manufacture or of copyright or trademark registration)
Stock number
Manufacturer
Country where pan was made
Licensor
Pan size (dimensions or volume)
Pan name (infrequent)

Not all pans have all of these elements. The same pan may have different elements or different values for those elements depending on its production run.

Most Wilton pans are stamped with identifying information, including the Wilton name. Older pans usually have the Wilton name in script; some have a fancier script with a star dotting the "i." Since the late 1970s, the name Wilton has usually been stamped in block letters, sometimes all upper case and sometimes not. Some pans from the early 1970s also have block lettering. The Wilton name is shown as Wilton, Wilton Enterprises, Wilton Enterprises, Inc., Wilton Industries, and Wilton Industries, Inc. When "Inc" is present, there may or may not be a comma and/or a period. The general chronology is that Wilton was used on early pans, then Wilton Enterprises, then Wilton Industries, Inc. However the use of these names overlap and there is not a clear cutoff point when one is replaced by another.

Below and on the next two pages are some examples of the information found on novelty pans.

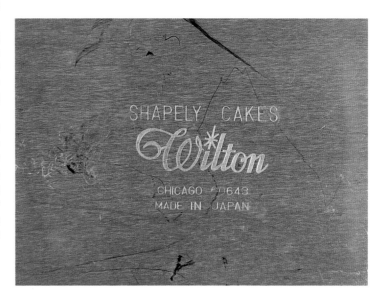

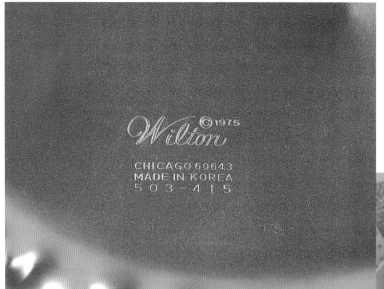

Wilton ©1975

CHICAGO 60643
MADE IN KOREA
5 0 3 – 4 1 5

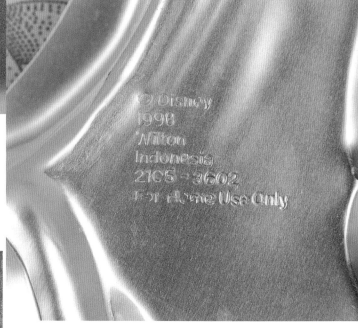

© Disney
1998
Wilton
Indonesia
2105 – 3602
For Home Use Only

© 1979 WILTON
WOODRIDGE, IL 60515
KOREA
502-2286

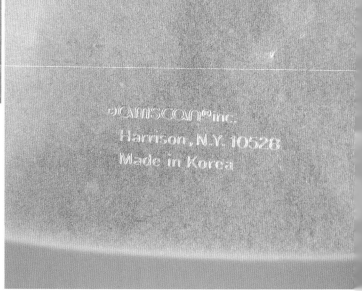

© AMSCAN® inc.
Harrison, N.Y. 10528
Made in Korea

How is this book organized?

I know that there are many ways collectors would like to be able to search for pans. Therefore, I have included indexes enabling you to find a pan by its stock number, its name, its key word, the company that owns the trademark (for licensed pans), the manufacturer, the date (when known), and the pan size.

I have tried to organize the pictures for viewing pleasure, grouping them loosely by theme. Each pan is shown just once, though some qualify for more than one theme. A bunny is an animal and also a holiday emblem. A bear with a stocking cap could be shown with winter-themed pans or with other bears. Confident that you will be able to find what you are looking for by using the indexes, I have simply placed each pan in the chapter that seems most fitting. I hope you will enjoy browsing as well as looking up specific pans.

What information appears in the picture captions?

For the pans shown, I have included the following details (as applicable to each pan):

• Company, pan size, stand-up/flat, type of mold if stand-up
• On pan: stock number, year, company, country where made, trademark owner if applicable, anything else on the pan
• For Wilton pans that appeared in Yearbooks: range of years, stock number(s), name(s) used if different from name above, price history
• For all pans: Estimated value (see price discussion below)

In addition, the same details for pans not shown are included at the end of each chapter.

The first Wilton publication to use "yearbook" in its title was the 1972 issue. There was no yearbook in 1973, and the 1974 yearbook was updated for 1975 without getting a new cover or title. A separate yearbook has been published each year since 1976. In addition to all of the yearbooks, I have consulted Wilton catalogs from 1959, 1964, 1966, 1969, and 1970. For simplicity, all Wilton publications issued periodically with decorating ideas and a catalog section are listed in the captions as "yearbooks" although not all of them had that title. The complete titles for each year appear in the Bibliography.

What do novelty pans cost?

People have been buying and using novelty cake pans for several decades, but the notion of collecting them is fairly new. Pricing has not settled into a stable pattern.

Garage sales and thrift stores are still a common source of novelty pans, and prices at these sources range from under $1 to $8 or so.

Dealers who specialize in kitchen collectibles may handle novelty cake pans, often in the range of $9 to $50, depending on the pan. Food crafting specialty stores sometimes offer discontinued pans, priced from $20 to $50, as well as current pans at their list prices (typically $9 to $20).

Internet auctions are an active market for novelty cake pans. Successful bids on eBay range from $2 to $100, with the majority of pans selling in the $4 to $10 range. The upper end of the price spectrum has been moving higher over the last year.

In short, there is no established convention for pricing novelty cake pans. Prices vary widely among different sources and also over fairly short periods of time. If you are wondering how to price a specific pan, or to predict what to expect to pay for a pan you want, here are some factors to consider:

1.   Generally, the upper limit for current pans (pans still being offered in catalogs) is the list price. Used pans sell for less.

2.   Discontinued pans on a theme of current interest tend to command higher prices, especially if there is no current pan on that theme. A renewed interest in firefighting sent the prices for Wilton's older *Little Fire Truck* pan climbing recently, until Wilton reissued that pan. The release of movie sequels or videos may also kindle a renewed interest in pans associated with the earlier movies. The licensed Star Wars™ pans enjoyed a resurgence of popularity after the release of new episodes, for example.

3.   Discontinued pans representing objects many people collect tend to be sought after, driving their prices up. Pans in this category include the Wilton *Frog* pan and *Cuddles the Cow*. While there are probably more people who adore cats than who adore cows or frogs, the cow and frog pans generally go for more money than the cat pans both because there are several cat pans to choose from and also because cat lovers may not see themselves as cat collectors.

4.   The very highest prices for novelty pans often are paid by people who have no interest in them as cake pans. Someone whose kitchen is decorated in a Poppin' Fresh™ motif or someone who has converted a spare room into a Star Wars shrine may consider pans on these themes important to their collections. Such pans may never see cake batter again! Often the paper that accompanies pans, especially colored graphics, is particularly important to these collectors.

5.   Condition and completeness are factors in comparing two of the same pans, but not determining factors in price among different pans. A pristine Santa pan with its insert and instruction booklet will sell for more than a scuffed Santa pan with no paperwork, but it will sell for less than a scuffed and paperless Poppin' Fresh pan.

6.   At this time, age of the pan does not seem to be a significant factor for price. Given a choice between dog-themed pans from the 1970s, 1980s, 1990s, or current, most people choose based on the design of the pan, not when it was made. Pricing reflects demand, and there is no consistently higher demand for older pans.

7.   Licensed-character pans are priced somewhat higher than non-licensed pans when they are issued. They may or may not retain that price premium when they are no longer current. The value is in the specific pan, not whether or not it is a licensed item.

8.   This book provides a very general "ballpark" estimate of the price range for each pan. The price given is for a pan with no major flaws and with its lay-on, if applicable. Paper goods (box, insert, instructions) with the pan often increase the value by $.50 to $2 for pans valued at less than $12, from $1 to $5 for pans valued between $12 and $40, and from $2 to $10 for pans valued at more than $40.

The estimated value shown is an educated guess based on careful observation of the market, but it is ultimately a guess. Pricing for aluminum novelty pans is far from stable or uniform. Neither the author nor the publisher can be responsible for any outcomes that result from consulting this guide.

Part II

The Pans

Chapter 2
Animals: Domestic, Wild, and Imaginary

These similar pans are both by Wilton. The one on the
right was offered in Yearbooks. The plainer version
on the left was not.

Left: *Cutie Cat, 1-2-3* (?)
Wilton Industries, full size
On pan: 2105-9424, 1989, Wilton, Korea
Estimated value: under $12

Right: *Kitty Cat Pan*
Wilton Industries, full size
Yearbooks 1988 through 1997, 2105-x-1009
$7.99 (1988); $8.99 (1989–1990); $9.99 (1991–1997)
On pan: 2105-1009, 1987, Wilton, Korea
Estimated value: under $12

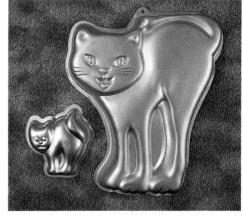

Left: *Cat Singles!*
Wilton Industries, individual serving
Yearbooks 1998 through 2000, 2105-x-1123, 2105-x-1117
(both stock numbers used in 1999 issue)
$1.99 (1998–2000)
Also available in colored non-stick 4-pan set, for $14.99
(cat is black)
On pan: no stamp
Courtesy of Denise Mayoff
Estimated value: under $12

Right: *Scary Cat*
Wilton Industries, full size
Yearbooks 1993 through 1994, 2105-x-5207
$7.99 (1993–1994)
On pan: 2105-5207, 1992, Wilton, Korea
Estimated value: under $12

Kitten
Wilton Industries, full size
Yearbooks 1981 through 1984, 2105-x-2479
$7.50 (1981); $7.95 (1982–1983); $6.95 (1984)
On pan: 502-1972, 1979, Wilton, no country
Estimated value: under $12

Left: *Cat*
Unknown (made in Portugal), full size
No stamp on pan; paper label
"Portugal"
Courtesy of Nila Pudwill
List price: $8

Right: *Sitting Dog with Bow*
Unknown (made in Portugal), full size
No stamp on pan; paper label
"Portugal"
Courtesy of Nila Pudwill
List price: $8

Puppy Dog
Wilton Industries, full size
Yearbooks 1988 through 1996, 2105-x-
2430, also called *Puppy*
$7.99 (1988); $8.99 (1989–1990);
$9.99 (1991–1996)
On pan: 2105-2430, 1986, Wilton,
Korea
Estimated value: under $12

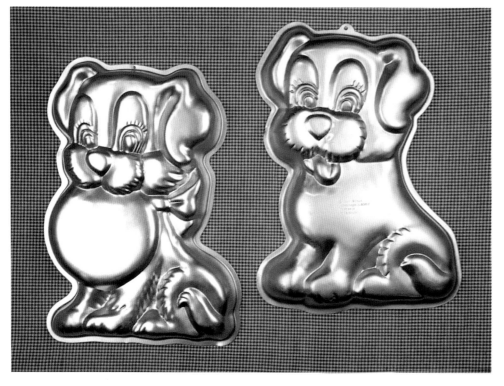

Left: *Playful Puppy*
Wilton Industries, full size
Yearbooks 1979 through 1984, 2105-x-5044
$5.50 (1979); $6.50 (1980); $7.25 (1981); $7.95
(1982–1983); $3.95 (1984, in Super Sale!
Section)
On pan: 502-7636, 1978, Wilton, Korea
Estimated value: under $12

Right: *Precious Puppy, 1-2-3*
Wilton Industries, full size
On pan: 2105-9434, 1991, Wilton, Indonesia
Estimated value: under $12

Left: *Dalmatian Pup*
Wilton Industries, full size
Yearbooks 1994 through 1999,
2105-x-9334, also called *Dalmatian*
$9.99 (1994–1999)
On pan: 2105-9334, 1993, Wilton,
Indonesia
Estimated value: under $12
Right: *Playful Pup*
Wilton Industries, full size
Yearbooks 2003, 2105-x-2064
$9.99 (2003)
On pan: 2105-2064, 2002, Wilton
Industries, Inc., China
List price: $10

Easter Bunny
Amscan, full size
On pan: no stock number, no year, Amscan
Inc., Harrison NY, Korea
Estimated value: under $12

Left: *Easter Bunny*
Wilton Industries, full size
Yearbooks 1981 through 1985, 2105-x-2495
$7.25 (1981); $7.95 (1982–1983); $5.95 (1984,
"Special Value!"); $5.99 (1985)
On pan: 502-1913, 1979, Wilton, Korea
Estimated value: under $12
Right: *Peek-A-Boo Bunny*
Wilton Industries, full size
Yearbooks 1993 through 1998, 2105-x-4395
$7.99 (1993–1998)
On pan: 2105-4395, 1992, Wilton, Indonesia
Courtesy of Nila Pudwill
Estimated value: under $12

Left: *Bunny in a Basket*
Wilton Industries, full size
Yearbook 2000, 2105-x-2037
$8.99 (2000)
On pan: 2105-2037, 1998, Wilton Industries, Inc.,
Indonesia
Estimated value: under $12

Right: *Special Delivery Bunny*
Wilton Industries, full size
Yearbooks 1992 through 1994, 2105-x-9001
$7.99 (1992–1994)
On pan: 2105-9001, 1991, Wilton, Indonesia
Estimated value: under $12

Quick as a Bunny, 1-2-3
Wilton Industries, full size
On pan: 2105-9408, 1989, Wilton, Korea
Courtesy of Nila Pudwill
Estimated value: under $12

Left: *Cottontail Bunny*
Wilton Industries, full size
Yearbooks 1987 through 1994 and 2001
through 2003, 2105-x-2015, 2105-x-175
$7.99 (1987–1994); $8.99 (2001–2003),
"Yearbook Flashback!" in 2001
On pan: 2105-2015, 1986, Wilton, Korea
List price: $9

Right: *Sunny Bunny*
Wilton Industries, full size
Yearbooks 1989 through 1993, 2105-x-2435
$8.99 (1989–1990); $7.99 (1991–1993)
On pan: 2105-2435, 1987, Wilton, Korea
Estimated value: under $12

Bunny Mold for 3-D Cake
Nordic Ware, full size, stand-up, snap-together
Nordic Ware booklet 11-71, c. 1970, stock
number 41200, Two Piece Bunny Mold, formed
aluminum
$2.49 (1971)
On pan: no stamp
Estimated value: under $12

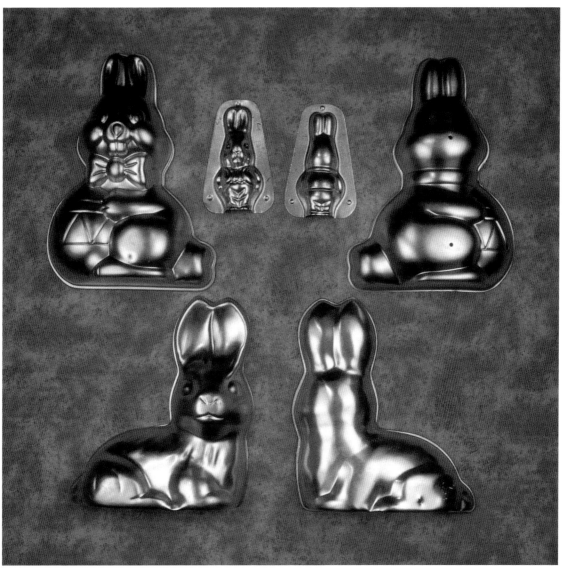

Top Left and Right: *Holiday Bunny*
Wilton Industries, full size, stand-up, snap-together
Yearbooks 1985 through 1988, 2105-x-5885
$9.99 (1985); $10.99 (1986–1988)
On pan: 502-3452, 1984, Wilton, Korea (stamp on front bottom)
Estimated value: under $12

Top Center: *Easter Bunny Mold*
Wilton Industries, individual serving, stand-up, clamp-together
Yearbooks 1974 through 1979, 518-x-284, also called *Bunny Mold* and *Easter
Bunny*, shown with chocolate molds 1974–1976 and with sugar molds 1977–1979
$2.25 (1974–1976); $1.95 (1977); $1.99 (1978); $2.50 (1979)

On pan: 518-284, 1974, Wilton (script), Korea
Estimated value: under $12

Bottom: *Bunny Cake Mold*
Wilton Industries, full size, stand-up, snap-together
Yearbooks 1972 through 1988; 502-x-2227, 2105-x-2223, also called *Bunny Pan*
$3.30 (1972); $4.25 (1974); $4.75 (1975); $5.50 (1976); $5.95 (1977); $7.99
(1978); $8.50 (1979); $9.50 (1980); $10.50 (1981); $9.95 (1982–1984); $9.99
(1985–1988)
On pan: 502-2243, no year, Wilton Enterprises, Inc., Korea
Estimated value: under $12

Left: *Funny Rabbit*
Unknown (made in Portugal), full size
On pan: no stamp, paper label "Portugal"
Courtesy of Nila Pudwill
List price: $8
Right: *Sitting Rabbit*
Unknown (made in Portugal), full size
On pan: no stamp, paper label "Portugal"
List price: $8

Insert for Ring Pan, *Rabbit*
This is a removable bottom for the Basic Ring pan, shown in
Chapter 7, Simple Shapes, page 132.
Wilton Industries, full size
Yearbooks 1977 through 1980, 503-x-466
$2.95 (1977 and 1979); $2.99 (1978); $3.50 (1980); through
1979, any 4 inserts, $9.95; 1980, any 4 inserts, $11.95
On pan: 503-466, 1976, Wilton (script), Korea
Estimated value: under $12

Left: *Bunny Face, 1-2-3*
Wilton Industries, full size
On pan: 2105-9433, 1992, Wilton,
Korea
Estimated value: under $12
Center: *Bunny Singles!*
Wilton Industries, individual serving
Yearbooks 1998 through 2000,
2105-x-1142
$1.99 (1998–2000)
On pan: no stamp
Estimated value: under $12
Right: *Funny Bunny Nonstick*
Wilton Industries, full size
Yearbooks 1999 through 2001,
2105-x-1518, also called *non-stick
Funny Bunny*
$9.99 (1999–2001)
On pan: 2105-1518, 1997, Wilton,
Indonesia
Courtesy of Nila Pudwill
Estimated value: under $12

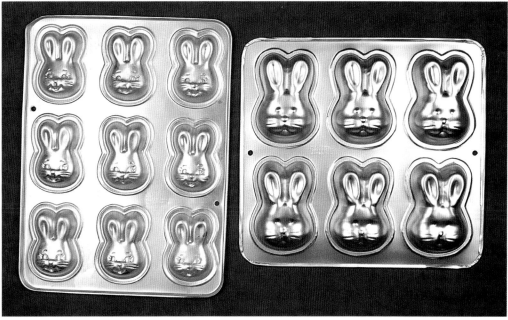

Left: *Bite-Size Bunny*
Wilton Industries, multiple cavity
Yearbooks 1997 through 2000, 2105-x-2120
$8.99 (1997–1998); $9.99 (1999–2000)
On pan: 2105-2120, 1996, Wilton Enterprises,
Indonesia
Estimated value: under $12

Right: *Mini Bunny*
Wilton Industries, multiple cavity
Yearbooks 1993 through 2003, 2105-x-4426,
also called *6 Cavity Mini Bunny,* and *Mini-Bunny*
$7.99 (1993–1995); $8.99 (1996–1998); $9.99
(1999–2003)
On pan: 2105-4426, 1992, Wilton, Indonesia
List price: $10

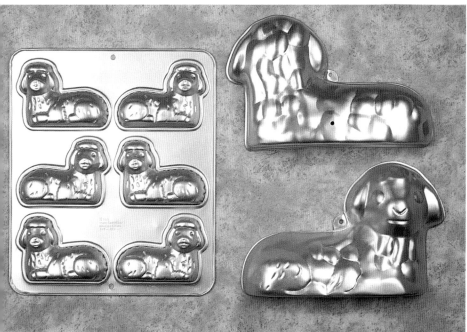

Left: *Mini Lamb*
Wilton Industries, multiple cavity
Yearbooks 1996 through 1997, 2105-x-1275
$9.99 (1996–1997)
On pan: 2105-1275, 1995, Wilton Enterprises,
Indonesia
Estimated value: under $12

Right: *Little Lamb / Stand-Up Lamb*
Wilton Industries, full size, stand-up, snap-
together
Yearbooks 1976 through 2003, 502-x-2014,
2105-x-2010, also called *Lamb*
Beginning 1999, each half has an extension of
the flange with a hole for hanging.
$4.95 (1976–1977); $6.50 (1978); $6.95
(1979); $7.95 (1980); $8.50 (1981): $8.95
(1982–1984); $8.99 (1985–1986); $9.99
(1987–1988); $10.99 (1989–2003)
On pan: 502-2014, 1972, Wilton (script), Korea
List price: $11

Adorable Lamb Pan
Wilton Industries, full size, stand-up, snap-together
Yearbook 1976, 502-x-386
$6.95 (1976)
On pan: 502-386, 1974, Wilton (script), Korea
Estimated value: under $12

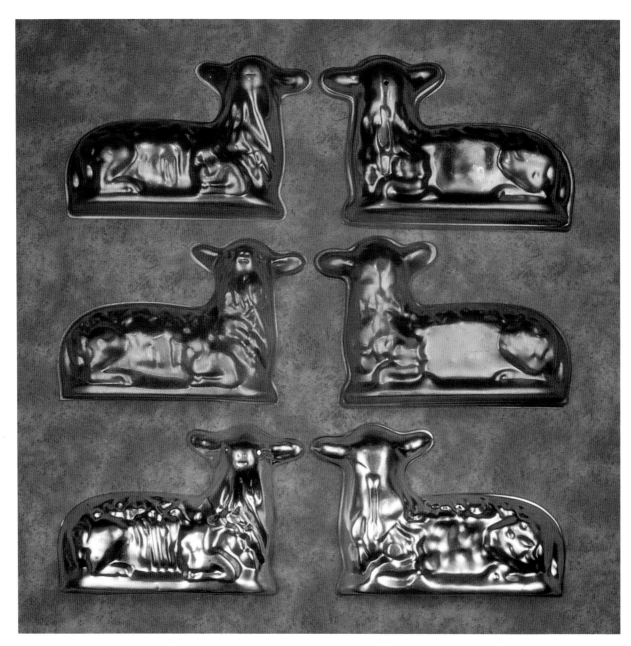

These three molds will make identical cakes. They are all included as an illustration of variations that can occur over the years, especially in a pan design that is not exclusive to one company.

Top: *Lamb Mold for 3-D Cake*
Nordic Ware, full size, stand-up, snap-together
Nordic Ware booklet 11-71, c. 1970, stock number 41300, Two Piece Lamb Mold, formed aluminum
$2.49 (c. 1970)
On pan: no stamp, has steam hole
Estimated value: under $12

Center: *Lamb Mold*
Wilton Industries, full size, stand-up, snap-together
Yearbooks 1959 through 1975, 201, BL-201, 502-x-2014, also called *Lamb Cake Mold* and *Two Piece Lamb Mold,* also in description: "Used in McCall's article on the Easter Lamb Cake"
$1.50 (1959–1966); $2.50 (1969–1972); $3.25 (1974); $3.50 (1975)
On pan: 502-2014, 1972, Wilton (script), Korea, no steam hole
Estimated value: under $12

Bottom: *Lamb Mold*
Unknown, full size, stand-up, snap-together
On pan: no stamp, no steam hole
Estimated value: under $12

Gentle Lamb
Wilton Industries, full size
Yearbooks 1991 through 1993, 2105-x-2515
$7.99 (1991–1993)
On pan: 2105-2515, 1990, Wilton, Korea
Estimated value: under $12

Left: *Gentle Lamb*
Wilton Industries, full size
Yearbook 1983, 2105-x-4269
$7.95 (1983)
On pan: 502-3444, 1981, Wilton, Korea
Estimated value: under $12

Right: *Lovable Lamb*
Wilton Industries, full size
Yearbooks 1988 through 1991;
2105-x-2514
$7.99 (1988 and 1991); $8.99 (1989–1990)
On pan: 2105-2514, 1987, Wilton, Korea
Estimated value: under $12

Left: *Precious Pony*
Wilton Industries, full size
Yearbooks 1987 through 1993, 2105-x-2914
$7.99 (1987–1988); $8.99 (1989–1990); $9.99 (1991–1993)
On pan: 2105-2914, 1986, Wilton, Korea
Estimated value: under $12

Right: Insert for Ring Pan, *Horse*
This is a removable bottom for the Basic Ring pan, shown in *Chapter 7, Simple Shapes*, page 132.
Wilton Industries, full size
Yearbooks 1976 through 1980, 503-x-288, 2105-x-2886, also called *The Champion*
$2.95 (1977 and 1979); $2.99 (1978); $3.50 (1980); through 1979, any 4 inserts, $9.95; 1980, any 4 inserts, $11.95
On pan: 503-288, 1974, Wilton (script), Korea
Estimated value: under $12

Cuddles the Cow
Wilton Industries, full size
Yearbooks 1989 through 1991, 2105-x-2875
$8.99 (1989–1990); $9.99 (1991)
On pan: 2105-2875, 1988, Wilton, Korea
Estimated value: $26 to $40

Left: Rocking Horse
Wilton Industries, full size
Yearbooks 1986 through 2003, 2105-x-2388
$8.49 (1986); $7.99 (1987–1988);
$8.99 (1989–1990); $9.99 (1991–2003)
On pan: 2105-2388, 1984, Wilton, Korea
List price: $10

Right: Carousel Horse
Wilton Industries, full size
Yearbooks 1992 through 2000, 2105-x-6507
$9.99 (1992–2000)
On pan: 2105-6507, 1990, Wilton, Korea
Estimated value: under $12

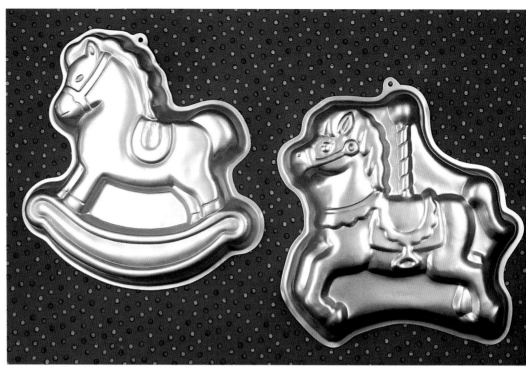

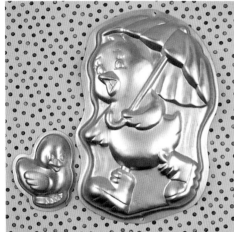

Left: Chick Singles!
Wilton Industries, individual serving
Yearbooks 1998 through 2000, 2105-x-1143
$1.99 (1998–2000)
On pan: no stamp
Estimated value: under $12

Right: Cheerful Chick
Wilton Industries, full size
Yearbook 2000, 2105-x-2106
$8.99 (2000)
On pan: 2105-2036, 1998, Wilton Industries, Inc., Indonesia
Estimated value: under $12

Left: Chick-In-Egg
Wilton Industries, full size
Yearbooks 1986 through 1988, 2105-x-2356
$6.49 (1986); $7.99 (1987–1988)
On pan: 2105-2356, 1985, Wilton, Korea
Estimated value: under $12

Right: Just Hatched Chick
Wilton Industries, full size
Yearbook 2003, 2105-x-2060
$8.99 (2003)
On pan: 2105-2060, 2002, Wilton Industries, Inc., China
List price: $9

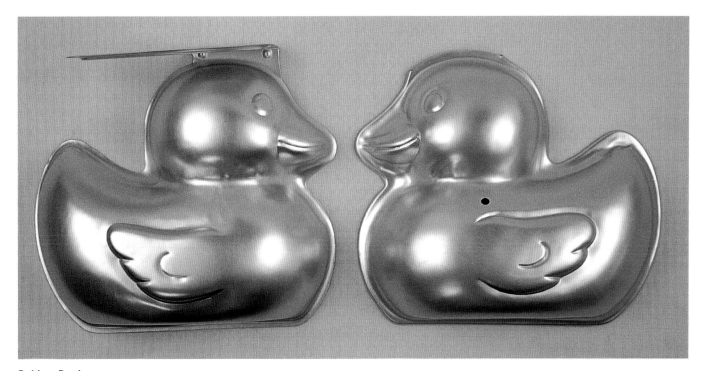

Rubber Ducky
Wilton Industries, full size, stand-up, snap-together
Yearbook 2003, 2105-x-2094, in description *3-D Rubber Ducky Pan,* in index
Rubber Ducky, 3-D
$12.99 (2003)
On pan: 2105-2094, 2002, Wilton Industries, Inc., China
List price: $13

Little Ducky
Wilton Industries, full size
Yearbooks 1990 through 1992, 2105-x-2029
$8.99 (1990); $7.99 (1991–1992)
On pan: 2105-2029, 1989, Wilton, Korea
Estimated value: under $12

Left: *Proud Rooster*
Wilton Industries, small
Yearbooks 1972 through 1976,
516-x-3403
$1.60 (1972); $2.25 (1974–1976)
On pan: 516-3403, 1972, Wilton
(script), Korea
Estimated value: under $12
Right: *Hen or Rooster Mold*
Mirro, small
On pan: no stock number, no year,
no company, no country, "3 1/2
cups"
Estimated value: under $12

Bird 'N Banner
Wilton Industries, full size
Yearbook 1989, 2105-x-2505
$8.99 (1989)
On pan: 502-2505, 1987, Wilton, Korea
Estimated value: $12 to $25

Goose/Country Goose
Wilton Industries, full size
Yearbooks 1989 through 1991, 2105-x-2499, described as *Goose*, listed
in index as *Country Goose*
$8.99 (1989–1990); $9.99 (1991)
On pan: 2105-2499, 1988, Wilton, Korea
Estimated value: under $12

Left: *Lovebirds*
Wilton Industries, small, stand-up, clamp-together
Yearbooks 1972 through 1976, 516-x-3500
$3.95 (1972); $4.25 (1974); $5.25 (1975–1976)
On pan: no stamp
Estimated value: $26 to $40
Right: *Little Boy Chick*
Wilton Industries, individual serving, stand-up, clamp-together

This is primarily a chocolate mold. Although Wilton has its usual stamp on this
pan, it was apparently not a Wilton exclusive.
Yearbooks 1974 through 1976, 518-x-306, also called *Boy Chick*
$2.25 (1974); $2.50 (1975–1976)
On pan: 518-306, 1974, Wilton (script), Korea
On pan: 16234, no year, F.Cluydts, Antwerp
Estimated value: under $12

Left: *Graduate Owl*
Amscan, full size
On pan: no stock number, no year, Amscan Inc.,
Harrison NY, Korea
Estimated value: $12 to $25

Right: *Mister Owl*
Wilton Industries, full size
Yearbooks 1979 through 1981, and 1984,
2105-x-5036
$5.50 (1979); $6.50 (1980); $7.50 (1981); $3.95
(1984, in Super Sale! section)
On pan: 502-7644, 1978, Wilton, Korea
Estimated value: $12 to $25

Stork
Amscan, full size
On pan: no stock number, no year,
Amscan Inc., Harrison NY, Korea
Courtesy of Nila Pudwill
Estimated value: under $12

Good News Stork
Wilton Industries, full size
Yearbooks 1984 through 1986,
2105-x-4587
$7.95 (1984); $7.99 (1985); $8.49
(1986)
On pan: 502-385, 1983, Wilton,
Korea
Estimated value: under $12

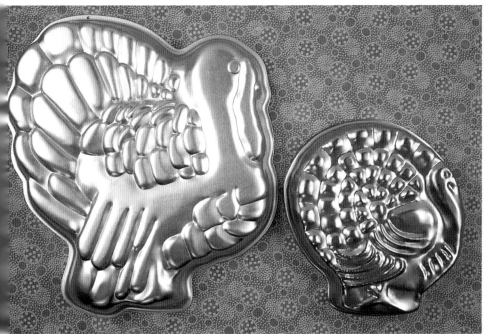

Left: *Turkey*
Wilton Industries, full size
Yearbooks 1980 through 1985, 2105-x-3114
$6.50 (1980); $7.25 (1981); $7.95 (1982–1983);
$5.95 (1984); $5.99 (1985, "special value")
On pan: 502-2634, 1979, Wilton, Korea
Estimated value: $12 to $25

Right: *Coppertone Turkey Mold*
Unknown, small
On pan: no stamp
Estimated value: under $12

Left: *Butterfly*
Unknown (made in Portugal), full size
On pan: no stamp, paper label "Portugal"
Courtesy of Nila Pudwill
List price: $8
Center: *Butterfly*
Unknown (made in Portugal), individual serving

List price: $3
Right: *Butterfly*
Unknown, small
On pan: no stamp
Shown in the 1961 *The Good Housekeeping Book of Cake Decorating*
Estimated value: under $12

Left: *Butterfly*
Wilton Industries, full size
Yearbooks 1989 through 1990, 2105-x-5409
$8.99 (1989–1990)
On pan: 502-5409, 1987, Wilton, Korea
Estimated value: $12 to $25
Center: *Butterfly Molds*
Wilton Industries, individual serving
Yearbooks 1969 through 1970, MO-2862
$1.25 (1969–1970, for package of 4, four sets #3.98)

On pan: no stamp
Courtesy of Nila Pudwill
Estimated value: $12 to $25
Right: *Butterfly Fancifill*
Wilton Industries, full size
Yearbooks 1980 through 1983, 2105-x-1219 also called *Fancifill Butterfly*
$6.50 (1980); $7.25 (1981); $7.95 (1982–1983)
On pan: 502-1158, 1979, Wilton, Korea
Courtesy of Nila Pudwill
Estimated value: $12 to $25

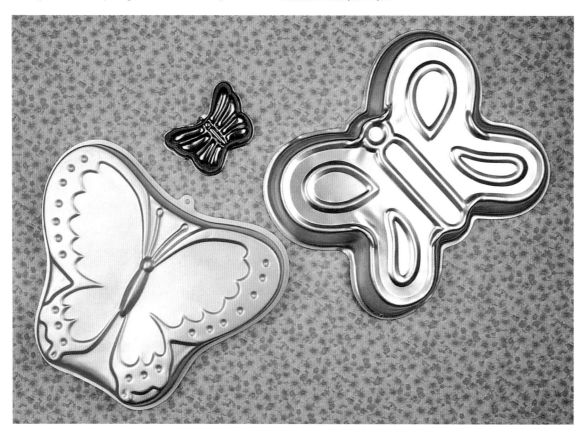

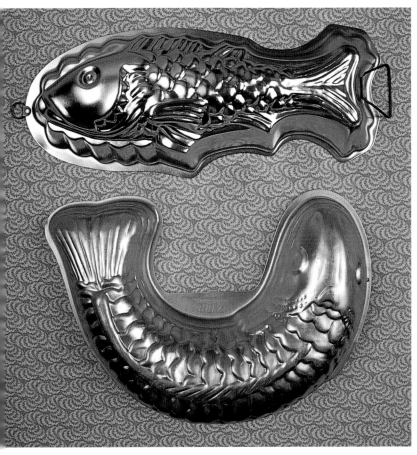

Top: *Fish*
Unknown, small
On pan: no stamp
Estimated value: under $12
Bottom: *Curved Fish*
Mirro, full size
On pan: 725M, no year, Mirro, USA
Estimated value: under $12

Lobster
Unknown, small
On pan: no stock number, no year, no
company, no country, "3 1/2 cups"
Courtesy of Nila Pudwill
Estimated value: under $12

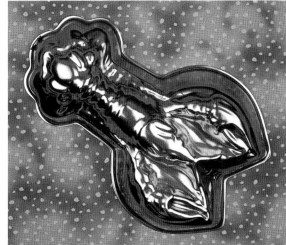

Top: *Coppertone Fish Mold*
Nordic Ware, full size, also sold by Wilton
Yearbooks 1964 through 1971, NA-244, 244
Nordic Ware booklet 11-71, c. 1970, stock number
30101, *Fish Mold, Copper anodized*
$1.98 (1964–1969, Wilton)
$2.49 (c. 1970, Nordic Ware)
On pan: no stamp
Estimated value: under $12
Bottom: *Fish*
Wilton Industries, small
Yearbooks 1964 through 1966, 313
$1.00 (1964–1966)
On pan: no stock number, no year, no company
name, Hong Kong
Estimated value: under $12

Left: *Flying Fish*
Wilton Industries, small
Yearbooks 1972 through 1976, 516-x-3209
On pan: 516-3203, 1972, Wilton (script), Korea
Estimated value: under $12

Right: *Big Fish*
Wilton Industries, full size
Yearbooks 1986 through 1988, 2105-x-2763
$8.49 (1986); $7.99 (1987–1988)
On pan: 2105-2763, 1984, Wilton, Korea
Estimated value: $12 to $25

Little Mouse
Wilton Industries, full size
Yearbooks 1988 through 1995, 2105-x-2380
$7.99 (1988); $8.99 (1989–1991); $9.99 (1992–1995)
On pan: 2105-2380, 1987, Wilton, Korea
Estimated value: under $12

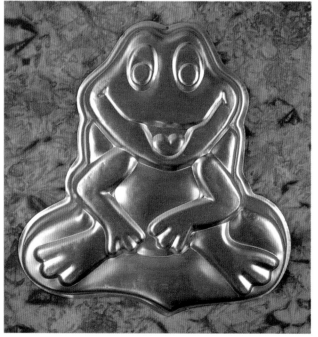

Frog
Wilton Industries, full size
Yearbooks 1981 through 1985, 2105-x-2452
$7.50 (1981); $7.95 (1982–1983); $6.95 (1984, "Special Value");
$6.99 (1985)
On pan: 502-1816, 1979, Wilton, Korea
Estimated value: $26 to $40

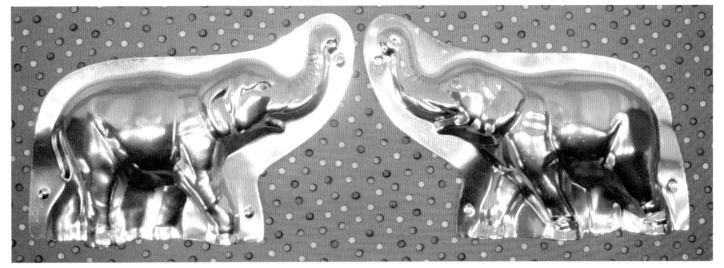

Elephant Chocolate Mold
Wilton Industries, small, stand-up,
clamp-together
Yearbooks 1972 through 1976, 516-x-
3100, also called *Trumpeting Elephant*
$3.95 (1972); $4.40 (1974–1976)
On pan: 516-3100, 1972, Wilton
(script), Korea
Courtesy of Jean Penn
Estimated value: over $40

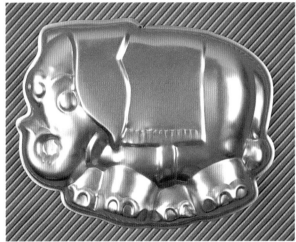

Happy Hippo
Wilton Industries, full size
Yearbooks 1976 through 1978,
502-x-712, 2105-x-743, also
called *Hippo*
$4.95 (1976–1977); $4.99 (1978)
On pan: 502-712, 1974, Wilton
(script), Korea
Estimated value: $12 to $25

Elephant
Wilton Industries, full size
Yearbooks 1976 through 1978, 502-x-720, 2105-x-743, also
called *Jolly Elephant*
$4.95 (1976–1977); $4.99 (1978)
On pan: 502-720, 1974, Wilton (script), Korea
Estimated value: $12 to $25

Lovable Animal
Wilton Industries, full size, stand-up, snap-together
Yearbooks 1975 through 1980, 502-x-135, also called *Stand-up Tiger*
$6.95 (1975); $7.25 (1976); $7.50 (1977 and 1979); $6.99 (1978); $8.50 (1980)
On pan: 502-135, 1974, Wilton (script), Korea
Estimated value: under $12

Left: *Mini Jungle Animals*
Wilton Industries, multiple cavity
Yearbooks 1996 through 1998, 2105-x-2096
$10.99 (1996–1998)
On pan: 2105-2096, 1995, Wilton Enterprises, Indonesia
Estimated value: under $12

Right: *Jungle Lion*
Wilton Industries, full size
Yearbooks 1995 through 1998, 2105-x-2095
$9.99 (1995–1998)
On pan: 2105-2095, 1994, Wilton Enterprises, Korea
Estimated value: under $12

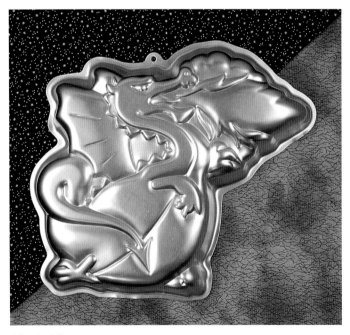

Mystical Dragon
Wilton Industries, full size
Yearbooks 1985 through 1986, 2105-x-1750,
2105-x-1720
$7.99 (1985); $8.49 (1986)
On pan: 2105-1750, 1984, Wilton, Korea
Estimated value: $26 to $40

Left: *Megasaurus*
Wilton Industries, full size
Yearbooks 2000 through 2003, 2105-x-2028
$9.99 (2000–2003)
On pan: 2105-2028, 1999, Wilton Industries, Inc., Korea
List price: $10

Right: *Partysaurus*
Wilton Industries, full size
Yearbooks 1988 through 2003, 2105-x-1280
$7.99 (1988); $8.99 (1989–1990); $9.99 (1991–2003)
On pan: 2105-1280, 1987, Wilton, Korea
List price: $10

Left: *Small Animal Molds:* **Squirrel, Duck, Pony, Rabbit**
Unknown, individual serving
On pan: no stamp
Estimated value: under $12
Center: *Noah's Ark*
Wilton Industries, full size
Yearbooks 2000 through 2003, 2105-x-2026
$9.99 (2000–2003)

On pan: 2105-2026, 1999, Wilton Industries, Inc., China
List price: $10
Right: *Ani-Mold Set*
Wilton Industries, individual serving
Yearbook 1964, 306, probably not a Wilton exclusive
$1.98 (1964, includes hangers and screws)
On pan: no stock number, no year, no company name, Japan
Estimated value: $12 to $25

Left: *Dinosaur, 1-2-3*
Wilton Industries, full size
On pan: 2105-9475, 1992, Wilton, Korea
Estimated value: under $12
Center: *Mini Dinosaur*
Wilton Industries, multiple cavity
Yearbooks 1994 through 1997, 2105-x-9331

$9.99 (1994–1995); $10.99 (1996–1997)
On pan: 2105-9331, 1993, Wilton, Indonesia
Estimated value: under $12
Right: *Friendly (?) Dinosaur, 1-2-3*
Wilton Industries, full size
On pan: 2105-9409, 1988, Wilton Enterprises, Korea
Estimated value: under $12

Ballerina Bear
Wilton Industries, full size
Yearbooks 1993 through 1997, 2105-x-2021
$9.99 (1993–1997)
On pan: 2105-2021, 1992, Wilton, Korea
Estimated value: under $12

Left: *Teddy (Mini Toy Cakes)*
Wilton Industries, small
Yearbooks 1976 through 1980, 508-x-477,
also called *Teddy Bear (minicakes)*
$6.25 (1976, price is for any 4 Mini Toy pans;
not sold individually); $1.95 (1977, $6.95 for
any 4 Mini Toy pans); $1.99 (1978, $6.99 for
any 4 minicakes); $2.30 (1979, $8.10 for any
4 minicakes); $2.95 (1980, $9.95 for any 4
minicakes)
On pan: 508-477, 1975, Wilton, Korea
Estimated value: under $12

Right: *Cuddly Bear*
Wilton Industries, full size
Yearbooks 1978 through 1982, and 1984,
502-x-7539, 2105-x-298
$5.50 (1978–1979); $6.50 (1980); $7.25 (1981);
$7.95 (1982); $3.95 (1984, in Super Sale!
section)
On pan: 502-7458, 1977, Wilton (script), Korea
Estimated value: under $12

Top Left: *Paw Print Singles!*
Wilton Industries, individual serving
Yearbooks 1998 through 1999, 2105-x-1118
$1.99 (1998–1999)
On pan: no stamp
Estimated value: under $12

Top Center: *Teddy Bear with Block*
Wilton Industries, full size
Yearbooks 1996 through 2003, 2105-x-8257
$9.99 (1996–2003)
On pan: 2105-8257, 1995, Wilton Enterprises,
Indonesia
List price: $10

Top Right: *Teddy Bear Singles!*
Wilton Industries, individual serving
Yearbooks 1998 through 2003, 2105-x-1109
$1.69 (1998); $1.99 (1999–2000); $2.49 (2001–
2003)
On pan: no stamp
List price: $2.50

Bottom Left: *Teddy Bear, 1-2-3*
Wilton Industries, full size
On pan: 2105-9402, 1986, Wilton, Korea
Estimated value: under $12

Bottom Right: *Huggable Teddy Bear*
Wilton Industries, full size
Yearbooks 1983 through 2003, 2105-x-4943
$7.95 (1983–1984); $7.99 (1985); $8.49 (1986);
$7.99 (1987–1988); $8.99 (1989–1990); $9.99
(1991–2003)
On pan: 502-3754, 1982, Wilton, China, stock
number on insert 2105-4943
List price: $10

Left: *Santa Bear Pan*
Wilton Industries, full size
Yearbooks 1992 through 1994, 2105-x-4432
$7.99 (1992–1994)
On pan: 2105-4432, 1991, Wilton, Indonesia
Estimated value: under $12

Right: *Bear-y Christmas*
Wilton Industries, full size
Yearbooks 1999 through 2000, 2105-x-3314
$8.99 (1999–2000)
On pan: 2105-3314, 1998, Wilton, Indonesia
Estimated value: under $12

Left: *Panda/Mini Stand-Up Bear*
Wilton Industries, small, stand-up, clamp-together
Yearbooks 1974 through 1986, and 1989 through 2003, 518-x-489, 2105-x-489
$2.50 (1974, 1975, 1977, "A Wilton Original" 1974); $2.65 (1976); $2.99 (1978); $3.50 (1979); $4.25 (1980–1981); $4.95 (1982–1984); $4.99 (1985-1993); $5.99 (1994–1997); $10.99 (1998–2003)
On pan: 518-489, no year, Wilton, China, stamped on back half
List price: $11

Top: *Teddy Bear StandUp*
Wilton Industries, full size, stand-up, clamp-together
Yearbooks 1987 through 1993, 2105-x-2325
$14.99 (1987–1988); $15.99 (1989–1992, additional baking core, $3.59); $16.99 (1993, baking core $4.49)
On pan: 2105-2325, 1986, Wilton, Korea
Estimated value: under $12

Bottom: *3-D Cuddly Bear / Panda*
Wilton Industries, full size, stand-up, clamp-together
Yearbooks 1974 through 2003, 502-x-501, 2105-x-603, described as "10 PC Pan Set," "2 PC Pan Set" and simply "Pan" or "Set" as Wilton fluctuated on how to count the heating core and the spring clips
$6.50 (1974); $7.50 (1975); $7.95 (1976–1977); $8.50 (1978); $9.50 (1979); $9.95 (1980); $10.95 (1981–1982); $11.95 (1983–1984); $12.99 (1985–1986); $14.99 (1987–1988); $15.99 (1989–1992); $16.99 (1993–1997); $17.99 (1998); $19.99 (1999–2003)
An additional baking core was also available for $3.59 (1987–1992) or $4.49 (1993–1996), with a note in the 1994 issue stating that the additional core is smaller than the one that comes with the pan. The core has not been sold separately since 1996.
On pan: 502-501, no year, Wilton, Korea, stamp on front half
List price: $20

Not Pictured

Little Dog
Wilton Industries, individual serving (chocolate mold)
Yearbooks 1974 through 1975, 518-x-349
$2.25 (1974–1975)
Estimated value: Unknown

Little Girl Chick
Wilton Industries, individual serving (chocolate mold)
Yearbooks 1974 through 1976, 518-x-322, also called *Girl Chick*
$2.25 (1974); $2.50 (1975–1976)
Estimated value: Unknown

Little Lamb
Wilton Industries, full size, or somewhat smaller (chocolate mold)
The lamb shape is very similar to the snap-together lamb pan sold by Wilton and Nordic Ware for cakes, but it has a wide flat flange and is a clip-together mold sold for molding chocolate. It has no stand for holding it upright in an oven.
Yearbooks 1972 through 1976; 516-x-3004
$3.95 (1972); $4.50 (1974); $5.50 (1975–1976)
Estimated value: $12 to $25

Merry Monkey
Wilton Industries, individual serving (chocolate mold)
Yearbooks 1974 through 1976, 518-x-446
$2.50 (1974–1976)
Estimated value: Unknown

Tom Turkey
Amscan, full size
Estimated value: $12 to $25

Left: *Petite Huggable Bear*
Wilton Industries, multiple cavity
Yearbooks 1995 through 1998, 2105-x-3655
$7.99 (1995); $8.99 (1996–1998)
On pan: 2105-3655, 1994, Wilton, Indonesia,
Estimated value: under $12

Right: *Mini Bear*
Wilton Industries, multiple cavity
Yearbooks 1992 through 2003, 2105-x-4497
$9.99 (1992–1995); $10.99 (1996–2003, "New" 2003)
On pan: 2105-4497, 1991, Wilton, Indonesia
List price: $11

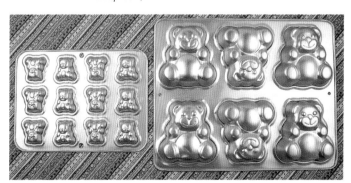

Chapter 3

People: Guys, Gals, and Dolls; Where They Live and How They Get Around

These pans with quite different finishes were both made in Korea for Wilton and sold over the same time period.

Left: *Pretty Lady*
Wilton Industries, full size
Yearbooks 1993 through 1996, 2105-x-2022
$9.99 (1993–1996)
On pan: 2105-2022, 1992, Wilton, Korea
Estimated value: under $12

Right: *Handsome Guy*
Wilton Industries, full size
Yearbooks 1993 through 1996, 2105-x-2023
$9.99 (1993–1996)
On pan: 2105-2023, 1992, Wilton, Korea
Estimated value: $12 to $25

Cute Baby
Wilton Industries, full size
Yearbooks 1995 through 1997, 2105-x-8461
$9.99 (1995–1997)
On pan: 2105-8461, 1994, Wilton, Korea
Courtesy of Nila Pudwill
Estimated value: under $12

Li'l Cowboy
Wilton Industries, full size
Yearbooks 1982 through 1984, 2105-x-4757
$7.95 (1982–1983); $6.95 (1984, "Special Value")
On pan: 502-3363, 1981, Wilton, Korea
Estimated value: $12 to $25

Merry Mermaid
Wilton Industries, full size
Yearbooks 1994 through 1996, 2105-x-6710
$9.99 (1994–1996)
On pan: 2105-6710, 1993, Wilton, Indonesia
Estimated value: under $12

Lil' Pirate
Wilton Industries, full size
Yearbooks 1994 through 1996, 2105-x-9333
$9.99 (1994–1996)
On pan: 2105-9333, 1993, Wilton, Indonesia
Estimated value: over $40

Spaceman
Wilton Industries, full size
Yearbooks 1979 through 1982, and 1984, 2105-x-255
$6.50 (1979–1980); $7.25 (1981); $7.95 (1982); $3.95
(1984, in Super Sale! section)
On pan: 502-2098, 1987, Wilton, Korea
Estimated value: $12 to $25

Troll
Wilton Industries, full size
Yearbooks 1994 through 1996, 2105-x-6712
$9.99 (1994–1996)
On pan: 2105-6712, 1992, Wilton, Korea
Estimated value: under $12

Toy Soldier
Wilton Industries, full size
Yearbooks 1981 through 1984, 2105-x-2037
$7.25 (1981); $7.95 (1982–1983); $3.95 (1984, in
Super Sale! section)
On pan: 502-5161, 1979, Wilton, Korea
Estimated value: under $12

Left: *Storybook Doll*
Wilton Industries, full size
Yearbooks 1969 through 1984, W-96, 502-x-968,
2105-x-964, also called *Rag Doll*, *Raggedy Doll*
$3.98 (1969, two for $7.15); $4.50 (1970–1971,
1973 and 1975, 1970 only, two for $8.10); $3.95
(1972); $4.25 (1974); $4.95 (1976–1977); $5.50
(1978); $5.95 (1979); $6.95 (1980); $7.75 (1981);
$7.95 (1982–1983); $6.95 (1984, "Special Value")
On pan: 502-968, 1971, Wilton (script), Korea
Estimated value: under $12
Right: *Rag Doll (Mini Toy Cakes)*
Wilton Industries, small
Yearbooks 1976 through 1980, 508-x-450, also
called *Rag Doll (minicake)*
$6.25 (1976, price is for any 4 Mini Toy pans; not
sold individually); $1.95 (1977, $6.95 for any 4
Mini Toy pans); $1.99 (1978, $6.99 for any 4
minicakes); $2.30 (1979, $8.10 for any 4
minicakes); $2.95 (1980, $9.95 for any 4
minicakes)
On pan: 508-450, 1975, Wilton (script), Korea
Estimated value: under $12

Rag Doll
Wilton Industries, full size, stand-up, clamp-together
Yearbooks 1974 through 1976, 502-x-208
$7.95 (1974); $8.25 (1975); $8.50 (1976, "2 piece")
On pan: 502-208, 1973, Wilton (script), Korea
Estimated value: under $12

Wizard
Wilton Industries, full size
Yearbooks 1985 through 1986, 2105-x-2633
$7.99 (1985); $8.49 (1986)
On pan: 502-2235, 1984, Wilton, Korea
Estimated value: $26 to $40

Storybook Doll
Wilton Industries, full size
Yearbooks 2002 through 2003, 2105-x-2048
$9.99 (2002–2003)
On pan: 2105-2048, 2001, Wilton Industries, Inc.,
Indonesia
List price: $10

Little Dolly
Wilton Industries, full size
On pan: 2105-9404, no year, Wilton, Korea
Estimated value: under $12

Left: *Darling Dolly, 1-2-3*
Wilton Industries, full size
On pan: 2105-9436, 1991, Wilton, Indonesia
Estimated value: under $12
Right: *Baby Doll*
Wilton Industries, full size
Yearbooks 2001 through 2003, 2105-x-573
$9.99 (2001–2003)
On pan: 2105-573, 2000, Wilton Industries, Inc., China
List price: $10

Left: *Happy Clown*
Wilton Industries, full size
Yearbooks 1990 through 1996,
2105-x-802
On pan: 2105-802, 1989, Wilton,
Korea
Estimated value: under $12
Center: *Jolly Clown*
Wilton Industries, full size
Yearbooks 1975 through 1981,
502-x-275, 2105-x-27544, also
called *Circus Clown*, *Clown*, *Funny
Clown*
$4.50 (1975); $4.95 (1976–1977);
$5.50 (1978–1979); $6.50 (1980);
$7.25 (1981)
On pan: 502-275, 1974, Wilton
(script), Korea
Estimated value: under $12
Right: *Circus Clown, 1-2-3*
Wilton Industries, full size
On pan: 2105-9474, 1992, Wilton,
Korea
Estimated value: under $12

Left: *Clown*
Unknown (made in Portugal), full size
On pan: no stamp, paper label "Portugal"
Courtesy of Nila Pudwill
List price: $8
Right: *Clown*
Unknown (made in Portugal), small
On pan: no stamp, paper label "Portugal"
Courtesy of Nila Pudwill
List price: $8

Mini Clown
Wilton Industries, multiple cavity
Yearbooks 1985 through 1986, 2105-x-5621
$6.99 (1985); $7.49 (1986)
On pan: 2105-5621, 1984, Wilton, Korea
Estimated value: under $12

Left: *Circus Clown*
Wilton Industries, full size
Yearbooks 1983 through 1989,
2105-x-3823
$7.95 (1983–1984); $7.99
(1985–1988); $8.99 (1989)
On pan: 502-3193, 1981,
Wilton, Korea
Estimated value: under $12
Right: *Clancy The Clown*
Amscan, full size
On pan: no stock number, no
year, Amscan Inc., Harrison NY,
Korea
Estimated value: under $12

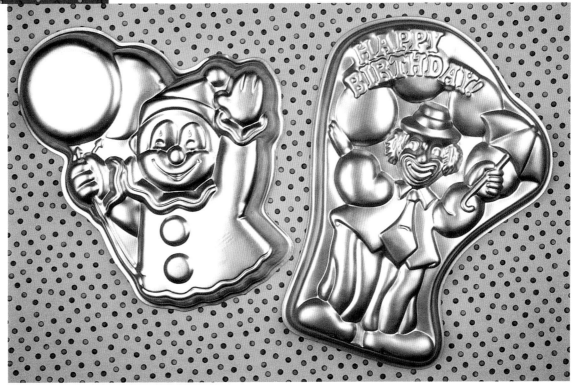

Left: *Cute Clown*
Wilton Industries, full size
Yearbooks 1994 through 2000, 2105-x-6711
$9.99 (1994–2000)
On pan: 2105-6711, 1993, Wilton, Indonesia
Estimated value: under $12
Center: *Juggling Clown*
Wilton Industries, full size

Yearbooks 2001 through 2003, 2105-x-572
$9.99 (2001–2003)
On pan: 2105-572, 2000, Wilton Industries, Inc., China
List price: $10
Right: *Circus Clown, 1-2-3*
Wilton Industries, full size
On pan: 2105-9401, 1986, Wilton, Korea
Estimated value: under $12

Left: *Gingerbread Boy*
Wilton Industries, full size
Yearbooks 1999 through 2002, 2105-x-3313
$8.99 (1999–2002)
On pan: 2105-3313, 1998, Wilton, Indonesia
Estimated value: under $12
Right: *Gingerbread Boy*
Wilton Industries, full size
Yearbooks 1986 through 1995, 2105-x-2072
$6.49 (1986); $7.99 (1987–1988); $8.99
(1989–1990); $7.99 (1991–1995)
On pan: 2105-2072, 1985, Wilton, Korea
Courtesy of Denise Mayoff
Estimated value: under $12

The slightly heavier pan with detailed contours has held up
better over the years than the very lightweight plain pan.
Left: *Gingerbread Man*
Wilton Industries, small
Yearbooks 1959 through 1970, HM-39, also called
Ginger Bread Man
$0.69 (1959–1966); $1.00 (1969); $1.25 (1970)
On pan: no stamp
Estimated value: under $12
Right: *Gingerbread Boy on Round*
Metalite (Canada), small
On pan: no stamp
Estimated value: under $12

Ginger Bread Mold
Nordic Ware, full size
Nordic Ware booklet 11-71, c. 1970,
stock number 31401, Ginger Bread
Mold, Copper anodized
$2.49 (c. 1970)
On pan: no stamp,
Courtesy of Nila Pudwill
Estimated value: under $12

Gingerbread Pair
Unknown, full size (together)
On pan: no stamp
Estimated value: under $12

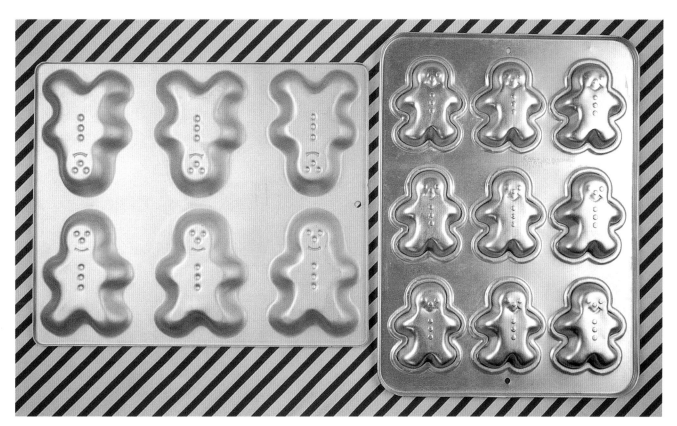

Left: *Mini Gingerbread Boy*
Wilton Industries, multiple cavity
Yearbooks 1991 through 2003, 2105-x-6503
$7.99 (1991–1995); $8.99 (1996–1999); $9.99 (2000–2003)
On pan: 2105-6503, 1990, Wilton, Korea
List price: $10

Right: *Bite-Size Gingerbread Boy*
Wilton Industries, multiple cavity
Yearbooks 1996 through 2003, 2105-x-926, 2105-x-0926
$8.99 (1996–1998); $9.99 (1999–2003)
On pan: 2105-926, 1995, Wilton Enterprises, Indonesia
List price: $10

T-Shirt
Wilton Industries, full size
Yearbooks 1980 through 1985, 1987 through 1988, 1994, and 2000
through 2003, 2105-x-2347
$6.50 (1980); $7.25 (1981); $7.95 (1982–1983); $6.95 (1984, "Special
Value!"); $6.99 (1985); $7.99 (1987–1988); $8.99 (1989–1990); $9.99
(1991–1994, 2000–2003, 2000, "Yearbook Flashback!")
On pan: 502-5617, 1979, Wilton, Korea
List price: $10

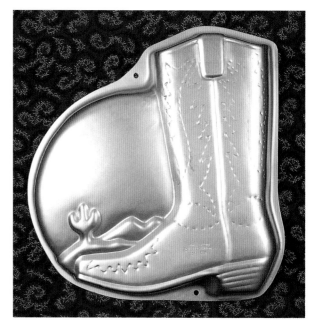

Western Boot
Wilton Industries, full size
Yearbooks 1996 through 1999, 2105-x-1238
$9.99 (1996–1999)
On pan: 2105-1238, 1995, Wilton, Indonesia
Estimated value: under $12

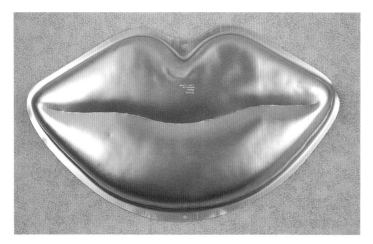

Hot Lips
Wilton Industries, full size
Yearbooks 1999 through 2001, 2105-x-2035
$9.99 (1999–2001)
On pan: 2105-2035, 1998, Wilton, Indonesia
Estimated value: under $12

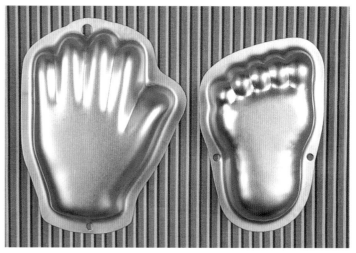

Left: Hand Singles!
Wilton Industries, individual serving
Yearbooks 1998 through 2000, 2105-x-1115
$1.99 (1998–2000)
On pan: no stamp
Estimated value: under $12
Right: Foot Singles!
Wilton Industries, individual serving
Yearbooks 1998 through 2000, 2105-x-1116
$1.99 (1998–2000)
On pan: no stamp
Estimated value: under $12

T-Nee-Bikini
Fancy Foods by Flo, full size
On pan: Patent D-221,577, 1971, Fancy Foods by Flo, USA
Estimated value: under $12

Enchanted Castle
Wilton Industries, full size
Yearbooks 1999 through 2003, 2105-x-2031
$9.99 (1999–2003)
On pan: 2105-2031, 1998, Wilton, China
List price: $10

Holiday House/Stand-Up House
Wilton Industries, full size, stand-up, open mold
Yearbooks 1983 through 1995 and 1998 through 2003; 2105-x-3311, 105-x-2282, 2105-x-2070 originally included icing colors, decorating tips, coupler, and bag; was called a "kit" through 1995
$7.95 (1983–1984); $7.99 (1985); $8.49 (1986); $8.99 (1987–1989); $9.99 (1990–1992); $11.95 (1993–1995); $9.99 (1998–2002); $12.99 (2003, "New!" [only packaging and name are new])
On pan: 502-3937, 1982, Wilton, Korea
On pan: 2105-2070, 2002, Wilton Industries, Inc., China
List price: $13

Left: *Classic House Pan*
Wilton Industries, full size
Yearbooks 1984 through 1985,
2105-x-5370
$7.95 (1984); $7.99 (1985)
On pan: 502-2464, 1983,
Wilton, Korea
Estimated value: under $12

Right: *Haunted House*
Wilton Industries, full size
Yearbooks 2001 through 2003,
2105-x-181
$8.99 (2001–2003)
On pan: 2105-181, 2000,
Wilton Industries, Inc., China
Courtesy of Nila Pudwill
List price: $9

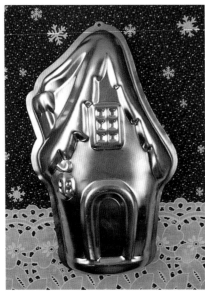

Gingerbread House
Unknown (made in Portugal), full size
On pan: no stamp, paper label "Portugal"
Courtesy of Nila Pudwill
List price: $8

The little houses shown below are each in four pieces that fit together without clamps. The box has twelve ideas for decorating the cake, month-by-month.

Left: *House*
Alumode, small, stand-up, open mold
On pan: no stock number, no year, no company name, PAT. PEND, box "Alumode, made in U. S. A."
Estimated value: under $12

Right: *Small house or barn*
Unknown, small, stand-up, open mold
On pan: no stock number, no year, no company name, PAT. PEND
Estimated value: under $12

Top: *Sports Car*
Wilton Industries, full size
Yearbooks 1981 through 1985,
2105-x-2428
$7.50 (1981); $7.95 (1982–1984);
$7.99 (1985)
On pan: 502-1948, 1979, Wilton,
Korea
Estimated value: under $12

Bottom: *Sporty Car*
Wilton Industries, full size
On pan: 2105-8423, 1989, Wilton,
Korea
Courtesy of Jean Penn
Estimated value: under $12

Comical Car
Wilton Industries, full size
Yearbooks 1977 through 1981, 502-x-236
$4.95 (1977); $5.50 (1978); $5.95 (1979); $6.95 (1980); $7.75 (1981)
On pan: 502-236, 1976, Wilton (script), Korea
Estimated value: under $12

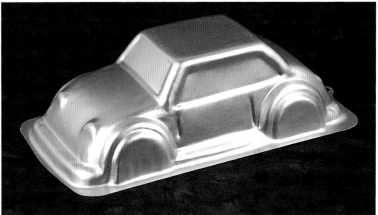

3-D Cruiser
Wilton Industries, full size, stand-up, open mold
Yearbooks 2002 through 2003, 2105-x-2043
$9.99 (2002–2003)
On pan: 2105-2043, 2001, Wilton Industries, Inc., China
List price: $10

Left: *Trail Rider*
Wilton Industries, full size
Yearbooks 1985 through 1988, 2105-x-5583
$7.99 (1985, 1987–1988); $8.49 (1986)
On pan: 502-4050, 1984, Wilton, Korea
Estimated value: under $12

Center: *Sports Utility Vehicle*
Wilton Industries, full size
Yearbooks 1999 through 2002, 2105-x-2034
$9.99 (1999–2002)

On pan: 2105-2034, 1998, Wilton, China
Estimated value: under $12

Right: *Van*
Wilton Industries, full size
Yearbooks 1979 through 1984, 2105-x-5184
$5.50 (1979); $6.50 (1980); $7.25 (1981); $7.95 (1982–1983); $6.95 (1984, "Special Value")
On pan: 502-7652, 1978, Wilton, Korea
Estimated value: under $12

Left: *Free-Wheelin' Truck*
Wilton Industries, full size
Yearbooks 1982 through 1985, 2105-x-1197
$7.95 (1982–1984); $7.99 (1985)
On pan: 502-1565, 1980, Wilton, Korea
Estimated value: under $12

Right *18-Wheeler Truck*
Wilton Industries, full size
Yearbooks 1987 through 1994, 2105-x-0018
$7.99 (1987–1988); $8.99 (1989–1990); $9.99 (1991–1994)
On pan: 2105-0018, 1986, Wilton, Korea
Estimated value: under $12

Little *Fire Truck/Firetruck*
Wilton Industries, full size
Yearbooks 1992 through 1997 and 2003, 2105-x-9110, 2105-x-2061
$9.99 (1992–1997, 2003, "Yearbook Flashback!")
On pan: 2105-9110, 1991, Wilton, Korea
On pan: 2105-2061, 2002, Wilton Industries, Inc., China
List price: $10

Tractor
Wilton Industries, full size
Yearbook 2003, 2105-x-2063
$9.99 (2003)
On pan: 2105-2063, 2002, Wilton Industries, Inc., China
List price: $10

Car (Mini Toy Cakes)
Wilton Industries, small
Yearbooks 1976 through 1980, 508-x-434, also called *Car (minicakes)*
$6.25 (1976, price is for any 4 Mini Toy pans; not sold individually); $1.95 (1977, $6.95 for any 4 Mini Toy pans); $1.99 (1978, $6.99 for any 4 minicakes); $2.30 (1979, $8.10 for any 4 minicakes); $2.95 (1980, $9.95 for any 4 minicakes)
On pan: 508-434, 1975, Wilton (script), Korea
Estimated value: under $12

Mini Locomotive
Wilton Industries, multiple cavity
Yearbooks 1994 through 1997, 2105-x-9332
$9.99 (1994–1995); $10.99 (1996–1997)
On pan: 2105-9332, 1993, Wilton, Indonesia
Estimated value: under $12

Top: *Race Car*
Wilton Industries, full size
Yearbooks 1998 through 2003, 2105-x-1350
$9.99 (1998–2003)
On pan: 2105-1350, 1997, Wilton, China
List price: $10
Bottom: *Race Car/Super Race Car*
Wilton Industries, full size
Yearbooks 1992 through 1996, 2105-x-6508, listed as *Super Race Car*, in index as *Race Car, Super*
$9.99 (1992–1996)
Estimated value: under $12

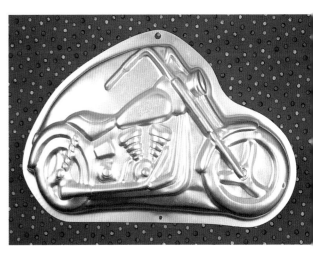

Motorcycle
Wilton Industries, full size
Yearbooks 2000 through 2003, 2105-x-2025
$9.99 (2000–2003)
On pan: 2105-2025, 1999, Wilton, Indonesia
List price: $10

Choo Choo Train
Wilton Industries, full size, stand-up, snap-together
Yearbooks 1976 through 2003, 502-x-836, 2105-x-2861, also called *2 Pc Choo Choo Train* and *3-D Choo Choo Train*
$5.95 (1976–1977); $5.99 (1978); $6.50 (1979); $7.50 (1980); $8.25 (1981); $8.95 (1982–1984); $8.99 (1985–1986); $9.99 (1987–1988); $10.99 (1989–2003)
On pan: 502-852, 1974, Wilton, Korea
Courtesy of Cheryl Thompson
List price: $11

Little Locomotive
Wilton Industries, full size
Yearbooks 1984 through 1985, 2105-x-4498
$7.95 (1984); $7.99 (1985)
On pan: 502-3649, 1983, Wilton, Korea
Estimated value: under $12

Little Train
Wilton Industries, full size
Yearbooks 1991 through 1997, 2105-x-6500
$9.99 (1991–1997)
On pan: 2105-6500, 1990, Wilton, Korea
Estimated value: under $12

Left: *Train (Mini Toy Cakes)*
Wilton Industries, small
Yearbooks 1976 through 1980, 508-x-493, 508W-493, also called *Train (minicake)*
$6.25 (1976, price is for any 4 Mini Toy pans; not sold individually); $1.95 (1977, $6.95 for any 4 Mini Toy pans); $1.99 (1978, $6.99 for any 4 minicakes); $2.30 (1979, $8.10 for any 4 minicakes); $2.95 (1980, $9.95 for any 4 minicakes)
On pan: 508-493, 1975, Wilton (script), Korea
Estimated value: under $12
Right: *Fun Train, 1-2-3*
Wilton Industries, full size
On pan: 2105-9433, 1991, Wilton, Indonesia
Estimated value: under $12

Cruise Ship
Unknown (made in Portugal), full size
On pan: no stamp, paper label "Portugal"
List price: $8

Sailboat
Wilton Industries, full size
Yearbooks 1985 through
1986, 2105-x-5532
$7.99 (1985); $8.49 (1986)
On pan: 502-3983, 1984,
Wilton, Korea
Estimated value: $12 to $25

Spaceship
Wilton Industries, full size
Yearbooks 1980 through 1984, 2105-x-1928
$5.95 (1980); $7.25 (1981); $7.95 (1982–1983); $6.95 (1984, "Special Value!");
plastic lay-on "Starship topper" was not included but sold separately for $1.70
to $1.95
On pan: 502-3584, 1979, Wilton, Korea
Estimated value: under $12

Up 'N Away Balloon
Wilton Industries, full size
Yearbooks 1983 through 1994, 2105-x-1898
$7.95 (1983–1984); $7.99 (1985–1988); $8.99
(1989–1990); $9.99 (1991–1994)
On pan: 502-3169, 1982, Wilton, Korea
Estimated value: under $12

Not Pictured

Baby Bootie Singles!
Wilton Industries, individual serving
Yearbooks 1998 through 2000, 2105-x-1144
$1.99 (1998–2000)
Estimated value: under $12

Dutch Boy
Wilton Industries, individual serving (chocolate mold)
Yearbooks 1974 through 1975, 518-x-209
$2.25 (1974–1975)
Estimated value: Unknown

Policeman Mold
Wilton Industries, individual serving (chocolate mold)
Yearbooks 1974 through 1975, 518-x-365
$2.25 (1974–1975)
Estimated value: $12 to $25

Chapter 4

Celebrations: Fun and Games, Food, Festivities

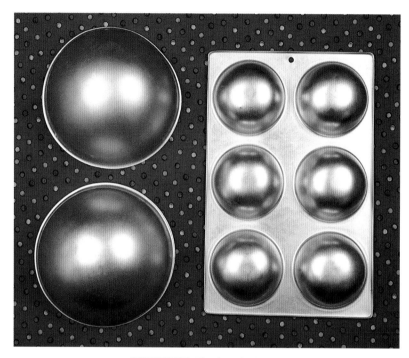

Left: *Sports Ball Pan Set*
Wilton Industries, full size, stand-up, join-after-baking
Yearbooks 1972 through 2003, 502-x-3002, 2105-x-6506,
2105-x-3002, also called *Bowling Ball, 4 PC. Sports Ball Pan*,
Ball Pan, *Ball Pan Set*, and *Ball-Shaped Pan*
$3.50 (1972); $3.75 (1974); $3.95 (1975–1976); $4.95
(1977); $5.50 (1978); $5.95 (1979); $6.50 (1980); $7.25
(1981); $7.95 (1982–1984); $7.99 (1985, and 1989–1990);
$8.49 (1986); $8.99 (1987–1988); $9.99 (1991–2003);
replacement ring stand was offered until 1997, for $.99
On pan: no stamp
List price: $10
Right: *Mini Ball*
Wilton Industries, multiple cavity
Yearbooks 1987 through 2003, 2105-x-1760, also called *6
Cavity Mini-Ball Pan*
$7.99 (1987–1988); $8.99 (1989–1990); $9.99 (1991–1995);
$10.99 (1996–2003)
On pan: 2105-1760, 1988, Wilton, China
List price: $11

Baseball Glove
Wilton Industries, full size
Yearbooks 1989 through 1997, 2105-x-1234
$8.99 (1989–1990); $9.99 (1991–1997)
On pan: 2105-1234, 1987, Wilton, Korea
Courtesy of Vicki Horton
Estimated value: under $12

Left: *Home Run Hitter*
Wilton Industries, full size
Yearbooks 1993 through 1999, 2105-x-2020
$9.99 (1993–1999)
On pan: 2105-2020, 1992, Wilton, China
Estimated value: under $12
Right: *Baseball Singles!*
Wilton Industries, individual serving
Yearbooks 1999 through 2000, 2105-x-1172
$1.99 (1999–2000)
On pan: no stamp
Estimated value: under $12

Left: *Soccer Ball*
Wilton Industries, full size
Yearbooks 2002 through 2003, 2105-x-2044
$9.99 (2002–2003)
On pan: 2105-2044, 2001, Wilton Industries, Inc., China
List price: $10
Center: *Soccer Singles!*
Wilton Industries, individual serving
Yearbooks 1999 through 2000, 2105-x-1177

$1.99 (1999–2000)
On pan: no stamp
Estimated value: under $12
Right: *SuperStar Shoe*
Wilton Industries, full size
Yearbooks 1981 through 1983, 2105-x-2444
$7.50 (1981); $7.95 (1982–1983)
On pan: 502-1964, 1978, Wilton, Korea
Estimated value: under $12

Left: *Tee It Up*
Wilton Industries, full size
Yearbooks 1999 through 2000, 2105-x-2032
$9.99 (1999–2000)
On pan: 2105-2032, 1998, Wilton, China
Estimated value: under $12
Center: *Golf Ball Singles!*
Wilton Industries, individual serving
Yearbooks 1999 through 2000, 2105-x-1176
$1.99 (1999–2000)

On pan: no stamp
Courtesy of Nila Pudwill
Estimated value: under $12
Right: *Golf Bag*
Wilton Industries, full size
Yearbooks 1988 through 1991, 2105-x-1836
$7.99 (1988); $8.99 (1989–1990); $9.99 (1991)
On pan: 2105-1836, 1987, Wilton, Korea
Estimated value: under $12

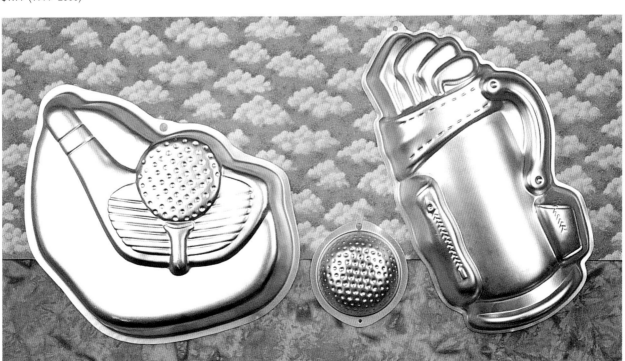

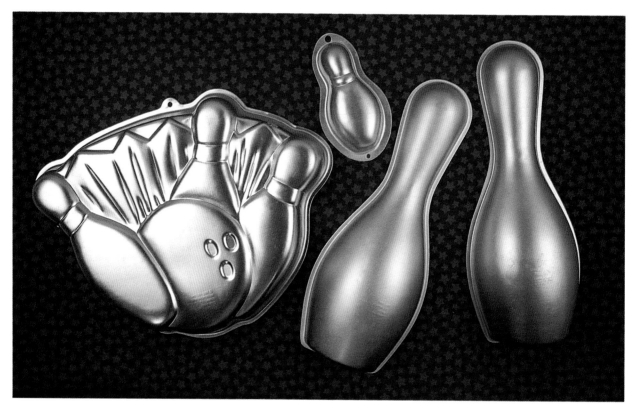

Left: *Bowling a Strike*
Wilton Industries, full size
Yearbooks 1992 through 1993, 2105-x-6505
$9.99 (1992–1993)
On pan: 2105-6505, 1990, Wilton, Korea
Estimated value: $12 to $25

Center: *Bowling Pin Singles!*
Wilton Industries, individual serving
Yearbooks 1999 through 2000, 2105-x-1174
$1.99 (1999–2000)
On pan: no stamp
Estimated value: under $12

Right: *Bowling Pin Set*
Wilton Industries, full size, stand-up, join-after-baking, also called *Bowling Pan Set, Bowling Pin Pan Set*
Yearbooks 1972 through 1991, 502-x-4424
$3.95 (1972); $4.95 (1974); $5.75 (1975); $5.95 (1976–1977); $6.50 (1978); $6.95 (1979); $7.95 (1980); $8.50 (1981); $8.95 (1982–1984); $8.99 (1985–1988); $9.99 (1989–1991); additional bake racks were offered through 1989 for $1.95 or $1.99 each; racks were not offered separately after 1989
On pan: 502-4424, 1972, Wilton (script), Korea, stamped on each half of pan
On pan: 502-4424, no year, Wilton, Korea, stamped on each half of pan
Estimated value: $12 to $25

Left: *First and Ten Football*
Wilton Industries, full size
Yearbooks 1991 through 2003, 2105-x-6504
$9.99 (1991–2003)
On pan: 2105-6504, 1990, Wilton, China
List price: $10

Center: *Football Singles!*
Wilton Industries, individual serving

Yearbooks 1999 through 2000, 2105-x-1175
$1.99 (1999–2000)
On pan: no stamp
Estimated value: under $12

Right: *Football*
Amscan, double
On pan: no stock number, no year, Amscan Inc., Harrison NY, Korea
Estimated value: under $12

Hockey Player
Wilton Industries, full size
Yearbooks 1999 through 2000, 2105-x-724
$9.99 (1999–2000)
On pan: 2105-724, 1998, Wilton, Indonesia
Estimated value: under $12

Top: *Football Helmet*
Wilton Industries, full size
Yearbooks 1980 through 1984, 2105-x-2738
$6.50 (1980); $7.25 (1981); $7.95 (1982–1983); $3.95
(1984, in Super Sale! section)
On pan: 502-2738, 1979, Wilton, Korea
Estimated value: under $12
Bottom: *Mini Football Helmet*
Wilton Industries, multiple cavity
Yearbooks 1985 through 1987, 2105-x-4308
$6.99 (1985); $7.49 (1986); $7.99 (1987)
On pan: 2105-4308, 1984, Wilton, Korea
Estimated value: under $12

Football Hero
Wilton Industries, full size
Yearbooks 1988 through 1991, 2105-x-4610
$7.99 (1988); $8.99 (1989–1990); $9.99 (1991)
On pan: 2105-4610, 1987, Wilton, Korea
Courtesy of Nila Pudwill
Estimated value: under $12

Top: *4 Leaf Clover Mold, Copper anodized*
Nordic Ware, full size
Nordic Ware booklet 11-71, c. 1970, stock number 31301, 4
Leaf Clover Mold, Copper anodized
$2.49 (c. 1970)
On pan: no stamp
Estimated value: under $12
Bottom: *4 Leaf Clover Mold with Teflon interior*
Nordic Ware, full size
Nordic Ware booklet 11-71, c. 1970, stock number 31301, 4
Leaf Clover Mold with Teflon interior, Lemon or Lime exterior
$3.49 (c. 1970)
On pan: no stamp
Courtesy of Denise Mayoff
Estimated value: under $12

Insert for Ring Pan, *Lucky Clover*
This is a removable bottom for the Basic Ring pan, shown in *Chapter 7, Simple
Shapes,* page 132.
Wilton Industries, full size
Yearbooks 1976 through 1980, 503-x-2533, 503-x-253, 2105-x-2533, also
called *Clover* and *Shamrock*
$2.25 (1976, with Ring Pan $5.95; with Ring and 5 other tops, $15.95); $2.95
(1977 and 1979); $2.99 (1978); $3.50 (1980); through 1979, any 4 inserts,
$9.95; 1980, any 4 inserts, $11.95
On pan: 503-253, 1974, Wilton, Korea
Estimated value: under $12

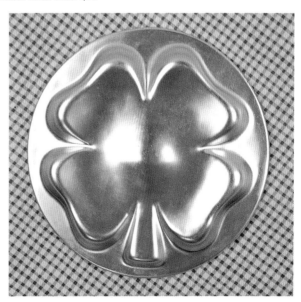

Left: *Two-Mix Horseshoe Pan*
Wilton Industries, double
Yearbooks 1988 through 1989, 2105-x-2530, also called *Horseshoe Pan*
$11.99 (1988–1989)
On pan: 2105-2530, 1986, Wilton, Korea
Estimated value: $12 to $25

Center Top: *Insert for Ring Pan, horseshoe*
This is a removable bottom for the Basic Ring pan, shown in *Chapter 7, Simple Shapes*, page 132.
Wilton Industries, full size
Yearbooks 1977 through 1980, 503-x-458, 2105-x-4307, also called *Winner's Circle*
$2.95 (1977 and 1979); $2.99 (1978); $3.50 (1980); through 1979, any 4 inserts $9.95; 1980 any 4 inserts $11.95
On pan: 503-458, 1975, Wilton (script), Korea
Estimated value: under $12

Center Bottom: *Horseshoe*
Unknown, full size
On pan: no stamp
Estimated value: under $12

Right: *Horseshoe*
Wilton Industries, full size
Yearbooks 1972 through 2003, 502-x-3258, 2105-x-3254
$3.95 (1972); $4.25 (1974); $4.75 (1975); $4.95 (1976–1977); $5.50 (1978–1979); $6.50 (1980); $7.25 (1981); $7.95 (1982–1984); $7.99 (1985); $8.49 (1986); $7.99 (1987–1988); $8.99 (1989–1990); $9.99 (1991–2003)
On pan: 502-3258, 1972, Wilton (script), Korea
On pan: 2105-3254, no year, Wilton, China
List price: $10

Slot Machine
Wilton Industries, full size
Yearbooks 1999 through 2000, 2105-x-2033
$9.99 (1999–2000)
On pan: 2105-2033, 1998, Wilton, Indonesia
Estimated value: under $12

Grand Slam
Wilton Industries, small
Yearbooks 1969 through 1980, W-97, 502-x-976, also called *Grand Slam Molds/Card Pan Set*
$3.50 (1969–1972, 2 sets for $6.00 in 1969 and 1970); $3.75 (1974); $4.25 (1975–1976); $4.95 (1977 and 1979); $4.99 (1978); $6.25 (1980)
On pan: 502-976, 1972, Wilton (script), Korea, same stock number on each pan
Estimated value: under $12

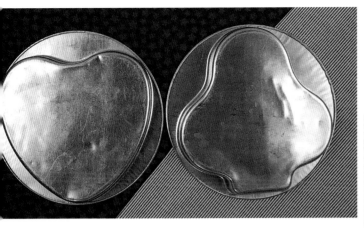

These pans are very lightweight and show considerable denting from use.

Left: *Heart On Round*
Metalite (Canada), full size
On pan: no stamp
Estimated value: under $12

Right: *Club on Round*
Metalite (Canada), full size
On pan: no stamp
Estimated value: under $12

Left: *Computer*
Wilton Industries, full size
Yearbooks 1998 through 2000, 2105-x-1519
$9.99 (1998–2000)
On pan: 2105-1519, 1997, Wilton, Indonesia
Estimated value: under $12

Right: *Computer*
Bakery Crafts, full size, with lay-on
On pan: CRT-1, 1984, Bakery Crafts, Cincinnati, Ohio, Korea
Courtesy of Nila Pudwill
Estimated value: under $12

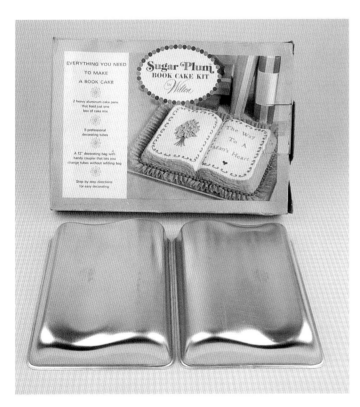

Book
Wilton Industries, full size
Yearbooks 1964 through 1978, W-94, 502-x-940, 2105-x-948, 502-x-940, also called *Book of Beauty*
$2.50 (1964–1969); $2.75 (1970, 2 sets, $5.00); $3 (1972); $3.25 (1974); $3.50 (1975); $3.95 (1976); $4.95 (1977); $5.50 (1978)
On pan: 502-940, 1971, Wilton (script), Korea
Estimated value: $12 to $25

Book
Marpol, full size
On pan: no stock number, no year, Marpol's Happy Face Products, Japan
Estimated value: under $12

Left: *Two-Mix Book Pan*
Wilton Industries, double
Yearbooks 1988 through 2003, 2105-x-2521
$11.99 (1988–1989); $12.99 (1990–2000); $13.99 (2001–2003)
On pan: 2105-2521, 1986, Wilton, "2 CAKE MIX SIZE PAN"
List price: $14

Right: *Book Pan*
Wilton Industries, full size
Yearbooks 1979 through 2003, 2105-x-972, also called *1-Pc Book Pan*
$5.50 (1979); $6.50 (1980); $7.25 (1981); $7.95 (1982–1983); $6.95 (1984, "Special Value"); $7.99 (1985); $8.49 (1986); $7.99 (1987–1988); $8.99 (1989–1990); $9.99 (1991–2003)
On pan: 2105-972, 1977, Wilton, China
List price: $10

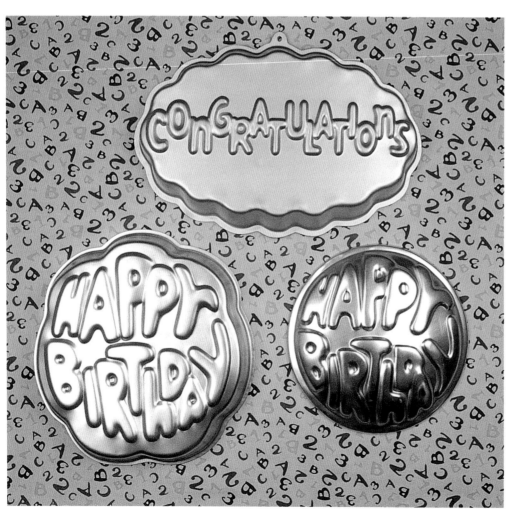

Top: *Congratulations*
Wilton Industries, full size
Yearbooks 1988 through 1991, 2105-x-3523
$7.99 (1988); $8.99 (1989–1990); $9.99 (1991)
On pan: 2105-3523, 1986, Wilton, Korea
Estimated value: under $12

Bottom Left: *Happy Birthday*
Wilton Industries, full size
Yearbooks 1982 through 1998, 2105-x-1073
$7.95 (1982–1983); $6.95 (1984, "Special Value!"); $7.99 (1985); $8.49 (1986); $7.99 (1987–1988); $8.99 (1989–1996); $9.99 (1997–1998)
On pan: 2105-1073, 1980, Wilton, China
Estimated value: under $12

Bottom Right: *Insert for Ring Pan, Birthday*
This is a removable bottom for the Basic Ring pan, shown in *Chapter 7, Simple Shapes,* page 132.
Wilton Industries, full size
Yearbooks 1976 through 1981 and 1984, 503-x-611, also called *Happy Birthday*
$2.25 (1976); $2.95 (1977 and 1979); $2.99 (1978); $3.50 (1980); $3.95 (1981); $1.00 (1984, in Super Sale! Section); through 1979, any 4 inserts, $9.95; 1980, any 4 inserts, $11.95
On pan: 503-611, 1975, Wilton (script), Korea
Estimated value: under $12

Rainbow Birthday Cake Pan
Amscan, full size
On pan: no stock number, no year, Amscan Inc., Harrison NY, Korea
Estimated value: under $12

Top: *Millennium Special 2000*
Wilton Industries, full size
Yearbook 2000, 2105-G_2017
$9.99 (2000)
On pan: 2105-2017, 1999, Wilton Industries, Inc., China
Estimated value: under $12
Bottom: *Mini Balloon*
Wilton Industries, multiple cavity
Yearbooks 1993 through 1997, 2105-x-2024
$9.99 (1993–1995); $10.99 (1996–1997)
On pan: 2105-2024, 1992, Wilton, Indonesia
Estimated value: under $12

Good Time Clock
Wilton Industries, full size
Yearbook 1992, 2105-x-9111
$9.99 (1992)
On pan: 2105-9111, 1991, Wilton, Korea
Courtesy of Nila Pudwill
Estimated value: under $12

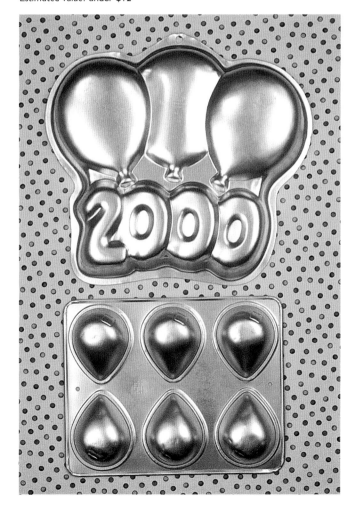

Zodiac Astrological Mold
Mirro, full size
On pan: no stock number, no year, no company name, no country, "6 CUPS," paper label "Mirro"
Courtesy of Nila Pudwill
Estimated value: under $12

Wilton sold its venerable piano kit for more than twenty years, offering first two versions then only the more elaborate one. The pans and the accessories were sold separately as well as together in a kit, and extra keyboards could also be purchased separately. The elaborate kit contains thirteen plastic pieces plus the two pans. Having been a popular kit for so many years there are plenty of piano pans in circulation. The plastic pieces are more fragile than the metal pans, and small enough to be easily lost. A full kit commands fairly high prices; the pans alone are not in high demand.

Piano
Wilton Industries, full size, stand-up, accessorize or stack, with lay-on

Yearbooks 1969 through 1990, W-809, W809, 501-x-8093, also called *Concert Grand Piano Cake Kit, Piano Cake Kit,* and *Piano Kit*

$4.50 (1969); $4.95 (1970); $5.25 (1972); $6.95 (1974); $7.50 (1975); $8.50 (1976–1977); $8.99 (1978); $8.95 (1979); $9.95 (1980); $10.95 (1981); $11.95 (1982–1984); $11.99 (1985–1986); $12.99 (1987–1990); the price of accessories kit (without the pans) ranged from $1.25 in 1970 to $7.49 in 1990; keyboards were generally $.25 each

On pan: 502-887, 1973, Wilton, Korea, stamped on both pans

On pan: no stock number, no year, Wilton (script, with star dotting the i), Japan, "Shapely Cakes," stamped on both pans

Estimated value: $26 to $40, with all plastic accessories

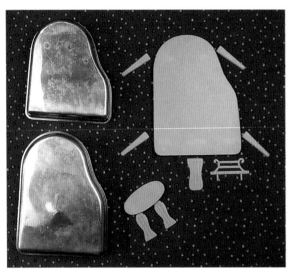

This is the less elaborate version of the piano kit. It sold for $1.25 without the pans. Paper keyboards were available at 6 for $.25.

Piano
Wilton Industries, full size, stand-up, accessorize or stack, with lay-on

Yearbooks 1966 through 1970, W-87, W87, W809, also called *Special piano Cake Kit Complete*

$2.98 (1966–1969); $3.50 (1970)

On pan: no stock number, no year, Wilton (script, with star dotting the i), Japan, "Shapely Cakes," stamped on both

Estimated value: $26 to $40

Wilton's first guitar pan had an even longer run than the piano kit. Its three plastic lay-ons, larger and sturdier than the piano's pieces, were less subject to loss or breakage. Perhaps more significantly, they are less integral to producing the finished cake—using them is optional. The plastic trim pieces were available separately throughout most of the pan's history, at prices ranging from $.50 to $1.59. The pan was sold without plastic pieces for $3.50 to $6.95 through 1980. During the late 1970s and early 1980s the pan is shown with a hanging clip.

Left: Guitar
Wilton Industries, full size, with lay-on

Yearbooks 1966 through 1993, W-85, 501-x-904, 501-x-858, also called *Guitar Kit, Guitar Pan Set, Swinging Guitar Kit*

$3.98 (1966–1969); $4.50 (1970 and 1975); $3.95 (1972); $4.75 (1974); $4.95 (1976); $5.50 (1977); $6.25 (1978); $6.95 (1979); $7.95 (1980); $8.50 (1981); $8.95 (1982–1984); $8.99 (1985–1990); $9.99 (1991–1993)

On pan: 502-933, 1977, Wilton, Korea

Estimated value: under $12, somewhat more with lay-ons and box or paper pieces

Right: Guitar
Wilton Industries, full size

Yearbooks 2001 through 2003, 2105-x-570

$9.99 (2001–2003)

On pan: 2105-570, 2000, Wilton Industries, Inc., Indonesia

List price: $10

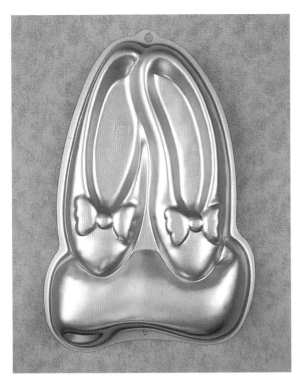

Ballet Slippers
Wilton Industries, full size
Yearbook 2003, 2105-x-2065
$9.99 (2003)
On pan: 2105-2065, 2002, Wilton Industries, Inc., Indonesia
List price: $10

Rockin' Juke Box
Wilton Industries, full size
Yearbooks 1984 through 1986, 2105-x-5311
$7.95 (1984); $7.99 (1985); $4.00 (1986, "Super Sale!")
On pan: 502-1387, 1983, Wilton, Korea
Estimated value: under $12

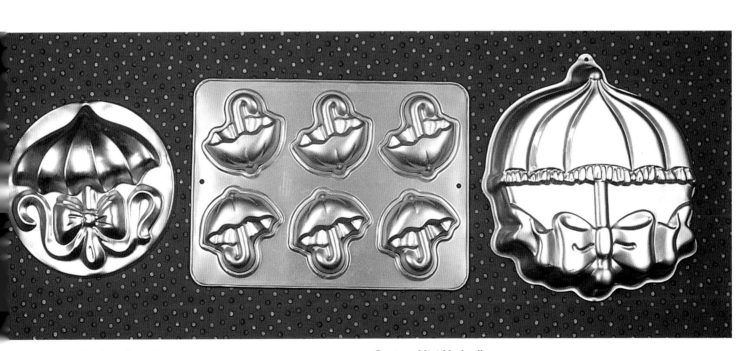

Left: *Insert for Ring Pan, Shower*
This is a removable bottom for the Basic Ring pan, shown in *Chapter 7, Simple Shapes*, page 132.
Wilton Industries, full size
Yearbooks 1976 through 1984, 503-x-570, 2105-x-5737, 2105-x-5702, also called *Shower Surprise*
$2.25 (1976); $2.95 (1977 and 1979); $2.99 (1978); $3.50 (1980); $3.95 (1981–1984); through 1979, any 4 inserts $9.95; 1980 any 4 inserts $11.95
On pan: 503-570, 1975, Wilton (script), Korea
Estimated value: under $12

Center: *Mini Umbrella*
Wilton Industries, multiple cavity
Yearbook 1996, 2105-x-8256
$10.99 (1996)
On pan: 2105-8255, 1995, Wilton Enterprises, Indonesia
Estimated value: under $12

Right: *Shower Umbrella*
Wilton Industries, full size
Yearbooks 1986 through 1988, 2105-x-2293
$8.49 (1986); $7.99 (1987–1988)
On pan: 2105-2293, 1984, Wilton, Korea
Estimated value: under $12

Left: *Graduate*
Wilton Industries, full size
Yearbooks 1996 through 2003,
2105-x-1800
$9.99 (1996–2003)
On pan: 2105-1800, 1995, Wilton
Enterprises, Indonesia
List price: $10

Right: *Topping Off Success*
Wilton Industries, full size
Yearbooks 2000 through 2003,
2105-x-2038
$8.99 (2000–2003)
On pan: 2105-2038, 1999, Wilton
Industries, Inc., Indonesia, "Topping
Off Success"
List price: $9

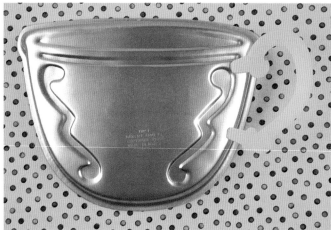

This pan originally came with two lay-on plastic handles.
Trophy
Bakery Crafts, full size, with lay-on
On pan: TRP-1, 1985, BAKERY CRAFTS, Korea
Courtesy of Nila Pudwill
Estimated value: under $12

Left: *Blue Ribbon*
Wilton Industries, full size
Yearbooks 1980 through 1984, 2105-x-2908
$6.50 (1980); $7.25 (1981); $7.95 (1982–1983);
$6.95 (1984, "Special Value!")
On pan: 502-2286, 1979, Wilton, Korea
On paper insert: 2105-2908, 1979, Wilton
Enterprises
Estimated value: under $12

Right: *Insert for Ring Pan, Blue Ribbon*
This is a removable bottom for the Basic Ring
pan, shown in *Chapter 7, Simple Shapes*, page
132.
Wilton Industries, full size
Yearbooks 1977 through 1980, 503-x-415,
2105-x-4668
$2.95 (1977 and 1979); $2.99 (1978); $3.50
(1980); through 1979, any 4 inserts $9.95; 1980
any 4 inserts $11.95
On pan: 503-415, 1975, Wilton (script), Korea
Estimated value: under $12

The coppertone of the pan on the right is so light it is hard to distinguish it from its silvertone counterpart.

Left: *Rose Mold Ring*, Silvertone
Unknown, full size
On pan: no stock number, no year, no company name, Hong Kong
Courtesy of Nila Pudwill
Estimated value: under $12

Right: *Rose Mold Ring*, Light Coppertone
AHC, full size
Yearbook 1964, 315, Rose Ring 5 Cups
$1.00 (1964)
On pan: 1968, A. H. C. St. Louis Mo, Hong Kong
Estimated value: under $12

Top Left: *Viennese Swirl Singles!*
Wilton Industries, individual serving
Yearbooks 1998 through 2001, 2105-x-1110
$1.69 (1998); $1.99 (1999–2000); $2.49 (2001)
On pan: no stamp
Estimated value: under $12

Top Center: *Viennese Swirl*
Wilton Industries, full size
Yearbooks 1990 through 2002, 2105-x-8252
$8.99 (1990); $9.99 (1991–2002)
On pan: 2105-8252, 1989, Wilton, Korea
Estimated value: under $12

Top Right: *Flower Singles!*
Wilton Industries, individual serving
Yearbooks 1998 through 2000, 2105-x-1119

$1.99 (1998–2000)
On pan: no stamp
Estimated value: under $12

Bottom Left: *Petal Pan Fancifill*
Wilton Industries, full size
Yearbooks 1980 through 1983, 2105-x-3092, also called *Fancifill Petal Pan*
$6.50 (1980); $7.25 (1981); $7.95 (1982–1983)
On pan: 502-4165, 1979, Wilton, Korea
Estimated value: under $12

Bottom Right: *Blossom Pan*
Wilton Industries, full size
Yearbooks 1976 through 1979, 502-x-437, also called *Big Bloom*
$4.50 (1976); $4.95 (1977); $5.50 (1978–1979)
On pan: 502-437, 1975, Wilton (script), Korea
Estimated value: $12 to $25

Left: *Coppertone Leaf*
Mirro, full size
On pan: no stock number, no year,
no company name, "SIX CUPS"
Estimated value: $12 to $25
Right: *Maple Leaf Singles!*
Wilton Industries, individual serving
Yearbooks 1999 through 2000,
2105-x-2000
$1.99 (1999–2000)
On pan: no stamp
Estimated value: under $12

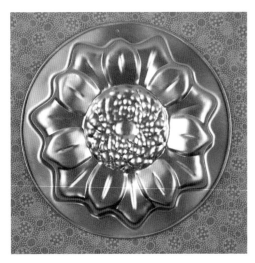

Sunflower
Unknown (made in Portugal), full size
On pan: no stamp, paper label "Portugal"
Courtesy of Nila Pudwill
List price: $8

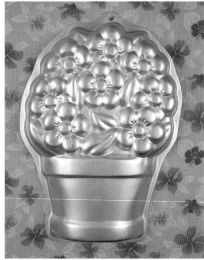

Flower Pot
Wilton Industries, full size
Yearbooks 1999 through 2003, 2105-x-2030
$9.99 (1999–2003)
On pan: 2105-2030, 1998, Wilton, China
List price: $10

Left and Right: *Morning Glory*
Wilton Industries, individual serving
Yearbooks 1969 through 1970, MO-2864
$1.25 for set of 4 pans, $3.98 for 4 sets
(1969–1970)
On pan: no stamp
Estimated value: under $12
Center: *Morning Glory*
Unknown, full size
Yearbook 1969, MO-755
$1.95 (1969)
On pan: no stock number, no year, no
maker, no country, "EIGHT CUPS"
Courtesy of Nila Pudwill
Estimated value: under $12

Left: *Hamburger*
Wilton Industries, full size
Yearbooks 1988 through 1991, 2105-x-3306
$7.99 (1988); $8.99 (1989–1990); $9.99 (1991)
On pan: 2105-3306, 1986, Wilton, Korea
Estimated value: under $12

Right: *Good Cheer Mug*
Wilton Industries, full size
Yearbooks 1985 through 1988, 2105-x-5496
$7.99 (1985, 1987, 1988); $8.49 (1986)
On pan: 502-3965, 1984, Wilton, Korea
Estimated value: under $12

Ice Cream Cone
Wilton Industries, multiple cavity
Yearbook 1989, 2105-x-3636
$8.99 (1989)
On pan: 2105-3636, 1987,
Wilton, Korea
Estimated value: under $12

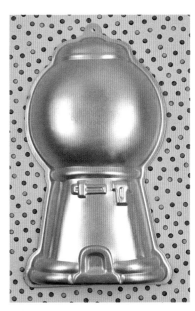

Gumball Machine
Wilton Industries, full size
Yearbooks 1989 through 1991, 2105-x-2858
$8.99 (1989–1990); $9.99 (1991)
On pan: 2105-2858, 1987, Wilton, Korea
Estimated value: under $12

Left: *Harvest Coppertone Mold*
Nordic Ware, full size, also sold by Wilton
Nordic Ware booklet 11-71, c. 1970, stock
number 30701, *Harvest Mold, Copper anodized*
Wilton Yearbook 1964–1969, NA-255, 255
$1.98 (1964–1969); $2.49 (c. 1971)
On pan: no stamp
Estimated value: under $12

Right: *Pumpkin Singles!*
Wilton Industries, individual serving
Yearbooks 1999 through 2001, 2105-x-2002
$1.99 (1999–2001)
On pan: no stamp
Estimated value: under $12

The Cornucopia is a popular harvest theme. Of the three that look to be the same shape, only one has an identifying stamp, with A. H. C. listed as the company. This shape also appears in Wilton books from the 1960s. Many designs of this era were not handled exclusively by one company.

Left: *Cornucopia*, yellow enameled
AHC
On pan: Copyright 1963, A. H. C., St. Louis, MO, Hong Kong, "5 CUPS"
Courtesy of Nila Pudwill
Estimated value: under $12

Top: *Cornucopia*, 6-cup coppertone
Wear-Ever, small
On pan: 2977, no year, WEAR-EVER, no country, "6 CUPS"
Courtesy of Nila Pudwill
Estimated value: under $12

Right: *Horn of Plenty*
Wilton Industries, small
Yearbooks 1964 through 1966, 319
$1.00 (1964–1966)
On pan: no stamp on pan, Hong Kong stamped on swivel hanger.
Estimated value: under $12

Bottom: *Coppertone Cornucopia*
unknown, small
On pan: no stamp on pan, Hong Kong stamped on swivel hanger.
Estimated value: under $12

The top of this mold represents several fruits in a heap.

Harvest Crown
Wilton Industries, small
Yearbook 1964, 621
$1.49 (1964)
On pan: no stock number, no year, no company name, Hong Kong, "6 CUPS CAPACITY"
Estimated value: under $12

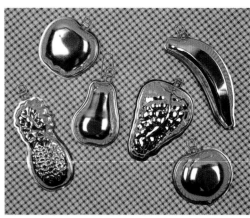

Individual Fruit Mold Set
Wilton Industries, individual serving
Yearbook 1964, 312
$1.98 (1964); originally included decorative wall hangers
On pan: no stock number, no year, no company, Japan
Estimated value: under $12

Left: *Fruit Round Mold*
Unknown, full size
On pan: no stamp
Estimated value: under $12

Right: *Fruit Oval Mold*
Unknown, full size
On pan: no stock number, no year, no company name, Italy
Estimated value: under $12

Left: *Pineapple,* **harvest gold**
AHC, small
On pan: no stock number, 1963 [hard to read, may be 1968], A. H. C. St. Louis Mo, Hong Kong, "4 CUPS"
Estimated value: under $12

Left Center: *Pineapple,* **coppertone**
Wilton Industries, small (probably not Wilton exclusive)
On pan: no stock number, 1963 [hard to read, may be 1968], A. H. C. St. Louis Mo, Hong Kong, "4 CUPS"
Estimated value: under $12

Center: *Pineapple* **Mold**
West Bend, small
On pan: no stock number, no year, WEST BEND,
Estimated value: under $12

Right Center: *Pineapple* **Mold**
Wilton Industries, small (probably not Wilton exclusive)
Yearbooks 1964 through 1966, 311
$1.00 (1964–1966)
On pan: no stock number, 1963 [hard to read, may be 1968], A. H. C. St. Louis Mo, Hong Kong, "4 CUPS"
Estimated value: under $12

Right: *Pineapple,* **avocado green**
AHC, full size
On pan: no stock number, 1963 [hard to read, may be 1968], A. H. C. St. Louis Mo, Hong Kong, "4 CUPS"
Estimated value: under $12

Fruit Basket Mold
Mirro, small, shown in *Joys of Jell-o,* c. 1970
On pan: no stock number, no year, Mirro, U. S. A. "3 1/2 cups"
Estimated value: under $12

Many manufacturers have offered versions of the classic melon shaped food mold.
Bottom: *Melon on Fluted Base*
Mirro, small
On pan: no stock number, no year, Mirro, USA
Estimated value: under $12

Top: *Traditional Melon-Shaped Mold*
Unknown, full size
On pan: no stamp on pan; original owner purchased in Korea
Estimated value: under $12

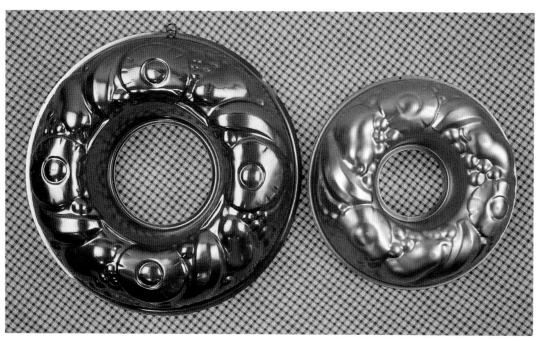

Left: *Large Fruit Ring Mold*
Unknown, full size
On pan: no stamp
Courtesy of Nila Pudwill
Estimated value: under $12

Right: *Deluxe Coppertone Fruit Ring Mold*
Nordic Ware, full size, also sold by Wilton
Nordic Ware booklet 11-71, c. 1970, stock number 30501, *Deluxe Ring Fruit Mold, Copper anodized*
Yearbooks 1964 through 1971, 253, NA- 253
$1.98 (1964–1969); $2.49 (c. 1970)
On pan: no stamp
Estimated value: under $12

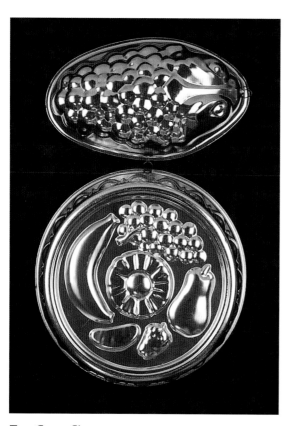

Top: *Grape Cluster*
Wilton Industries, small
Yearbooks 1972 through 1976, 516-x-3306
$1.60 (1972); $2.25 (1974–1976)
On pan: 516-3306, 1972, Wilton (script), Korea
Estimated value: under $12

Bottom: *Coppertone Fruit Salad Mold*
Nordic Ware, full size, also sold by Wilton
Yearbooks 1964 through 1971, 259, A-259
Nordic Ware booklet 11-71, c. 1970, stock number 31101, *Fruit Salad Mold, Copper anodized*
$1.98 (1964–1969); $2.49 (c. 1970)
On pan: no stamp
Estimated value: under $12

Not Pictured

Basketball Singles!
Wilton Industries, individual serving
Yearbooks 1999 through 2000, 2105-x-1173
$1.99 (1999–2000)
Estimated value: under $12

Blossom Pans
Wilton Industries, individual serving
Yearbooks 1974 through 1981, 508-x-1007
$4.75 (1974); $5.95 (1975–1977); $6.50 (1978); $7.50 (1979); $8.95 (1980); $9.95 (1981)
Estimated value: $12 to $25

Ear of Corn
Unknown, small
Estimated value: under $12

Melon
Has leaves and stem on one end
Wilton Industries, full size
Yearbook 1964, 623
$1.49 (1964)
Estimated value: Unknown

Mini Molds
Wilton Industries, individual serving
Set of six molds, each with different fruit, deeply embossed
Yearbooks 1974 through 1976, 516-x-803
$4.85 (1974–1975), $3.95 (1976)
Estimated value: Unknown

Pineapple
Three-piece mold of a standing pineapple
Wilton Industries, full size, stand-up, clamp-together
Yearbooks 1972 through 1975, 516-x-3705, also called *The Pineapple*
$3.50 (1972), $2.95 (1974–1975)
Estimated value: $26 to $40

***Rose Mold*, round, fluted sides**
Nordic Ware, full size, also sold by Wilton
Yearbooks 1964 through 1969, NA-257, 257, also called *Coppertone Rose Mold Pan*
Nordic Ware booklet 11-71, c. 1970, stock number 30901, Rose Mold, Copper anodized
$1.98 (1964–1969); $2.49 (c. 1970)
Estimated value: under $12

Chapter 5

Holidays and Seasons

This is one example of heart-shaped pans sold in sets and individually by several pan companies.

Heart Set
Wilton Industries, mixed sizes in set
Yearbooks 1976 through 2003, 504-x-207, 2105-x-606, 2105-x-2131, also called *4 PC. Heart Pan Set, Heart Pan Set*
$13.95 (1976); $14.95 (1977); $15.99 (1978); $18.95 (1979); $21.50 (1980); $22.95 (1981–1984); $24.99 (1985–1994); $29.99 (1995–2003)
On pan: 2105-606, 2000, Wilton Industries, Inc., China, all pans stamped the same
List price: $30

Happiness Heart
Wilton Industries, full size
Yearbooks 1966 through 1995, W-95, W 95, 502-x-956, 502-x-951, 2105-x-956, also called *2 PC. Happiness Heart Pan Set, Heart Pans*

$2.50 (1966–1969); $3.00 (1970); $3.50 (1972); $3.95 (1974); $4.75 (1975); $4.95 (1976–1977); $5.50 (1978); $5.95 (1979); $6.95 (1980); $7.75 (1981); $7.95 (1982–1983); $5.95 (1984, "special Value!"); $5.99 (1985); $6.49 (1986); $7.99 (1987–1988); $8.99 (1989–1990); $7.99 (1991–1995)
On pan: 502-951, no year, Wilton, Korea
Estimated value: under $12

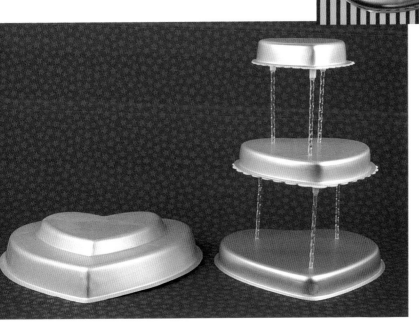

Left: *Double Tier Heart*
Wilton Industries, full size
Yearbooks 1982 through 1996, 2105-x-1699
$7.95 (1982–1983); $6.95 (1984, "Special Value!"); $7.99 (1985 and 1987–1988); $8.49 (1986); $8.99 (1989–1990); $9.99 (1991–1996)
On pan: 502-2695, no year, Wilton, Korea
Estimated value: under $12

Right: *Heart Mini-Tier*
Wilton Industries, full size
Yearbooks 1972 through 1995, 501-x-408, 2105-x-409
$3.50 (1972); $4.75 (1974); $5.50 (1975); $5.95 (1976–1977); $6.99 (1978); $7.95 (1979); $8.95 (1980); $9.95 (1981); $10.95 (1982–1984); $10.99 (1985–1991); $11.99 (1992–1995); prices listed are for pans and plastic parts; separator plates and pillars were also sold separately from $1.00 to $2.99
On pan: 502-3053, no year, Wilton, Korea, same stamp on all 3 pans, plastic parts made in Hong Kong
Courtesy of Nila Pudwill
Estimated value: $12 to $25

Left: *Cupid Pan*
Wilton Industries, full size
Yearbooks 2001 through 2002, 2105-x-173
$8.99 (2001–2002)
On pan: 2105-173, 2000, Wilton Industries, Inc., China
Estimated value: under $12

Right: *Puffed Heart*
Wilton Industries, full size
Yearbooks 1987 through 2003, 2105-x-214, 2105-x-172
$7.99 (1987–1988); $8.99 (1989–2003), 2000 listed as "New!" [no change in pan]
On pan: 2105-172, 1999, Wilton Industries, Inc., China
List price: $9

Left: *Be Mine*
Wilton Industries, full size
Yearbooks 1984 through 1985, 2105-x-4331
$5.95 (1984, "New!" and "Special Value!"); $5.99 (1985)
On pan: 502-2790, 1983, Wilton, Korea
Courtesy of Nila Pudwill
Estimated value: under $12

Right: *Cupid's Delight*
Wilton Industries, full size
Yearbook 1984, 2105-x-3279
$5.95 (1984, "New!" and "Special Value!")
On pan: 502-4262, 1982, Wilton, Korea
Estimated value: under $12

Left: *Cupid's Heart*
Wilton Industries, full size
Yearbooks 1985 through 1986, 2105-x-4911
$5.99 (1985); $6.49 (1986)
On pan: 2105-4911, 1984, Wilton, Korea
Estimated value: under $12

Top: *Individual Heart Mold*
Unknown, individual serving
On pan: no stamp
Estimated value: under $12

Center: *Fanciful Heart Singles!*
Wilton Industries, individual serving
Yearbooks 1998 through 1999, 2105-x-1137

$1.99 (1998–1999)
On pan: no stamp
Estimated value: under $12

Bottom: *Fancy Heart Singles!*
Wilton Industries, individual serving
Yearbooks 1998 through 2003, 2105-x-1105, also spelled *Fanci Heart*
$1.69 (1998); $1.99 (1999–2000); $2.49 (2001–2003)
On pan: no stamp
List price: $2.50

Right: *Hearts Entwined*
Blue Ribbon Bakeware Co., Downers Grove IL, full size
On pan: no stamp
Estimated value: under $12

Left: *Double Heart Fancifill*
Wilton Industries, full size
Yearbooks 1980 through 1984, 2105-x-2517, also called *Double Heart Pan,
Fancifill Double Heart Pan*
$6.50 (1980); $7.25 (1981); $7.95 (1982–1983); $3.95 (1984 in Super Sale!
section)
Estimated value: $12 to $25
Center: *Lacy Heart*
Amscan, full size
On pan: no stock number, no year, Amscan Inc., Harrison NY, Korea
Estimated value: under $12

Right: *Insert for Ring Pan, Heart*
This is a removable bottom for the Basic Ring pan, shown in *Chapter 7, Simple
Shapes,* page 132.
Wilton Industries, full size
Yearbooks 1977 through 1980, 503-x-407, 2105-x-4821, also called *Sweetheart*
$2.95 (1977 and 1979); $2.99 (1978); $3.50 (1980); through 1979, any 4 inserts
$9.95; 1980 any 4 inserts $11.95
On pan: 503-407, 1976, Wilton (script), Korea
Estimated value: under $12

Left: *Embossed Heart*
Wilton Industries, full size
Yearbooks 1995 through 2003, 2105-x-9340
$7.99 (1995); $8.99 (1996–2000); $9.99 (2001–2003)
On pan: 2105-9340, 1993, Wilton, Indonesia
List price: $10
Right: *Double Heart with Embossing*
Unknown (made in Portugal), full size
On pan: no stamp, paper label "Portugal"
Courtesy of Nila Pudwill
List price: $8

Left: *Heart with Cherry*
West Bend, small
On pan: no stock number, no year, WEST BEND
Estimated value: under $12
Center: *Sweetheart/Fancy Heart Mold*
Nordic Ware, full size, also sold by Wilton
Yearbooks 1964 through 1970, 252, NA-252, also called *Coppertone Sweetheart
Mold*
Nordic Ware booklet 11-71, c. 1970, stock number 30401, *Fancy Heart Cake
Pan*
Nordic Ware online catalog, 2002
$1.98 (1964–1970); $2.49 (c. 1970); $11.50 (2002)
On pan: no stamp
List price $11.50
Right: *Heart mold, small embossed coppertone*
Unknown, small
On pan: no stamp
Estimated value: under $12

Top: *Petite Heart*
Wilton Industries, multiple cavity
Yearbooks 1994 through 2003, 2105-x-2432
$7.99 (1994–1995); $8.99 (1996–2003)
On pan: 2105-2432, 1996, Wilton, China
List price: $9

Center: *Mini Heart*
Wilton Industries, multiple cavity
Yearbooks 1974 through 2003, 508-x-1104, 2105-x-11044, also called, *Heart Cupcake Pan*, *Heart Minicake*, and *Heart Mini-Cake*
$3.00 (1974); $3.25 (1975); $3.95 (1976–1977); $4.50 (1978); $4.95 (1979); $5.95 (1980); $6.50 (1981); $6.95 (1982–1984); $6.99 (1985); $7.49 (1986); $7.99 (1987, 1988, 1991–1995); $8.99 (1989, 1990, 1996–1998); $9.99 (1999–2003)
On pan: 2105-11044, 1994, Wilton, Indonesia
List price: $10

Bottom: *Mini Embossed Heart*
Wilton Industries, multiple cavity
Yearbooks 1996 through 2003, 2105-x-8255
$10.99 (1996–2003)
On pan: 2105-8255, 1994, Wilton, Indonesia
List price: $11

I Love You
Wilton Industries, full size
Yearbooks 1989 through 1990, 2105-x-215
$8.99 (1989–1990)
On pan: 2105-215, 1987, Wilton, Korea
Courtesy of Nila Pudwill
Estimated value: under $12

Heart Ring
Wilton Industries, full size
Yearbooks 1991 through 2000, 2105-x-3219
$12.99 (1991–2000)
On pan: 2105-3219, 1989, Wilton, Korea
Estimated value: under $12

Left: *Heart Quartet*
Wilton Industries, full size
Yearbooks 1990 through 1992, 2105-x-1414
$8.99 (1990); $7.99 (1991–1992)
On pan: 2105-1414, 1989, Wilton, Korea
Estimated value: under $12

Right: *Heart mold, deep with arrow*
Wear-Ever, full size
On pan: 294 1/2, no year, WEAR-EVER, USA
Estimated value: under $12

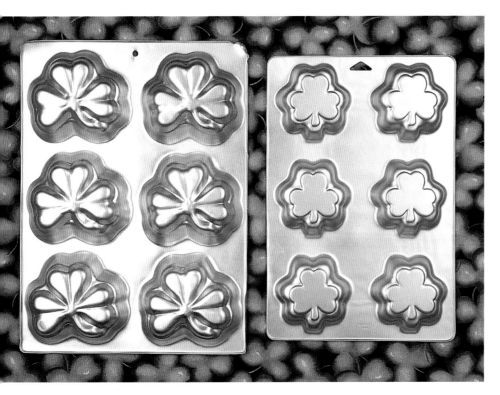

Left: *Mini Shamrock*
Wilton Industries, multiple cavity
Yearbooks 1985 through 1986, 2105-x-3459
$6.99 (1985); $7.49 (1986)
On pan: 508-1465, 1983, Wilton, Korea
Estimated value: under $12
Right: *Shamrock minis*
Amscan, multiple cavity
On pan: no stock number, no year, Amscan Inc.,
Harrison NY, Korea
Estimated value: under $12

Easter Basket
Wilton Industries, full size
Yearbooks 1982 through 1984, 2105-x-4374
$7.95 (1982–1983); $3.95 (1984 in Super Sale!
section)
On pan: 502-1727, 1980, Wilton, Korea
Estimated value: under $12

Left: *Cross /Bevelled Cross*
Wilton Industries, full size
Yearbooks 1972 through 2003, 502-x-2502, 2105-x-2509
$3.95 (1972); $4.25 (1974); $4.50 (1975); $4.95 (1976–1977);
$5.50 (1978–1979); $6.50 (1980); $7.25 (1981); $7.95 (1982–
1983); $5.95 (1984, "Special Value!"); $5.99 (1985); $6.49
(1986); $7.99 (1987, 1988, 1991–1993); $8.99 (1989, 1990,
1994, 1995); $9.99 (1996–2003)
On pan: 502-2502, 1972
On pan: 502-2502, no year
Courtesy of Cheryl Thompson
List price: $10
Right: *Cross Singles!*
Wilton Industries, individual serving
Yearbooks 1999 through 2000, 2105-x-1146
$1.99 (1999–2000)
On pan: no stamp
Courtesy of Denise Mayoff
Estimated value: under $12

Left: *Shamrock*
Unknown, full size
On pan: no stamp
Estimated value: under $12
Top Left: *Shamrock, Coppertone*
Unknown, small
On pan: no stamp
Estimated value: under $12
Top Right: *Shamrock*
Wear-Ever, small
On pan: 2971, no year, WEAR-EVER, USA
Estimated value: under $12

Right: *Shamrock Singles!*
Wilton Industries, individual serving
Yearbooks 1998 through 2001, 2105-x-1140
$1.99 (1998–2000); $2.49 (2001)
On pan: no stamp
Estimated value: under $12
Bottom: *Shamrock*
Amscan, full size
On pan: no stock number, no year, Amscan Inc., Harrison NY, Korea
Courtesy of Nila Pudwill
Estimated value: under $12

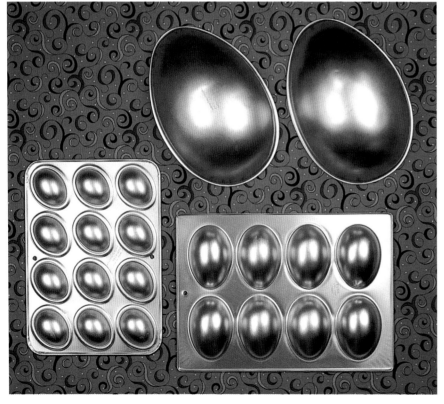

Left: *Petite Egg*
Wilton Industries, multiple cavity
Yearbooks 1995 through 2003, 2105-x-4794
$7.99 (1995); $8.99 (1996–1998); $9.99 (1999); $8.99 (1999–2003)
On pan: 2105-4794, 1993, Wilton, Indonesia
List price: $9
Top: *Egg Pan Set*
Wilton Industries, full size, stand-up, join-after-baking
Yearbooks 1972 through 2003, 502-x-2121, 2105-x-700, 2105-x-4793, also called *3 Pc. 3-D Egg Pan Set, 3-D Egg Pan, 3-D Egg Pan Set, Egg-Shaped Cake Pans*
$2.00 (1972); $4.50 (1974); $4.75 (1975); $4.95 (1976); $5.95 (1977); $7.50 (1978); $7.95 (1979); $8.95 (1980); $9.95 (1981–1984); $9.99 (1985–1988): $10.99 (1989–1993); $9.99 (1994–2003); rings available separately until 1996, for $.99 and $1.49
On pan: 2105-4793, no year, Wilton Enterprises, Indonesia, stamp on one egg half
List price: $10
Right: *Mini Egg*
Wilton Industries, multiple cavity
Yearbooks 1972 through 2003, 508-x-2119, 2105-x-2118, also called *8 Cavity Mini Egg Pan, Egg Cupcake Pan, Egg Minicake Pan, Egg Mini-Cake Pan, Egg-Shaped Cupcake Pans, Mini Egg Pan*
$2.75 (1972); $5.95 (1974, for set of two, not offered individually); $6.95 (1975); $7.25 (1976); $3.95 (1977); $4.99 (1978); $4.95 (1979); $5.95 (1980); $6.50 (1981); $6.95 (1982–1984); $6.99 (1985); $7.49 (1986); $7.99 (1987–1988); $8.99 (1989–1998); $9.99 (1999–2003)
On pan: 508-2119, 1971, Wilton (script), Korea
On pan: 2105-2118, no year, Wilton, China
List price: $10

Top Left: *Easter Eggs*
Amscan, multiple cavity
On pan: no stock number, no year, Amscan Inc.,
Harrison NY, Korea
Estimated value: under $12

Top Right: *Egg Singles!*
Wilton Industries, individual serving
Yearbooks 1998 through 2000, 2105-x-1141
$1.99 (1998–2000)
On pan: no stamp
Estimated value: under $12

Bottom Left: *Decorated Egg*
Wilton Industries, full size
Yearbooks 2001 through 2003, 2105-x-174
$8.99 (2001–2003)
On pan: 2105-174, 2000, Wilton Industries, Inc.,
China
Estimated value: under $12

Bottom Right: *Happy Easter Egg*
Wilton Industries, full size
Yearbooks 1984 through 1985, 2105-x-3749
$5.95 (1984, "New!" and "Special Value!");
$5.99 (1985)
On pan: 502-3495, 1983, Wilton, Korea
Estimated value: under $12

Top: *Patriotic Flag*
Wilton Industries, full size
On pan: 2105-1850, no year, Wilton, Korea, paper insert has © 1985 Wilton
Enterprises, Inc
Estimated value: under $12

Bottom: *13-Star Flag*
Wilton Industries, full size
Yearbooks 1975 through 1980, 502-x-283, 2105-x-2827 also called *Original Old
Glory, Star-Spangled Flag*
$4.50 (1975); $4.95 (1976–1977); $4.99 (1978); $5.50 (1979); $6.50 (1980)
On pan: 502-283, 1974, no company, no country
Estimated value: under $12

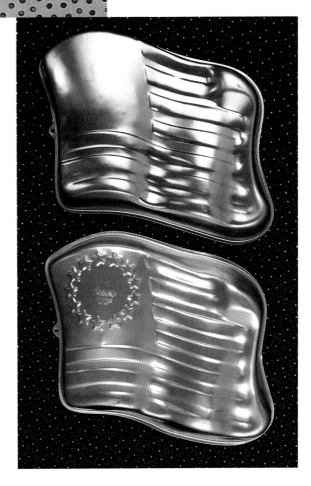

81

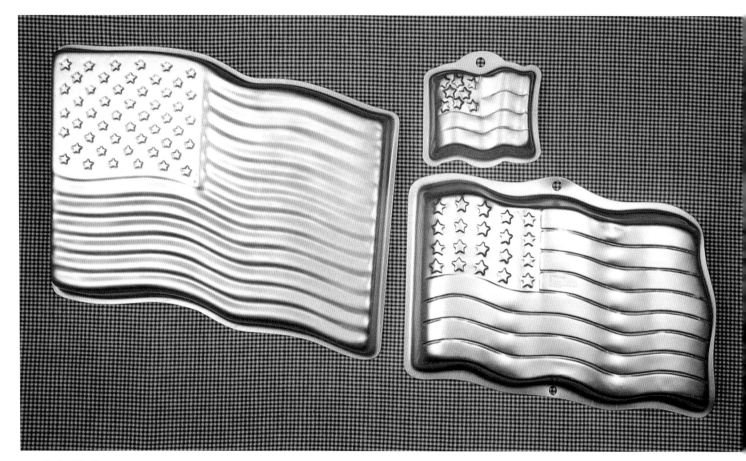

Left: *US Flag*
Amscan, full size
On pan: no stock number, no year, Amscan Inc., Harrison NY, Korea
Estimated value: under $12
Top Right: *Flag Singles!*
Wilton Industries, individual serving
Yearbooks 1998 through 2001, 2105-x-1132
$1.99 (1998–2000); $2.49 (2001)
On pan: no stamp
Estimated value: under $12
Bottom Right: *Stars & Stripes*
Wilton Industries, full size
Yearbooks 2001 through 2003, 2105-x-183, also spelled *Stars and Stripes*
$8.99 (2001–2003)
On pan: 2105-183, 2000, Wilton Industries, Inc., Indonesia
List price: $9

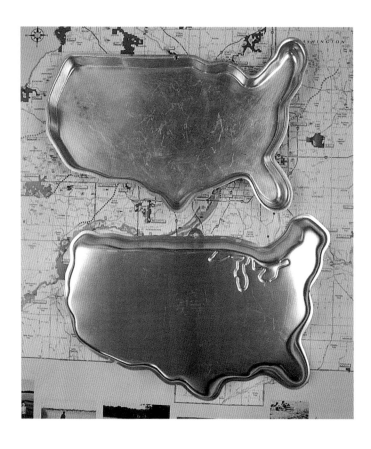

Almost all novelty pans are reverse-image when seen from the open side, so that the cake image will be oriented correctly when the cake is turned out of the pan. Note that the top pan here is shallow and is not reverse-image. The food is apparently intended to be served in the pan rather than turned out on a platter.
Top: *USA*
Meyco Imports, small
On pan: no stock number, no year, Meyco Imports, Hong Kong
Courtesy of Denise Mayoff
Estimated value: under $12
Bottom: *USA*
Wilton Industries, full size
Yearbooks 1990 through 1991, 2105-x-8251
$8.99 (1990); $9.99 (1991)
On pan: 2105-8251, 1989, Wilton, Korea
Estimated value: under $12

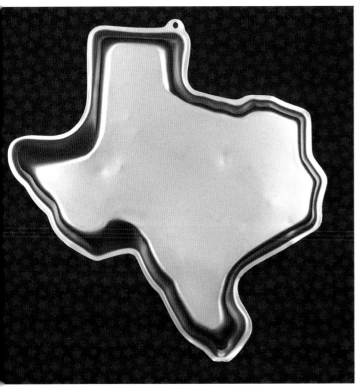

Lone-Star State
Wilton Industries, full size
Yearbook 1988, 2105-x-7925
$8.99 (1988)
On pan: no stamp
Courtesy of Denise Mayoff
Estimated value: $12 to $25

American Eagle Mold
AHC, full size
On pan: no stock number, no year, AHCI, St. Louis Mo, Hong Kong, "10 CUPS"
Estimated value: under $12

Silver Dollar Molds
Unknown, individual serving
On pan: no stock number, no year, no company name, Hong Kong
Estimated value: under $12

Left: *Liberty Bell Mold*
AHC, full size
On pan: no stock number, no year, AHCI, St. Louis Mo, Hong Kong, "10 CUPS"
Estimated value: under $12
Right: *Statue of Liberty*
AHC, full size
On pan: no stock number, no year, AHCI, St. Louis Mo, Hong Kong, "10 CUPS"
Estimated value: under $12

Left: *Scarecrow*
Wilton Industries, full size
Yearbooks 1999 through 2003, 2105-x-2001
$8.99 (1999–2003)
On pan: 2105-2001, 1998, Wilton, Indonesia
List price: $9
Right: *Scarecrow*
Wilton Industries, full size
Yearbooks 1990 through 1993, 2105-x-801
$8.99 (1990); $7.99 (1991–1993)
On pan: 2105-801, 1989, Wilton, Korea
Estimated value: under $12

Top: *Petite Jack-O-Lantern*
Wilton Industries, multiple cavity
Yearbooks 1995 through 2003, 2105-x-8462
$7.99 (1995); $8.99 (1996–2003)
On pan: 2105-8462, 1994, Wilton, Indonesia
List price: $9
Bottom: *Mini Pumpkin*
Wilton Industries, multiple cavity
Yearbooks 1984 through 2003, 2105-x-1499
$6.95 (1984); $6.99 (1985); $7.49 (1986); $7.99 (1987, 1988,
1991–1995); $8.99 (1989, 1990, 1996–1998); $9.99 (1999–2003)
On pan: 508-1040, 1983, Wilton, Korea
List price: $10

Jack-O-Lantern Stand-Up
Wilton Industries, full size, stand-up, snap-
together
Yearbooks 1996 through 2003, 2105-x-3150 also
called *Stand-Up Jack-O-Lantern Pan Set*
$9.99 (1996–2003)
On pan: 2105-3150, 1995, Wilton Enterprises,
China
List price: $10

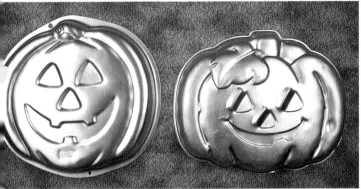

Left: *Jack-O-Lantern*
Wilton Industries, full size
Yearbooks 1982 through 2003, 2105-x-3068
$7.95 (1982–1983); $5.95 (1984, "Special Value"); $5.99 (1985); $6.49 (1986);
$7.99 (1987–1988); $8.99 (1989–1990); $7.99 (1991–1998); $8.99 (1999–
2003); also available in a non-stick version, 1999 through 2001, for $9.99
On pan: 2105-3068, 1995, Wilton, Indonesia
List price: $9
Right: *Decorative Pumpkin*
Amscan, full size
On pan: no stamp
Estimated value: under $12

Left: *Ghostly Greeting*
Amscan, full size
On pan: no stock number, no year, Amscan Inc., Harrison NY, Korea
Estimated value: under $12
Right: *Haunted Pumpkin*
Wilton Industries, full size
Yearbooks 1999 through 2002, 2105-x-3070
$8.99 (1999–2002)
On pan: 2105-3070, 1998, Wilton, Indonesia
Estimated value: under $12

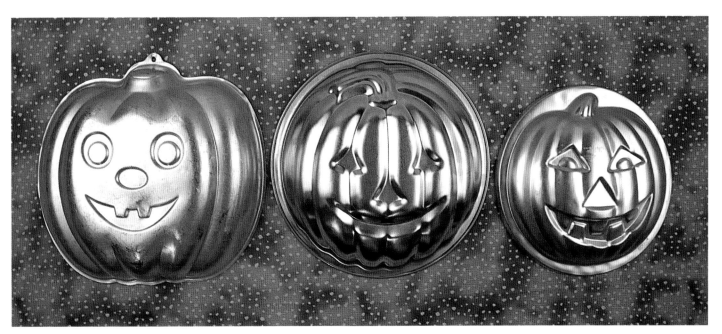

Left: *Party Pumpkin, 1-2-3*
Wilton Industries, full size
On pan: 502-9414, 1987, Wilton, Korea
Estimated value: under $12
Center: *Pumpkin* (**Domed**)
Unknown (made in Portugal), full size
On pan: no stamp, paper label "Portugal"
List price: $8

Right: *Insert for Ring Pan, Pumpkin*
This is a removable bottom for the Basic Ring pan, shown in *Chapter 7, Simple Shapes*, page 132.
Wilton Industries, full size
Yearbooks 1976 through 1981, 503-x-598, 2105-x-5982 also called *Jack-O-Lantern*
$2.95 (1977 and 1979); $2.99 (1978); $3.50 (1980); through 1979, any 4 inserts, $9.95; 1980, any 4 inserts, $11.95
On pan: 503-598, 1976, Wilton (script), Korea
Estimated value: under $12

Top Left: *Bat Singles!*
Wilton Industries, individual serving
Yearbooks 1998 through 2000, 2105-x-1122
$1.99 (1998–2000), also available in colored non-stick 4-pan set, for $14.99 (bat is black)
On pan: no stamp
Estimated value: under $12

Top Right: *Scary Ghost*
Wilton Industries, full size
Yearbooks 1983 through 1984, 2105-x-4889
$7.95 (1983); $5.95 (1984)
On pan: 502-2499, 1982, Wilton, Korea
Estimated value: under $12

Bottom Right: *Jack-O-Lantern Singles!*
Wilton Industries, individual serving
Yearbooks 1998 through 2000, 2105-x-1120
$1.99 (1998–2000), also available in set of 4
colored non-stick pans for $14.99 (orange)
On pan: no stamp
Estimated value: under $12

Bottom Left: *Over the Hill Tombstone*
Wilton Industries, full size
Yearbooks 1996 through 2003, 2105-x-1237
$9.99 (1996–2003)
On pan: 2105-1237, 1995, Wilton, Indonesia
List price: $10

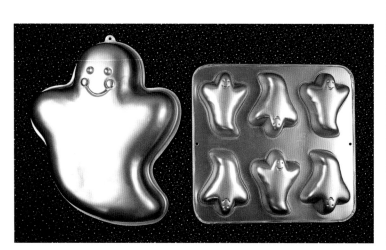

Left: *Playful Ghost, 1-2-3*
Wilton Industries, full size
On pan: 2105-9427, 1991, Wilton, Indonesia
Estimated value: under $12

Right: *Mini Ghost*
Wilton Industries, multiple cavity
Yearbooks 1992 through 2003, 2105-x-3845
$7.99 (1992–1995); $8.99 (1996–1998); $9.99 (1999–2003)
On pan: 2105-3845, 1991, Wilton, Indonesia
List price: $10

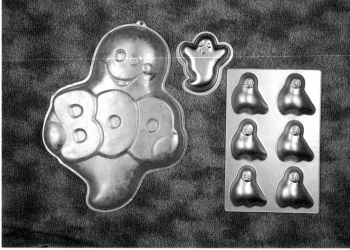

Left: *Boo Ghost*
Wilton Industries, full size
Yearbooks 1989 through 1994, 2105-x-1031
$8.99 (1989–1990); $7.99 (1991–1994)
On pan: 2105-1031, 1988, Wilton, Korea
Courtesy of Denise Mayoff
Estimated value: under $12

Center: *Ghost Singles!*
Wilton Industries, individual serving
Yearbooks 1998 through 2000, 2105-x-1121
$1.99 (1998–2000), also available in colored non-stick 4-pan set, for $14.99
(orange)
On pan: no stamp
Courtesy of Nila Pudwill
Estimated value: under $12

Right: *Ghosts*
Amscan, multiple cavity
On pan: no stock number, no year, Amscan Inc., Harrison NY, Korea
Estimated value: under $12

Smiling Skull
Wilton Industries, full size
Yearbooks 2002 through 2003, 2105-x-2057
$8.99 (2002–2003)
On pan: 2105-2057, 2001, Wilton Industries, Inc.,
China
List price: $9

Cute Witch
Wilton Industries, full size
Yearbook 1994, 2105-x-9330
$7.99 (1994)
On pan: 2105-9330, 1993, Wilton, Indonesia
Estimated value: under $12

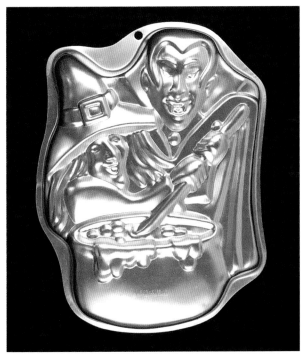

Monster Party Pan
Wilton Industries, full size
Yearbooks 2000 through 2001, 2105-x-2039
$8.99 (2000–2001)
On pan: 2105-2039, 1999, Wilton, China
Estimated value: under $12

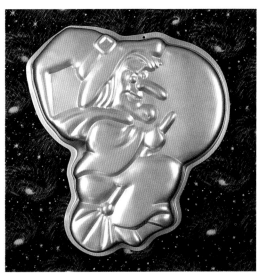

High Flyin' Witch
Wilton Industries, full size
Yearbooks 1982 through 1984, and 1986, 2105-x-4773
$7.95 (1982–1983); $5.95 (1984, "Special Value"); $4.00
(1986 "Super Sale!")
On pan: 502-3398, 1981, Wilton, Korea
Estimated value: under $12

Left: _Whimsical Witch_
Wilton Industries, full size
Yearbook 2003, 2105-x-2068
$8.99 (2003)
On pan: 2105-2068, 2002, Wilton Industries,
Indonesia
List price: $9
Right: _Wicked Witch_
Wilton Industries, full size
Yearbooks 1991 through 1993, 2105-x-4590
$7.99 (1991–1993)
On pan: 2105-4590, 1990, Wilton, Korea
Estimated value: under $12

Happy Chanukah
Amscan, full size
On pan: no stock number, no year,
Amscan Inc., Harrison NY, Korea
Courtesy of Denise Mayoff
Estimated value: under $12

Snowman
Wilton Industries, full size
Yearbooks 1990 through 2003, 2105-x-803
$8.99 (1990); $7.99 (1991–2000); $8.99 (2001–2003)
On pan: 2105-803, 1989, Wilton, China
List price: $9

Left: _Snowman_
Unknown (made in Portugal), full
size
On pan: no stamp, paper label
"Portugal"
Courtesy of Nila Pudwill
List price: $8
Right: _Snowman_
Wilton Industries, full size
Yearbooks 1981 through 1984,
2105-x-1618
$7.25 (1981); $7.95 (1982–1983);
$5.95 (1984)
On pan: 502-1646, 1980, Wilton,
Korea
Courtesy of Vicki Horton
Estimated value: under $12

Left: *Snowflake*
Wilton Industries, full size
Yearbook 2003, 2105-x-2067
$8.99 (2003)
On pan: 2105-2067, 2002, Wilton Industries, Inc., China
List price: $9

Top: *Snowflake Singles!*
Wilton Industries, individual serving

Yearbooks 1998 through 1999, 2105-x-1130
$1.99 (1998–1999), also offered as part of a set of 4 colored non-stick pans, for 14.99
On pan: no stamp,
Estimated value: under $12

Right: *Colored Snowflake Molds*
Unknown, individual serving
On pan: no stamp
Estimated value: under $12

Left: *Mini Snowman*
Wilton Industries, multiple cavity
Yearbooks 1993 through 2003, 2105-x-472
$7.99 (1993–1995); $8.99 (1996–1998); $9.99 (1999–2003)
On pan: 2105-472, 1992, Wilton, Indonesia
List price: $9

Right: *Snowman Singles!*
Wilton Industries, individual serving
Yearbooks 1998 through 2000, 2105-x-1125
$1.99 (1998–2000), also offered as part of a set of 4 colored non-stick pans for $14.99
On pan: no stamp
Estimated value: under $12

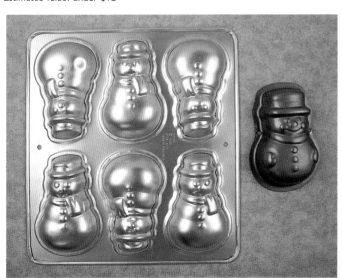

Noel Candle
Wilton Industries, full size
Yearbooks 1982 through 1984, 2105-x-4706
$7.95 (1982–1983); $3.95 (1984 in Super Sale! section)
On pan: 502-3304, 1981, Wilton, Korea
Estimated value: under $12

Left: *Snowman Stand-up*
Wilton Industries, full size, stand-up, join-after-baking
Yearbooks 1985 through 1990, 2105-x-1394 also called *Stand-Up Snowman Pan Kit*
$7.99 (1985); $8.49 (1986); $8.99 (1987–1989); $9.99 (1990)
On pan: 2105-1394, 1984, Wilton, Korea
Estimated value: under $12

Right: *Snowman Stand-up*
Wilton Industries, full size, stand-up, snap-together
Yearbooks 2001 through 2003, 2105-x-2047, also called
Stand-Up Snowman Pan Set
$9.99 (2001–2003)
On pan: 2105-2047, 2000, Wilton Industries, Indonesia
List price: $10

Left: *Christmas Stocking*
Unknown (made in Portugal), full size
On pan: no stamp, paper label "Portugal"
Courtesy of Nila Pudwill
List price: $8

Center: *Stocking Singles!*
Wilton Industries, individual serving
Yearbooks 1998 through 2000, 2105-x-1126
$1.99 (1998–2000), also offered as part of a set of 4 colored non-stick pans, for $14.99
On pan: no stamp
Estimated value: under $12

Right: *Holiday Stocking*
Wilton Industries, full size
Yearbooks 2000 through 2001, 2105-x-2040
$8.99 (2000–2001)
On pan: 2105-2040, 1999, Wilton Industries, Inc., Indonesia
Estimated value: under $12

Left: *Joyful Angel*
Wilton Industries, full size
Yearbooks 1984 and 1986, 2105-x-2797
$5.95 (1984, "New" and "Special Value"); $4.00 (1986, "Super Sale")
On pan: 502-4246, 1983, Wilton, Korea
Estimated value: $12 to $25

Top Right: *Angel Singles!*
Wilton Industries, individual serving
Yearbooks 1998 through 2000, 2105-x-9802, 2105-x-1131
$1.99 (1998–2000), also offered as part of a set of 4 colored non-stick pans for $14.99
On pan: no stamp
Estimated value: under $12

Bottom Right: *Angel Mold*
Unknown, individual serving
On pan: no stamp
Estimated value: under $12

Left: *Smiling Santa*
Wilton Industries, full size
Yearbooks 1997 through 2001, 2105-x-3310
$7.99 (1997–1998); $8.99 (1999); $7.99
(2000–2001)
On pan: 2105-3310, no year, Wilton
Enterprises, Inc., China
Estimated value: under $12

Right: *Santa Face*
Amscan, multiple cavity
On pan: no stock number, no year, Amscan
Inc., Harrison NY, Korea
Estimated value: under $12

Santa in Chimney Stand-Up Cake Mold
Nordic Ware, full size, stand-up, snap-together
Nordic Ware booklet 11-71, c. 1970, stock
number 41300, *Two Piece Santa Mold,* formed
aluminum
$2.49 (c. 1970)
On pan: no stamp, on box, made in USA
Estimated value: under $12

Wreath
Wilton Industries, full size
Yearbooks 1981 through 1984, 2105-x-1502
$7.25 (1981); $7.95 (1982–1983); $3.95 (1984,
in Super Sale! section)
On pan: 502-1484, 1980, Wilton, Korea
Estimated value: under $12

Left: *Mini Santa*
Wilton Industries, multiple cavity
Yearbooks 1984 through 1986, 2105-x-4692
$6.95 (1984); $6.99 (1985); $7.49 (1986)
On pan: 502-3878, 1983, Wilton, Korea
Estimated value: under $12

Right: *Insert for Ring Pan, Santa*
This is a removable bottom for the Basic Ring
pan, shown in *Chapter 7, Simple Shapes,* page 132.
Wilton Industries, full size
Yearbooks 1976 through 1980, and 1984, 503-x-
555, 22105-x-5559, 22105-x-387, 2105-x-5559
$2.95 (1977 and 1979); $2.99 (1978); $3.50
(1980); $3.95 (1984, in Super Sale! Section,
includes Basic Ring); through 1979, any 4 inserts,
$9.95; 1980, any 4 inserts, $11.95
On pan: 503-555, 1974, Wilton (script), Korea
Estimated value: under $12

Left: *Santa*
Wilton Industries, full size
Yearbooks 1980 through 1984, 2105-x-3319
$6.50 (1980); $7.25 (1981); $7.95 (1982–1983);
$3.95 (1984, in Super Sale! section)
On pan: 502-2308, 1979, Wilton, Korea
Courtesy of Vicki Horton
Estimated value: under $12

Right: *Jolly Santa*
Wilton Industries, full size
Yearbooks 1988 through 1994, 2105-x-1225
$7.99 (1988, 1991–1994); $8.99 (1989–1990)
On pan: 2105-1225, 1987, Wilton, Korea
Courtesy of Nila Pudwill
Estimated value: under $12

Left: *Santa Stand Up*
Wilton Industries, full size, stand-up, join-after-baking
Yearbooks 1986 through 1989, 2105-x-6007
$10.99 (1986–1989)
On pan: 502-6007, 1985, Wilton, Korea
Estimated value: under $12

Right: *Santa*
Unknown, full size, stand-up, snap-together
On pan: no stamp, no steam hole
Estimated value: under $12

Left: *Santa Checking List*
Wilton Industries, full size
Yearbooks 1996 through 1998, 2105-x-3323
$7.99 (1996–1998)
On pan: 2105-3323, 1995, Wilton Enterprises, Indonesia
Estimated value: under $12

Right: *Santa's List*
Wilton Industries, full size
Yearbooks 1983 through 1985, 2105-x-1995
$7.95 (1983); $5.95 (1984, "Special Value"); $5.99 (1985)
On pan: 502-4203, 1982, Wilton, Korea
Estimated value: under $12

Old World Santa
Wilton Industries, full size
Yearbooks 2000 through 2001, 2105-x-2041
$8.99 (2000–2001); $9.99 for non-stick version
On pan (non stick version): 2105-1520, 1999, Wilton Industries, Inc., Indonesia
Courtesy of Vicki Horton
Estimated value: under $12

Poinsettia
Wilton Industries, full size
Yearbooks 1998 through 2003, 2105-x-3312
$8.99 (1998–2003)
On pan: 2105-3312, 1997, Wilton, China
List price: $9

Left: *Rudy Reindeer*
Wilton Industries, full size
Yearbooks 1989 through 2003, 2105-x-180, 2105-x-1224
$8.99 (1989–1990); $7.99 (1991–1993); $8.99 (1994 and 2001–2003, in 2001, "Yearbook Flashback!")
On pan: 2105-1224, 1988, Wilton, Korea
List price: $9

Right: *Santa's Sleigh*
Wilton Industries, full size
Yearbooks 1985 through 1987, 2105-x-3235
$5.99 (1985); $6.49 (1986); $7.99 (1987)
On pan: 2105-3235, 1984, Wilton, Korea
Estimated value: under $12

Left: *Santa with Gift*
Amscan, full size
On pan: no stock number, no year, Amscan
Inc., Harrison NY, Korea
Courtesy of Nila Pudwill
Estimated value: under $12
Right: *Santa's Treasures*
Wilton Industries, full size
Yearbooks 1994 through 1996, 2105-x-9338
$7.99 (1994–1996)
On pan: 2105-9338, Wilton, Indonesia
Estimated value: under $12

Top: *Candy Cane Pan*
Wilton Industries, full size
Yearbooks 2002 through 2003, 2105-x-2056
$8.99 (2002–2003)
On pan: 2105-2056, 2001, Wilton Industries, Inc., China
List price: $9
Bottom: *Candy Cane Singles!*
Wilton Industries, individual serving
Yearbooks 1998 through 2000, 2105-x-1128
$1.99 (1998–2000); also offered as part of a set of 4
colored non-stick pans for $14.99
On pan: no stamp
Estimated value: under $12

Tree Cake and Mold Set
Mirro, mixed sizes in set (larger molds make a full-size layer cake)
On pan: 1190M, no year, Mirro, USA (stamp on large pans; no stamp on small molds)
Estimated value: under $12, more with original box

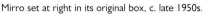

Mirro set at right in its original box, c. late 1950s.

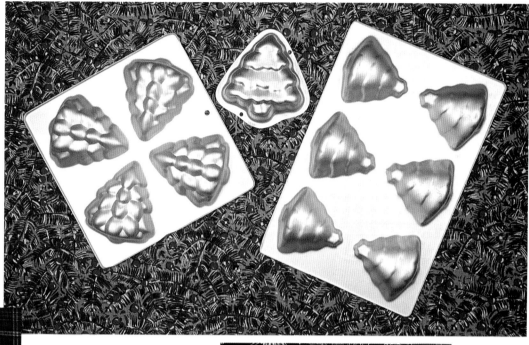

Left: *Christmas Tree Little Cakes*
Wilton Industries, multiple cavity
On pan: 2105-9496, 1990, Wilton, Korea
Courtesy of Vicki Horton
Estimated value: under $12

Center: *Tree Singles!*
Wilton Industries, individual serving
Yearbooks 1998 through 2000,
2105-x-1124
$1.99 (1998–2000), also offered as part
of a set of 4 colored non-stick pans for
$14.99
On pan: no stamp
Estimated value: under $12

Right: *Trees*
Amscan, multiple cavity
On pan: no stock number, no year,
Amscan Inc., Harrison NY, Korea

Treeliteful/Christmas Tree
Wilton Industries, full size
Yearbooks 1972 through 2003, 502-x-1107, 2105-x-425
$3.50 (1972); $3.95 (1974); $4.25 (1975); $4.35 (1976); $4.95 (1977); $5.50
(1978–1979); $6.50 (1980); $7.25 (1981); $7.95 (1982–1983); $5.95 (1984,
"Special Value"); $5.99 (1985); $6.49 (1986); $7.99 (1987, 1988 and 1991–
1998); $8.99 (1989, 1990, 1999–2002); $5.99 (2003); also offered with non-
stick finish in 2000 and 2001 for $9.99
On pan: 502-1107, no year, Wilton, Korea
On pan: 2105-425, no year, Wilton, China
List price: $6

Christmas Tree Mold (coppertone)
Nordic Ware booklet 11-71, c. 1970, stock number 30301, *Christmas Tree Mold*,
Copper anodized, full size, also sold by Wilton
Yearbooks 1964 through 1971, 250, NA-250,
$1.98 (1964–1970); $2.49 (c. 1970)
On pan: no stamp
Courtesy of Nila Pudwill
Estimated value: under $12

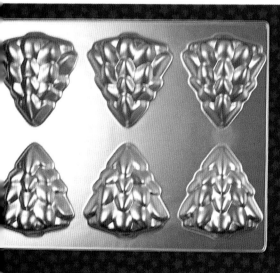

Left: *Mini Christmas Tree*
Wilton Industries, multiple cavity
Yearbooks 1985 through 1997,
2105-x-1779
$6.99 (1985); $7.49 (1986); $7.99
(1987–1988); $8.99 (1989–1990);
$7.99 (1991–1995); $8.99
(1996–1997)
On pan: 2105-1779, 1984, Wilton,
Korea
Courtesy of Nila Pudwill
Estimated value: under $12

Right: *Petite Christmas Tree*
Wilton Industries, multiple cavity
Yearbooks 1995 through 2003,
2105-x-8463
$7.99 (1995); $8.99 (1996–2003)
On pan: 2105-8463, 1994, Wilton,
Indonesia
Courtesy of Nila Pudwill
List price: $9

Three-Layer Tree
Unknown, full size, stand-up, accessorize or stack
On pan: no stamp; small recipe paper with it says C-162, MADE IN U.S.A.
Estimated value: under $12

Candlelit Tree Pan Set
Wilton Industries, full size, stand-up, clamp-together, includes plastic stand
Yearbooks 1974 through 1986, 501-x-6074, 2105-x-719, also called *3D Tree Pan, Christmas Tree Kit*
$7.25 (1974); $8.25 (1975); $8.75 (1976); $8.95 (1977 and 1979); $8.99 (1978); $9.95 (1980); $10.95 (1981–1982); $11.95 (1983–1984); $12.99 (1985–1986)
On pan: 502-607, 1973, Wilton (script), Korea
Estimated value: under $12

Left: *Stand-up Tree Pan set*
Wilton Industries, full size, stand-up, clamp-together
Yearbooks 1997 through 2002, 2105-x-750, also called *2 PC. Stand-up Tree Pan*
$16.99 (1997–2002)
On pan: no stamp
Estimated value: under $12

Right: *Holiday Tree*
Wilton Industries, full size, stand-up, join-after-baking
Yearbooks 1987 through 1990, 2105-x-1510
$8.99 (1987–1988); $9.99 (1989–1990)
On pan: 2105-1510, 1986, Wilton, Korea
Courtesy of Nila Pudwill
Estimated value: under $12

Left: *Christmas Tree, 1-2-3/Step-by-Step*
Wilton Industries, full size
Yearbook 2003, 2105-x-2058, (sold as 1-2-3 pan
for several years before appearing in yearbook
with a name change)
$5.99 (2003)
On pan: 2105-9410, 1986, Wilton, Korea
List price: $6
Right: *Christmas Tree*
Unknown (made in Portugal), full size
On pan: no stamp, paper label "Portugal"
List price: $8

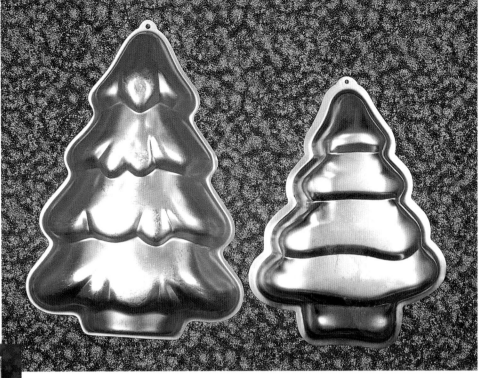

Treats 4 You!
Wilton Industries, individual serving
Yearbook 1998
$14.99 (1998)
On pan: no stamp, on box 1997, Wilton Enterprises,
Indonesia
Estimated value: under $12

Decorated Christmas Tree
Unknown, full size
On pan: no stamp, paper label "Italy"
Estimated value: under $12

Left: *Twin Parti Bell,* **orange exterior**
Nordic Ware, full size, also offered in lime
exterior
Nordic Ware booklet 11-71, c. 1970, stock
number 3083, *Twin Parti Bell Mold with Teflon
Interior*
$3.49 (c. 1970)
On pan: no stamp
Estimated value: under $12
Right: *Christmas Tree Mold,* **lime
exterior**
Nordic Ware, full size, also offered in orange
exterior
Nordic Ware booklet 11-71, c. 1970, stock
number 3033, *Christmas Tree Mold with Teflon
Interior*
$3.49 (c. 1970)
On pan: no stamp

Top: *Bell Pans*
Wilton Industries, full size
Yearbooks 1959 through 1983, 205, BL-205, 502-x-2057, 2105-x-220, 2105-x-2057, also called *Bell Pans (set of 2), Bell-shaped molds, 2-PC. Bell Molds, Two Piece Bell Mold Set, Bell Pan Set*
$1.50 (1959–1966); $2.50 (1969–1972); $3.95 (1974–1975); $4.95 (1976–1977); $5.50 (1978); $5.95 (1979); $6.95 (1980); $7.75 (1981); $7.95 (1982-1983)
Estimated value: under $12

Bottom: *Bell*
Wilton Industries, full size, stand-up, clamp-together
Yearbooks 1972 through 1978, 516-x-3608, 2105-x-3602, also called *Bell Pan Set*
$3.95 (1972); $4.25 (1974); $4.50 (1975–1977); $5.99 (1978)
On pan: 516-3608, 1971, Wilton (script), Korea
Estimated value: under $12

Mini Bell
Wilton Industries, multiple cavity
Yearbooks 1990 through 1991, 2105-x-8254
$8.99 (1990); $9.99 (1991)
On pan: 2105-8254, 1989, Wilton, Korea
Estimated value: under $12

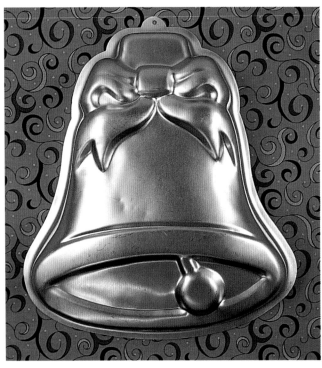

Bell with Bow
Unknown (made in Portugal), full size
On pan: no stamp, paper label "Portugal"
Courtesy of Nila Pudwill
List price: $8

Top Left: *Coppertone Twin Parti Bell Mold*
Nordic Ware, full size, also sold by Wilton
Yearbooks 1964 through 1971, 256, NA-256, also called *Bell Mold*
Nordic Ware booklet 11-71, c. 1970, stock number 30801, *Twin Parti Bell Mold*,
copper anodized
$1.98 (1964–1970)
$2.49 (c. 1970)
On pan: no stamp
Courtesy of Vicki Horton
Estimated value: under $12

Top Right: *Coppertone Bell Mold*
Unknown, individual serving
On pan: no stamp
Estimated value: under $12

Bottom Right: *Double Bell*
Wilton Industries, full size
Yearbooks 1980 through 1983, and 1987 through 1991, 2105-x-1537
$6.50 (1980); $7.25 (1981); $7.95 (1982–1983); $7.99 (1987–1988); $8.99
(1989–1990); $9.99 (1991)
On pan: 502-1220, 1979, Wilton, Korea
Estimated value: under $12

Bottom Left: *Bell Singles!*
Wilton Industries, individual serving
Yearbooks 1998 through 2000, 2105-x-9800, 2105-x-1129
$1.99 (1998–2000), also offered as part of a set of 4 colored non-stick pans for
$14.99
On pan: no stamp
Estimated value: under $12

Not Pictured

Christmas Tree
Wilton Industries, individual serving (chocolate mold)
Yearbooks 1974 through 1976, 518-x-268
$2.25 (1974–1976)
Estimated value: Unknown

Coppertone Holiday Mold Set
Lamb, bunny, and Santa in chimney, done as one-piece molds, but same design
as stand-up versions.
Wilton Industries, full size
Yearbook 1964, 2024
$4.39 (1964 "complete in display carton") also sold individually for $1.49
Estimated value: Unknown

Cross, 2 mix
Wilton Industries, double
Yearbooks 1988 through 1989, 2105-x-2510, also called *Two-Mix Cross Pan*
$11.99 (1988–1989)
Estimated value: $12 to $25

Heart Angel Food
Wilton Industries, full size
Yearbooks 1992 through 2000, 2105-x-6509
$12.99 (1992–1995); $13.99 (1996–2000)
Estimated value: Unknown

Heart Angel Food
Wilton Industries, small
Yearbooks 1995 through 2000; 2105-x-9339
$9.99 (1995–1997); $10.99 (1998–2000)
Estimated value: Unknown

Heart Angel Food Singles!
Wilton Industries, individual serving
Yearbooks 1998 through 1999, 2105-x-1138
$2.49 (1998–1999)
Estimated value: $12 to $25

Sweetheart Mold with Teflon Interior (Lemon or Orange Exterior)
Nordic Ware, full size
Yearbooks 1971 through 1971
Nordic Ware booklet 11-71, c. 1970, stock number 3043
$3.49 (c. 1970)
Estimated value: Unknown

Chapter 6
Licensed Images

Left: *Minnie Mouse*™
Wilton Industries, full size, licensed, Disney, with lay-on
Yearbooks 1972 through 1980, 515-x-809, 2105-x-336, also
called *Minnie*
$4.50 (1972); $4.75 (1974); $4.95 (1975–1977); $5.99
(1978); $6.50 (1979); $7.50 (1980); plastic eyes and lashes
were included 1972–1976 and extras were also sold
separately for $.25 1972–1974
On pan: 515-809, no year, Wilton Enterprises, Korea, Walt
Disney Productions
Estimated value: under $12
Right: *Minnie Mouse*
Wilton Industries, full size, licensed, Disney
Yearbooks 1999 through 2003, 2105-x-3602
$10.99 (1999–2003)
On pan: 2105-3602, 1998, Wilton, Indonesia, Disney
List price: $11

Left: *Mickey Mouse*™
Wilton Industries, full size, licensed, Disney
Yearbooks 1979 through 1984, 2105-x-395, also called *Full-Figure Mickey Mouse*
$6.50 (1979); $7.50 (1980); $8.25 (1981); $8.95 (1982–1983); $6.95 (1984,
"special Value!")
On pan: 515-1805, 1978, Wilton, Korea, Walt Disney Productions
Estimated value: under $12
Center: *Mickey Mouse*
Wilton Industries, full size, licensed, Disney
Yearbooks 1985 through 1986, 2105-x-4358

$8.99 (1985–1986)
On pan: 502-2987, 1983, Wilton, Korea, Walt Disney Productions, Inc.
On insert: 2105-4358, 1984
Estimated value: under $12
Right: *Mickey Mouse*
Wilton Industries, full size, licensed, Disney
Yearbooks 1996 through 2001, 2105-x-3601
$9.99 (1996–1998); $10.99 (1999–2001)
On pan: 2105-3601, 1995, Wilton Enterprises, Indonesia
Estimated value: under $12

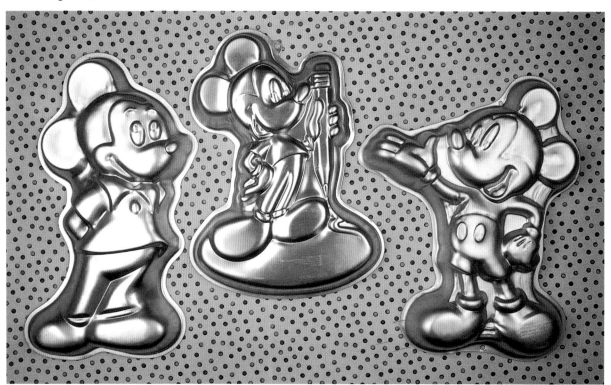

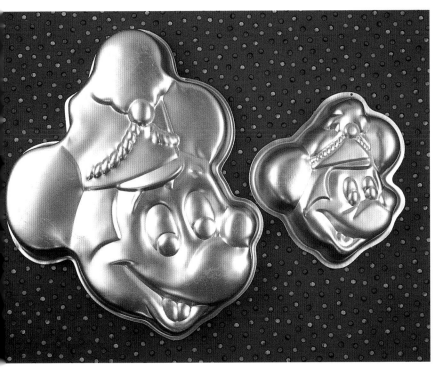

Left: *Mickey Mouse*
Wilton Industries, full size, licensed, Disney, with lay-on
Yearbooks 1972 through 1981, 515-x-302, 2105-x-328, also
called *Mickey*
$4.50 (1972); $4.75 (1974); $4.95 (1975–1977); $5.99
(1978); $5.95 (1979); $6.95 (1980); $7.75 (1981); plastic
eyes and nose were included 1972–1976 and extras were
also sold separately for $.25 1972–1974
On pan: 515-302, no year, Wilton Enterprises, Korea, Walt
Disney Productions
Estimated value: under $12
Right: *Mini Disney Mickey*
Wilton Industries, small, licensed, Disney
Yearbooks 1977 through 1980, 515-x-329, also called *Mickey,
Mini Mickey Mouse*
$1.95 (1977); $1.99 (1978); $2.30 (1979); $2.95 (1980); any
4 mini Disney Pans were offered at $6.95 to $9.95
On pan: 515-329, 1976, Wilton Enterprises, Korea, Walt
Disney Productions
Estimated value: under $12

Top Left: *Mickey Mouse*
Unknown, small, licensed, Disney, sold at Disney
World
On pan: no stock number, no year, "Disney," no
country, paper label Portugal,
Courtesy of Denise Mayoff
Estimated value: under $12
Top Center: *Mickey Mouse*
Wilton Industries, small, licensed, Disney, with
lay-on
On pan: 3005-696, no year, Wilton, Korea, Walt
Disney Productions
Estimated value: under $12, at higher end with
plastic lay-on
Top Right: *Mickey Singles!*
Wilton Industries, individual serving, licensed,
Disney
Yearbooks 1997 through 2001, 2105-x-1136
$1.99 (1997–1998); $2.19 (1999–2000); $2.49
(2001)
On pan: no stamp
Estimated value: under $12
Bottom Right: *Mini Mickey Mouse*
Wilton Industries, multiple cavity, licensed, Disney
Yearbooks 1996 through 2001, 2105-x-3600, also
called *Mickey Mini Pan, Mickey Mouse Mini Pan*
$10.99 (1996–1998); $11.99 (1999–2001)
On pan: 2105-3600, 1995, Wilton Enterprises,
Indonesia
Estimated value: under $12
Bottom Left: *Mickey Face*
Wilton Industries, full size, licensed, Disney
Yearbooks 2002 through 2003, 2105-x-3603
$10.99 (2002–2003)
On pan: 2105-3603, 2001, Wilton, China, Disney
List price: $11

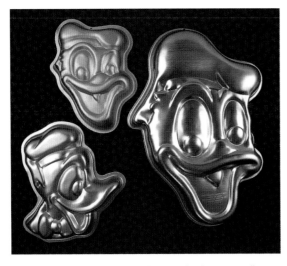

Note that the Yearbook stock number is the same for the two small pans, even though the pans are clearly different designs.

Left: *Mini Disney Donald Duck*™
Wilton Industries, small, licensed, Disney
Yearbooks 1979 through 1980, 515-x-515, also called *Mini Donald Duck*
$2.30 (1979); 2.95 (1980); any 4 mini Disney Pans were offered at $6.95 to $9.95
On pan: 515-1503, 1977, Wilton, Korea, Walt Disney Productions
Estimated value: $12 to $25

Center: *Mini Disney Donald Duck*
Wilton Industries, small, licensed, Disney
Yearbooks 1977 through 1978, 515-x-515, also called *Donald Duck, Mini Donald Duck*
$1.95 (1977); $1.99 (1978); any 4 mini Disney Pans were offered at $6.95 to $9.95
On pan: 515-515, 1976, Wilton Enterprises, Korea, Walt Disney Productions
Estimated value: under $12

Right: *Donald Duck*
Wilton Industries, full size, licensed, Disney, with lay-on
Yearbooks 1972 through 1981, 515-x-507, 501-x-5078, 2105-x-360 also called *Donald*
$4.50 (1972); $4.75 (1974); $4.95 (1975–1977); $5.99 (1978); $6.50 (1979); $6.95 (1980); $7.75 (1981); plastic eyes were included 1972–1976 and extras were also sold separately for $.25 1972–1974
On pan: 515-507, no year, Wilton Enterprises, Korea, Walt Disney Productions
Estimated value: under $12

Left: *Donald Duck*
Wilton Industries, full size, licensed, Disney
Yearbooks 1981 through 1983, 2105-x-2703, also called *Full-Figure Donald Duck*
$8.25 (1981); $8.95 (1982–1983)
On pan: 502-7245, no year, Wilton, Korea, Walt Disney Productions
Estimated value: under $12

Right: *Donald Duck*
Wilton Industries, full size, licensed, Disney
Yearbooks 1984 through 1986, 2105-x-4556
$8.95 (1984); $8.99 (1985–1986)
On pan: 502-3681, 1983, Wilton, Korea, Walt Disney Productions, Inc.
Estimated value: under $12

The full-size pans of Disney character heads originally came with black plastic lay-ons for the eyes, nose, and sometimes ears. These were only offered for a few years and then the pans were sold without them. It is rare to find a full set intact.

Left: *Pluto*™
Wilton Industries, full size, licensed, Disney, with lay-on
Yearbooks 1972 through 1980, 515-x-604, 2105-x-352
$4.50 (1972); $4.75 (1974); $4.95 (1975–1977); $5.99 (1978); $6.50 (1979); $7.50 (1980)); plastic eyes and ear were included 1972–1976 and extras were also sold separately for $.25 1972–1974
On pan: 515-604, no year, Wilton Enterprises, Korea, Walt Disney Productions
Estimated value: $12 to $25

Top: *Mini Disney Goofy*™
Wilton Industries, small, licensed, Disney
Yearbooks 1977 through 1980, 515-x-1104, also called *Goofy, Mini Goofy*
$1.95 (1977); $1.99 (1978); $2.30 (1979); $2.95 (1980); any 4 mini Disney Pans were offered at $6.95 to $9.95
On pan: 515-1104, 1976, Wilton Enterprises, Korea, Walt Disney Productions
Estimated value: under $12

Right: *Goofy*
Wilton Industries, full size, licensed, Disney, with lay-on
Yearbooks 1972 through 1980, 515-x-1007, 501-x-1005, 2105-x-344
$4.50 (1972); $4.75 (1974); $4.95 (1975–1977); $5.99 (1978); $6.50 (1979); $7.50 (1980)); plastic eyes, ear and nose were included 1972–1976 and extras were also sold separately for $.25 1972–1974
On pan: 515-1007, no year, Wilton Enterprises, Korea, Walt Disney Productions
Estimated value: $12 to $25

Bottom: *Mini Disney Pluto*
Wilton Industries, small, licensed, Disney
Yearbooks 1977 through 1980, 515-x-612
$1.95 (1977); $1.99 (1978); $2.30 (1979); $2.95 (1980);, any 4 mini Disney Pans were offered at $6.95 to $9.95
On pan: 515-1007, no year, Wilton Enterprises, Korea, Walt Disney Productions
Estimated value: under $12

Any 4 mini Disney Pans were offered at $6.95 to $9.95

Left: *Mini Disney Jiminy Cricket*™
Wilton Industries, small, licensed, Disney
Yearbooks 1977 through 1980; 515-x-221, 515-x-205
$1.95 (1977); $1.99 (1978); $2.30 (1979); $2.95 (1980);
On pan: 515-205, 1976, Wilton Enterprises, Korea, Walt Disney
Productions
Estimated value: under $12

Top: *Mini Disney Dumbo*™
Wilton Industries, small, licensed, Disney
Yearbooks 1977 through 1980, 515-x-434
$1.95 (1977); $1.99 (1978); $2.30 (1979); $2.95 (1980);
On pan: 515-434, 1976, Wilton Enterprises, Korea, Walt Disney
Productions
Estimated value: $12 to $25

Right: *Mini Disney Pinocchio*™
Wilton Industries, small, licensed, Disney
Yearbooks 1977 through 1980, 515-x-701
$1.95 (1977); $1.99 (1978); $2.30 (1979); $2.95 (1980)
On pan: 515-701, 1976, Wilton Enterprises, Korea, Walt Disney
Productions
Estimated value: under $12

Bottom: *Mini Disney Bambi*™
Wilton Industries, small, licensed, Disney
Yearbooks 1977 through 1980, 515-x-469
$1.95 (1977); $1.99 (1978); $2.30 (1979); $2.95 (1980)
On pan: 515-469, 1976, Wilton Enterprises, Korea, Walt Disney
Productions
Estimated value: under $12

Left: *Winnie the Pooh*™
Wilton Industries, full size, licensed, Disney
Yearbooks 1972 through 1976, 515-x-401, 2105-x-379, also
spelled *Winnie-the-Pooh*
The pan shown in the 1972 yearbook is not tinted; the later
issues show a goldtone pan
$4.50 (1972); $4.75 (1974); $4.95 (1975–1976)
On pan: 515-401, no year, Wilton Enterprises, Korea, Walt Disney
Products
Estimated value: under $12

Right: *Pooh with Honey Pot,* **small, golden**
Wilton Industries, small, licensed, Disney
On pan: 3005-203, 1976, Wilton Enterprises, Korea, Walt Disney
Productions
Estimated value: $12 to $25

Pooh Stand-up
Wilton Industries, full size, stand-up, clamp-together, licensed,
Disney
Yearbooks 1999 through 2003, 2105-x-3002
$17.99 (1999–2003)
On pan: 2105-3002, 1998, Wilton, Indonesia, Disney, on front
stand
List price: $18

Left: *Winnie the Pooh*
Wilton Industries, full size, licensed, Disney
Yearbooks 1996 through 2001, 2105-x-3000, some-
times listed in index under Pooh, sometimes Winnie
$9.99 (1996–1998); $10.99 (1999–2001)
On pan: 2105-3000, 1995, Wilton, Indonesia, Disney
Courtesy of Cheryl Thompson
Estimated value: under $12

Right: *Pooh #1*
Wilton Industries, full size, licensed, Disney
Yearbooks 1999 through 2001, 2105-x-3003
$10.99 (1999–2001)
On pan: 2105-3003, 1998, Wilton, Indonesia, Disney
Estimated value: under $12

Left: *Pooh Face*
Wilton Industries, full size, licensed, Disney
Yearbooks 2002 through 2003, 2105-x-3004
$10.99 (2002–2003)
On pan: 2105-3004, 2001, Wilton Industries, Inc., China, Disney
List price: $11

Right: *Pooh Singles!*
Wilton Industries, individual serving, licensed, Disney
Yearbooks 1998 through 2002, 2105-x-1135
$1.99 (1998); $2.19 (1999–2000); $2.49 (2001–2002)
On pan: no stamp
Estimated value: under $12

Little Mermaid™
Wilton Industries, full size, licensed, Disney, with lay-on
Yearbooks 1999 through 2000, 2105-x-3400
$10.99 (1999–2000)
On pan: 2105-3400, no year, Wilton, China, Disney
Courtesy of Denise Mayoff
Estimated value: $26 to $40

Left: *Tigger*™
Wilton Industries, full size, licensed, Disney
Yearbooks 1998 through 2003, 2105-x-3001
$9.99 (1998); $10.99 (1999–2003)
On pan: 2105-3001, no year, Wilton, Indonesia, Disney
List price: $11

Right: *Tigger Singles!*
Wilton Industries, individual serving, licensed, Disney
Yearbooks 1998 through 2000, 2105-x-1145
$1.99 (1998); $2.19 (1999–2000)
On pan: no stamp
Estimated value: under $12

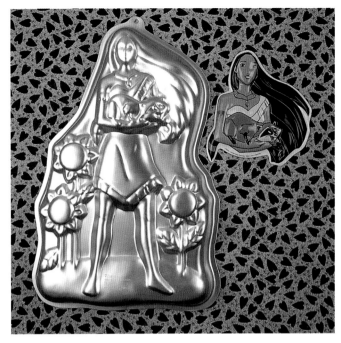

Esmeralda ™
Wilton Industries, full size, licensed, Disney, with lay-on
Yearbooks 1997 through 1998, 2105-x-3800
$10.99 (1997–1998)
On pan: 2105-3800, 1996, Wilton, Indonesia, Disney
Estimated value: under $12

Pocahontas ™
Wilton Industries, full size, licensed, Disney, with lay-on
Yearbooks 1996 through 1998, 2105-x-3700
$9.99 (1996–1998)
On pan: 2105-3700, 1995, Wilton Enterprises, Korea, Disney
Estimated value: under $12

Hercules ™
Wilton Industries, full size, licensed, Disney, with lay-on
Yearbooks 1998 through 1999; 2105-x-3300
$10.99 (1998–1999)
On pan: 2105-3300, no year, Wilton, China, Disney
Estimated value: under $12

Flik Bug's Life ™
Wilton Industries, full size, licensed, Disney
Yearbooks 2000 through 2001, 2105-x-3203
$10.99 (2000–2001)
On pan: 2105-3203, 1998, Wilton, China, Disney/Pixar
Estimated value: under $12

Left: *Eleroo*™
Wilton Industries, full size, licensed, Disney
Yearbook 1987, 2105-x-1950
$8.99 (1987)
On pan: 2105-1950, 1985, Wilton Enterprises, Inc., Korea, Hasbro Inc. Walt Disney Productions, "This mold not intended for commercial use"
Estimated value: under $12
Right: *Bumblelion*™
Wilton Industries, full size, licensed, Disney
Yearbook 1987, 2105-x-1875
$8.99 (1987)
On pan: 2105-1875, 1985, Wilton Enterprises, Hasbro, Inc. Walt Disney Productions, "This mold not intended for commercial use."
Estimated value: under $12

Left: *Mini Big Bird*™
Wilton Industries, multiple cavity, licensed, Sesame Workshop
Yearbook 1986, 2105-x-2384
$7.99 (1986)
On pan: 2105-2384, 1984, Wilton, Korea, Muppets, Inc.
Estimated value: under $12
Top: *Big Bird small pan*
Wilton Industries, small, licensed, Sesame Workshop, with lay-on
On pan: 3005-602, 1971, 1977, Wilton Enterprises, Korea, Muppets, Inc.

Left: *101 Dalmatians*™
Wilton Industries, full size, licensed, Disney
Yearbooks 1998 through 2000, 2105-x-3250
$9.99 (1998); $10.99 (1999–2000)
On pan: 2105-3250, 1996, Wilton, Indonesia, Disney
Estimated value: under $12
Right: *101 Dalmatians Singles!*
Wilton Industries, individual serving, licensed, Disney
Yearbooks 1998 through 2000, 2105-x-1133
$1.99 (1998); $2.19 (1999–2000)
On pan: no stamp
Estimated value: under $12

Estimated value: under $12
Right: *Big Bird face*
Wilton Industries, full size, licensed, Sesame Workshop
Yearbooks 1978 through 1984, 2105-x-646
$5.99 (1978); $5.95 (1979); $6.95 (1980); $7.75 (1981); $7.95 (1982–1983); $2.00 (1984 in Super Sale! section)
On pan: 502-7407, 1971, 1977, Wilton Enterprises, Korea, Muppets, Inc.
Estimated value: under $12

Left: *Big Bird*
Wilton Industries, full size, licensed, Sesame Workshop
Yearbooks 1984 through 1989, 2105-x-3653
$8.95 (1984); $8.99 (1985–1989)
On pan: 502-3401, 1983, Wilton, Korea, Muppets, Inc.
Estimated value: under $12

Right: *Big Bird*
Wilton Industries, full size, licensed, Sesame Workshop
Yearbooks 1990 through 1991, 2105-x-0805
$8.99 (1990); $9.99 (1991)
On pan: 2105-805, 1989, Wilton Enterprises, Korea, Muppets, Inc.
Estimated value: under $12

Left: *Big Bird with Banner*
Wilton Industries, full size, licensed, Sesame Workshop
Yearbooks 1992 through 2001, 210B-x-3654, 2105-x-3654
$9.99 (1992–1998); $10.99 (1999–2001)
On pan: 2105-3654, no year, Wilton Enterprises, China, Jim Henson Productions, Inc.
Estimated value: under $12

Right: *Big Bird Full Figure*
Wilton Industries, full size, licensed, Sesame Workshop
Yearbooks 1979 through 1983, 2105-x-123
$6.50 (1979); $7.50 (1980); $8.25 (1981); $7.95 (1982); $8.95 (1983)
On pan: 502-2065, 1971, 1977, Wilton, Korea, Muppets, Inc.
Estimated value: under $12

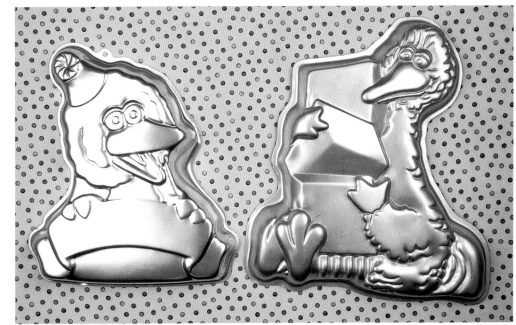

Left: *Big Bird Happy Birthday, 1-2-3*
Wilton Industries, full size, licensed, Sesame Workshop, with lay-on
On pan: 2105-9407, 1988, Wilton Enterprises, Korea, Muppets, Inc.
Estimated value: under $12

Right: *Big Bird, 1-2-3*
Wilton Industries, full size, licensed, Sesame Workshop, with lay-on
On pan: 2105-9476, 1988, Wilton Enterprises, Korea, Muppets, Inc.
Estimated value: under $12

Top Left: *Sesame Street*™ *Mini Pan*
Wilton Industries, multiple cavity, licensed,
Sesame Workshop
Yearbooks 1995 through 1996, 2105-x-8472
$9.99 (1995); $10.99 (1996)
On pan: 2105-8472, 1994, Wilton, Indonesia, Jim
Henson Productions, Inc.
Estimated value: under $12

Top Right: *Cookie Monster*™ *small*
Wilton Industries, small, licensed, Sesame
Workshop
On pan: 3005-629, 1971, 1977, Wilton
Enterprises, Korea, Muppets, Inc.
Estimated value: under $12

Bottom Left: *Cookie Monster*
Wilton Industries, full size, licensed, Sesame
Workshop
Yearbooks 1978 through 1982, and1984, 2105-x-638
$5.99 (1978); $6.50 (1979); $7.50 (1980); $8.25
(1981); $8.95 (1982); $3.95 (1984, in Super Sale!
section)
On pan: 502-7415, 1971, 1977, Wilton
Enterprises, Korea, Muppets, Inc.
Estimated value: under $12

Bottom Right: *Cookie Monster*
Wilton Industries, full size, licensed, Sesame
Workshop
Yearbooks 1983 through 1996, 2105-x-4927
$8.95 (1983–1984); $8.99 (1985–1990); $9.99
(1991–1996)
On pan: 502-3738, 1982, Wilton Enterprises,
Korea, Muppets, Inc.
Estimated value: under $12

Left: *Ernie*™
Wilton Industries, full size, licensed, Sesame Workshop
Yearbooks 1984 through 1991, 2105-x-3173
$8.95 (1984); $8.99 (1985–1990, "New!" and "He's back by popular de-
mand."); $9.99 (1991)
On pan: 502-3614, 1983, Wilton, Korea, Muppets, Inc.
Estimated value: under $12

Right: *Ernie and Bert*™
Wilton Industries, full size, licensed, Sesame Workshop
Yearbooks 1978 through 1983, 502-x-7555, 2105-x-999 also called *Bert and
Ernie*
$5.99 (1978); $6.50 (1979); $7.50 (1980); $8.25 (1981); $8.95 (1982–1983)
On pan: 502-7423, 1971, 1977, Wilton, Korea, Muppets, Inc.
Estimated value: under $12

Oscar the Grouch*™*
Wilton Industries, full size, licensed, Sesame Workshop
Yearbooks 1978 through 1983, 502-x-7548, 2105-x-2665
$5.99 (1978); $6.50 (1979); $7.50 (1980); $8.25 (1981); $8.95 (1982–1983)
On pan: 502-7512, 1971, 1977, Wilton Enterprises, Korea, Muppets, Inc.
Estimated value: under $12

Left: *Elmo*™
Wilton Industries, full size, licensed, Sesame Workshop
Yearbook 2003, 2105-x-3461
$10.99 (2003)
On pan: 2105-3461, 2002, Wilton Industries, China, Sesame Workshop
List price: $11

Center: *Elmo Singles!*
Wilton Industries, individual serving, licensed, Jim Henson Productions, Inc.
Yearbooks 1999 through 2000, 2105-x-3460
$2.19 (1999–2000)

On pan: no stamp
Courtesy of Nila Pudwill
Estimated value: under $12

Right: *Elmo*
Wilton Industries, full size, licensed, Sesame Workshop
Yearbooks 1997 through 2002, 2105-x-4298
$9.99 (1997–1998); $10.99 (1999–2002)
On pan: 2105-4298, 1996, Wilton, Indonesia, Henson
Estimated value: under $12

Left: *Bugs Bunny*™
Wilton Industries, full size, licensed, Warner Bros.
Yearbooks 1993 through 1996, 2105-x-2553
$9.99 (1993–1996)
On pan: 2105-2553, 1992, Wilton, Korea, Warner Bros. Inc.
Estimated value: under $12

Center: *Bugs Bunny*
Wilton Industries, small, licensed, Warner Bros., with lay-on
On pan: 3005-262, 1979, Wilton, Korea, Warner Bros. Inc.
Estimated value: under $12

Right: *Bugs*
Wilton Industries, full size, licensed, Warner Bros.
Yearbooks 2002 through 2003, 2105-x-3204
$10.99 (2002–2003)
On pan: 2105-3204, 2001, Wilton Industries, Inc., China, Warner Bros.
List price: $11

The Count™
Wilton Industries, full size, licensed, Sesame Workshop
Yearbooks 1978 through 1980, and 1983, 1984, and 1986,
502-x-7474, 2105-x-2673
$5.99 (1978); $6.50 (1979); $7.50 (1980); $8.95 (1983); $2.00 (1984, in Super Sale! section); $4.00 (1986, "Super Sale!")
On pan: 502-7512, 1971, 1977, Wilton Enterprises, Korea, Muppets, Inc.
Estimated value: under $12

Left: *Bugs Bunny*
Wilton Industries, full size, licensed, Warner Bros.
Yearbooks 1990 through 1992, 2105-x-8253
$8.99 (1990); $9.99 (1991–1992)
On pan: 2105-8253, 1989, Wilton Enterprises, Korea, Warner Bros. Inc.
Estimated value: under $12

Center: *Bugs Bunny Singles!*
Wilton Industries, individual serving, licensed, Warner Bros.
Yearbooks 1998 through 1999, 2105-x-1134
$1.99 (1998); $2.19 (1999)
On pan: no stamp
Estimated value: under $12

Right: *Bugs Bunny*
Wilton Industries, full size, licensed, Warner Bros.
Yearbooks 1979 through 1983, 2105-x-5087
$6.50 (1979); $7.50 (1980); $8.25 (1981); $8.95 (1982–1983)
On pan: 2105-8253, 1989, Wilton Enterprises, Korea, Warner Bros. Inc.
Estimated value: under $12

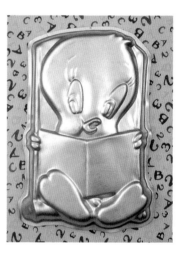

***Porky Pig*™**
Wilton Industries, full size, licensed, Warner Bros.
Yearbook 1985, 2105-x-2371
$8.99 (1985)
On pan: 502-3533, 1983, Wilton, Korea, WARNER BROS., INC.
Estimated value: $26 to $40

***Tweety*™**
Wilton Industries, full size, licensed, Warner Bros.
Yearbooks 1980 through 1984, 2105-x-1383
$7.50 (1980); $8.25 (1981); $8.95 (1982–1983); $6.95 (1984, "Special Value!")
On pan: 502-7687, 1978, no company name, Korea, Warner Bros., Inc.
Estimated value: under $12

Left: *Bugs Bunny*
Wilton Industries, full size, licensed, Warner Bros.
Yearbooks 1984 through 1986, 2105-x-3351
$8.95 (1984); $8.99 (1985); $4.00 (1986, "Super Sale!")
On pan: 502-3517, 1983, Wilton, Korea, Warner Bros, Inc.
Estimated value: under $12

Right: *Bugs Bunny*
Wilton Industries, full size, licensed, Warner Bros.
Yearbooks 1997 through 2000, 2105-x-3200
$9.99 (1997–1998); $10.99 (1999–2000)
On pan: 105-3200, 1996, Wilton Industries, Inc., Indonesia, Warner Bros., left edge of pan, stamp faint
Estimated value: under $12

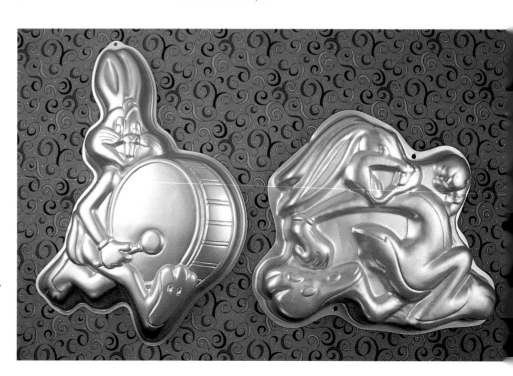

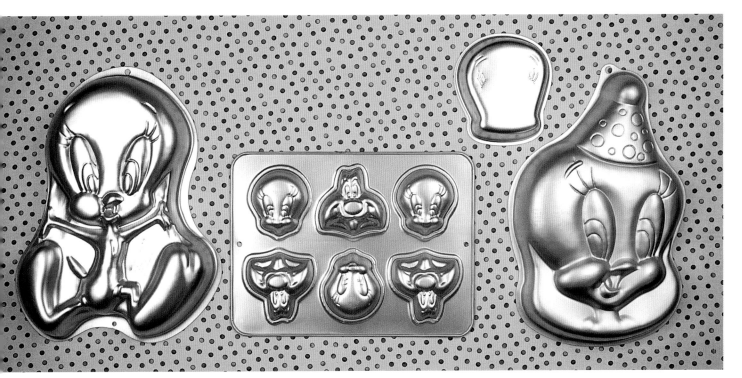

Left: *Tweety*
Wilton Industries, full size, licensed, Warner Bros.
Yearbooks 1999 through 2002, 2105-x-3201
$10.99 (1999–2002)
On pan: 2105-3201, no year, Wilton, Indonesia, Warner Bros
Estimated value: under $12

Center: *Sylvester*™ *and Tweety Mini*
Wilton Industries, multiple cavity, licensed, Warner Bros.
Yearbooks 1995 through 2000, 2105-x-8471
$9.99 (1995); $10.99 (1996–1999); $11.99 (2000)
On pan: 2105-8471, 1994, Wilton, Indonesia, Warner Brothers
Estimated value: under $12

Top Right: *Tweety Bird Mini*
Wilton Industries, individual serving, with lay-on
On pan: 3005-246, 1979, Wilton,
Estimated value: under $12

Right: *Tweety*
Wilton Industries, full size, licensed, Warner Bros.
Yearbook 2003, 2105-x-3205
$10.99 (2003)
On pan: 2105-3205, 2002, Wilton Industries, China, Warner Bros.
List price: $11

***Harry Potter*™**
Wilton Industries, full size, licensed, Warner Bros.
Yearbook 2003, 2105-x-5000
$10.99 (2003)
On pan: 2105-5000, 2001, Wilton Industries Inc., China,
Warner Bros.
List price: $11

***Tasmanian Devil*™**
Wilton Industries, full size, licensed, Warner Bros.
Yearbooks 1996 through 2002, 2105-x-1236
$9.99 (1996–1998, 1997: "New!"); $10.99 (1999–2002)
On pan: 2105-1236, 1995, Wilton Enterprises, Indonesia,
Warner Brothers
Estimated value: under $12

Yosemite Sam™
Wilton Industries, full size, licensed, Warner Bros.
Yearbooks 1982 through 1984, and 1986, 2105-x-3207
$8.95 (1982–1983); $6.95 (1984, "Special Value!"); $4.00 (1986, "Super Sale!")
On pan: 502-2908, 1981, Wilton Enterprises, Korea, Warner Bros., Inc.
Estimated value: under $12

Snoopy™
Wilton Industries, full size, licensed, United Feature Syndicate, Inc., with lay-on
Yearbooks 1986 through 1987, 2105-x-1319
$8.99 (1986–1987)
On pan: 502-1319, 1958, 1965, Wilton Enterprises, Korea, United Feature Syndicate, Inc. [year applies to character copyright, not pan]
Estimated value: $26 to $40, less without lay-on

Popeye™
Wilton Industries, full size, licensed, King Features Syndicate, Inc.
Yearbooks 1982 through 1983, 2105-x-1944
$8.95 (1982–1983)
On pan: 502-1719, 1980, Wilton, Korea, King Features Syndicate, Inc.
Estimated value: under $12

Charlie Brown™
Wilton Industries, full size, licensed, United Feature Syndicate, Inc., with lay-on
Yearbooks 1986 through 1987, 2105-x-1317
$8.99 (1986–1987), extra plastic faceplate $1.99 1985 only
On pan: 2105-1317, 1950, Wilton Enterprises, Korea, United Feature Syndicate, Inc. [year applies to character copyright, not pan]
Estimated value: $26 to $40, less without lay-on

Cathy™
Wilton Industries, full size, licensed, Universal Press Syndicate
Yearbooks 1984 through 1986, 2105-x-4641
$8.95 (1984); $8.99 (1985); $4.00 (1986, "Super Sale!")
On pan: 502-3894, 1983, Wilton, Korea, Universal Press
Syndicate
Estimated value: under $12

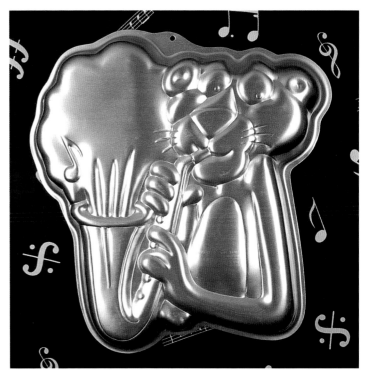

Pink Panther™
Wilton Industries, full size, licensed, United Artists
Yearbooks 1983, 1984, and 1986, 2105-x-2576
$8.95 (1983–1984); $4.00 (1986, "Super Sale!")
On pan: 502-3902, 1982, Wilton Industries, Inc., Korea, United Artists
Estimated value: $12 to $25

Ziggy™
Wilton Industries, full size, licensed, Universal Press Syndicate
Yearbooks 1979 through 1984, 2105-x-5053
$6.50 (1979); $7.50 (1980); $8.25 (1981); $8.95 (1982–1983);
$6.95 (1984, "Special Value!")
On pan: 502-7628, 1976, Wilton, Korea, Universal Press Syndicate
Estimated value: under $12

Pink Panther
Wilton Industries, full size, licensed, United Artists
Yearbooks 1978 through 1982, 502-x-4513,
2105-x-4528
$5.99 (1978); $6.50 (1979); $7.50 (1980); $8.25
(1981); $8.95 (1982)
On pan: 502-4548, 1977, Wilton, Korea, UAC Geoffrey
Estimated value: under $12

Left: *Garfield™ the Cat, 1-2-3*
Wilton Industries, full size, licensed,
United Feature Syndicate, Inc.
On pan: 502-9403, 1978, Wilton
Enterprises, Korea, United Feature
Syndicate, Inc. [year is for copyright
by United Features]
Estimated value: under $12
Right: *Garfield Stand-up*
Wilton Industries, full size, stand-up,
clamp-together, licensed, United
Feature Syndicate, Inc., with lay-on
Yearbooks 1985 through 1991,
2105-x-3147, also called *Garfield
Stand-up Cake Pan Set*
$12.99 (1985–1986), $14.99
(1987–1991), 1985–1986 extras
faceplates offered for $1.99
On pan: 2105-3147, 1978 1981,
Wilton, no country, United Feature
Syndicate, Inc
Estimated value: under $12

Top: *Garfield*
Wilton Industries, full size, licensed, United Feature Syndicate, Inc., with lay-on
Yearbooks 1985 through 1995, 2105-x-2447, also called *Garfield One-Mix Pan,
Garfield Pan (Flat), Garfield Pan (One-Mix)*
$8.99 (1985–1988); $9.99 (1989–1995)
On pan: 2105-2447, 1978, 1981, Wilton, Korea, United Feature Syndicate, Inc.
[year is for copyright by United Features]
Estimated value: under $12
Bottom: *Mini Garfield*
Wilton Industries, multiple cavity, licensed, United Feature Syndicate, Inc.
Yearbooks 1993 through 1996, 2105-x-2550
$9.99 (1993–1996)
On pan: 2105-2550, no year, Wilton, Indonesia, no licensor
Estimated value: under $12

Bart Simpson™
Wilton Industries, full size, licensed, Twentieth
Century Fox Film Corporation
Yearbook 1992, 2105-x-9431
$9.99 (1992)
On pan: 2105-9002, 1990, Wilton, Indonesia,
Twentieth Century Fox Film Corp. "Matt
Groening The Simpsons"
Estimated value: under $12

Alf™
Wilton Industries, full size, licensed, Alien
Productions, with lay-on
Yearbooks 1989 through 1990, 2105-x-2705
$9.99 (1989–1990)
On pan: 2105-2705, 1988, Wilton Enterprises,
Korea, Alien Productions
Estimated value: under $12

Biker Mice from Mars™
Wilton Industries, full size, licensed, Brentwood Television Funnies, Inc.
Yearbooks 1995 through 1996, 2105-x-2711
$9.99 (1995–1996)
On pan: 2105-2711, 1994, Wilton Enterprises, Indonesia, Brentwood
Television Funnies, Inc.
Estimated value: under $12

Marvin the Martian™
Wilton Industries, full size, licensed, Warner Bros.
Yearbooks 1999 through 2001, 2105-x-3202
$10.99 (1999–2001)
On pan: 2105-3202, 1998, Wilton, Indonesia, Warner
Bros.
Estimated value: under $12

Left: *Teenage Mutant Ninja Turtles™ Face, Mini*
Wilton Industries, multiple cavity, licensed, Mirage Studio, USA
Yearbooks 1995 through 1996, 2105-x-8473
$9.99 (1995); $10.99 (1996)
On pan: 2105-8473, 1994, Wilton, Indonesia, Mirage Studios "Exclusively licensed by Surge Licensing"
Estimated value: under $12

Center: *Teenage Mutant Ninja Turtles*
Wilton Industries, full size, licensed, Mirage Studio, USA
Yearbooks 1992 through 1996, 2105-x-4436, also called *Teenage Mutant Ninja Turtles Face, Teenage Mutant Ninja Turtles Head*
$9.99 (1992–1996)
On pan: 2105-4436, 1991, Wilton, Indonesia, no licensor
Estimated value: under $12

Right: *Teenage Mutant Ninja Turtles*
Wilton Industries, full size, licensed, Mirage Studio, USA
Yearbooks 1990 through 1996, 2105-x-3075, also called *Teenage Mutant Ninja Turtles Michelangelo*
$9.99 (1990–1996)
On pan: 2105-3075, 1989, Wilton, Korea, Mirage Studios "Exclusively licensed by Surge Licensing"
Estimated value: under $12

G. I. Joe™
Wilton Industries, full size, licensed, Hasbro Inc., with lay-on
Yearbooks 1987 through 1989, 2105-x-2950
$8.99 (1987–1989); extra facemaker $1.99
On pan: 2105-2950, 1986, Wilton, Korea
Estimated value: under $12

Left: *Holly Hobbie*™
Wilton Industries, full size, licensed, American Greetings Corp
Yearbooks 1976 through 1984, 502-x-194, 2105-x-778
$4.95 (1976); $5.95 (1977); $5.99 (1978); $6.50 (1979); $7.50 (1980); $8.25
(1981); $8.95 (1982–1984)
On pan: 502-194, 1975, Wilton Enterprises, Korea, American Greetings
Corporation
Estimated value: under $12

Center Left: *Holly Hobbie*
Wilton Industries, small, licensed, American Greetings Corp
Yearbooks 1977 through 1980, 502-x-313, also called *Holly Hobbie MiniPan*
$3.50 (1977); $3.99 (1978); $4.50 (1979); $5.50 (1980)
On pan: 502-313, 1976, Wilton Enterprises, Korea, American Greetings
Corporation
Estimated value: under $12

Center Right: *Holly Hobbie*
Wilton Industries, small, licensed, American Greetings Corp
On pan: 3005-513, no year, Wilton Enterprises, Korea, American Greetings
Corporation
Estimated value: under $12

Right: *Robby Hobbie*™
Wilton Industries, small, licensed, American Greetings Corp
Yearbooks 1977 through 1980, 502-x-321, also called *Robby Hobbie MiniPan*
$3.50 (1977); $3.99 (1978); $4.50 (1979); $5.50 (1980)
On pan: 502-321, 1976, Wilton Enterprises, Korea, American Greetings
Corporation
Estimated value: under $12

Lamb Chop™
Wilton Industries, full size, licensed, Shari Lewis Enterprises, Inc.
Yearbooks 1995 through 1996, 2105-x-8468
$9.99 (1995–1996)
On pan: 2105-8468, 1993, Wilton, Korea, Shari Lewis Enterprises, Inc.
Estimated value: under $12

Precious Moments™
Wilton Industries, full size, licensed, Precious Moments
Yearbooks 1994 through 1998, 2105-x-9365
$9.99 (1994–1998)
On pan: 2105-9365, 1993, Wilton, Korea, Precious Moments, Inc.
Estimated value: $12 to $25

Left: Cabbage Patch™ Preemie
Wilton Industries, full size, licensed,
Original Appalachian Artworks, Inc.
Yearbook 1986, 2105-x-1990
$8.99 (1986)
On pan: 2105-1990, 1985, Wilton,
Korea, O.A.A., Inc.
Estimated value: under $12

Center: Cabbage Patch Stand-up
Wilton Industries, full size, stand-up,
clamp-together, licensed, Original
Appalachian Artworks, Inc.
Yearbook 1986, 2105-x-1988
$12.99 (1986)
On pan: 2105-1988, 1984, Wilton,
Korea, O.A.A. Inc. (on inside of back
piece)
Estimated value: under $12

Right: Cabbage Patch Kids
Wilton Industries, full size, licensed,
Original Appalachian Artworks, Inc.
Yearbooks 1986 through 1987,
2105-x-1984 Cabbage Patch Kids Pan
$8.99 (1986–1987)
On pan: 2105-1984, 1984, Wilton,
Korea, O.A.A.
Estimated value: under $12

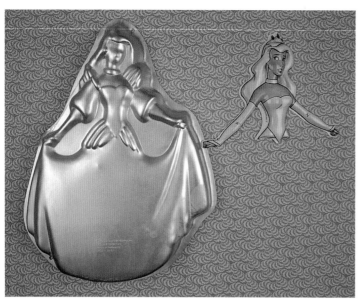

Swan Princess™
Wilton Industries, full size, licensed, Nest Productions Inc., with lay-on
Yearbooks 1995 through 1996, 2105-x-3951
$9.99 (1995–1996)
On pan: 2105-3951, 1994, Wilton Enterprises, Indonesia, Nest Production Inc.
Estimated value: under $12

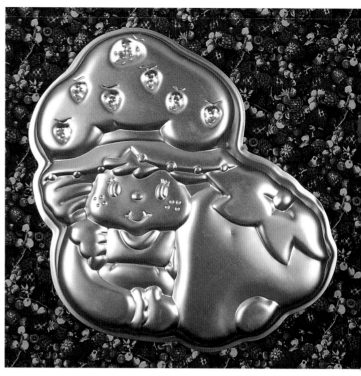

Strawberry Shortcake™
Wilton Industries, full size, licensed, American Greetings Corp
Yearbooks 1983 through 1986, 2105-x-4458
$8.95 (1983–1984); $8.99 (1985–1986)
On pan: 502-3835, 1981, Wilton Enterprises, Korea, American Greetings
Corporation
Estimated value: under $12

Rainbow Brite™
Wilton Industries, full size, licensed, Hallmark Cards, Inc.
Yearbooks 1985 through 1988, 2105-x-4798
$8.99 (1985–1988)
On pan: 2105-4798, 1983, Wilton, Korea, Hallmark Cards, Inc.
Estimated value: under $12

Powerpuff Girls™
Wilton Industries, full size, licensed, Cartoon Network
Yearbooks 2002 through 2003, 2105-x-9902 also called *The Powerpuff Girls*
$10.99 (2002–2003)
On pan: 2105-9902, 2000, no company name, no country, Cartoon Network
List price: $11

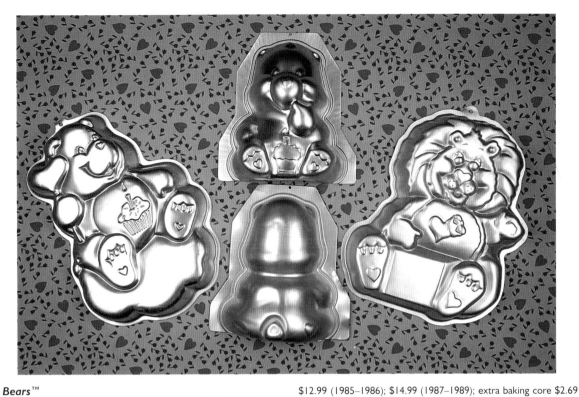

Left: *Care Bears*™
Wilton Industries, full size, licensed, Those Characters From Cleveland, Inc.
Yearbooks 1985 through 1989, 2105-x-1793
$8.99 (1985–1989)
On pan: 2105-1793, 1983, Wilton Enterprises, Korea, American Greetings Corp.
Estimated value: under $12
Center: *Care Bears Stand-up*
Wilton Industries, full size, stand-up, clamp-together, licensed, Those Characters From Cleveland, Inc.
Yearbooks 1985 through 1989, 2105-x-2350

$12.99 (1985–1986); $14.99 (1987–1989); extra baking core $2.69
On pan: 2105-2350, 1984, Wilton Enterprises, Korea, American Greetings Corporation (inside of back)
Estimated value: $12 to $25
Right: *Brave Heart Lion*™
Wilton Industries, full size, licensed, American Greetings Corp
Yearbook 1986, 2105-x-3197
$8.99 (1986)
On pan: 2105-3197, 1984, Wilton Enterprises, Korea, American Greetings Corp
Estimated value: under $12

Left: *Party Popple*™
Wilton Industries, full size, licensed, Those Characters From Cleveland, Inc.
Yearbooks 1987 through 1988, 2105-x-2056
$8.99 (1987–1988)
On pan: 2105-2056, 1985, Wilton Enterprises, Korea, Those Characters From Cleveland
Estimated value: under $12
Center: *Popples, 1-2-3*
Wilton Industries, full size, licensed, Those Characters From Cleveland, Inc., with lay-on

On pan: 2105-9406, 1985, Wilton Enterprises, Korea, Those Characters from Cleveland, Inc.
Estimated value: under $12
Right: *P. C. Popple*™
Wilton Industries, full size, licensed, Those Characters From Cleveland, Inc.
Yearbooks 1987 through 1988, 2105-x-2060
$8.99 (1987–1988)
On pan: 2105-2060, 1985, Wilton Enterprises, Korea, Those Characters From Cleveland
Estimated value: under $12

Left: *Montgomery Good News Moose*™
Wilton Industries, full size, licensed, American Greetings Corp
Yearbook 1986, 2105-x-1968
$8.99 (1986)
On pan: 2105-1968, 1985, Wilton, Korea, A.G.C.
Estimated value: under $12

Right: *Dotty Dog*™
Wilton Industries, full size, licensed, American Greetings Corp
Yearbook 1986, 2105-x-3975
$8.99 (1986)
On pan: 2105-3975, 1985, Wilton, Korea, A.G.C.
Estimated value: under $12

Veggie Tales™
Wilton Industries, full size, licensed, Big Idea Productions
Yearbooks 2002 through 2003, 2105-x-9904
$10.99 (2002–2003)
On pan: 2105-9904, 2001, Wilton Industries, Inc., China, Big Idea Productions, Inc.
List price: $11

Pokémon™
Wilton Industries, full size, licensed, Nintendo
Yearbooks 2001 through 2003, 2105-x-37
$10.99 (2001–2003)
On pan: 2105-37, 1995, 1996, 1998, Wilton, China, Nintendo [years appear to be for character copyright]
List price: $11

Super Mario Brothers™
Wilton Industries, full size, licensed, Nintendo
Yearbooks 1990 through 1994, 2105-x-2989, also called *Super Mario Bros.*
$9.99 (1990–1994)
On pan: 2105-2989, 1983, Wilton, Korea, Nintendo of America
Estimated value: under $12

Blue's Clues™
Wilton Industries, full size, licensed, Viacom International Inc.
Yearbooks 2000 through 2003, 2105-x-3060
$10.99 (2000–2003)
On pan: 2105-3060, 1999, Wilton, China, Viacom
List price: $11

Teletubbies™
Wilton Industries, full size, licensed, Ragdoll Productions (UK) Limited
Yearbooks 2000 through 2001, 2105-x-3065
$10.99 (2000–2001)
On pan: 2105-3065, 1999, Wilton, China, Ragdoll Productions (UK)
Limited
Estimated value: under $12

RugRats™
Wilton Industries, full size, licensed, Viacom International Inc.
Yearbooks 2000 through 2001, 2105-x-3050
$10.99 (2000–2001)
On pan: 2105-3050, 1998, Wilton, Indonesia, Viacom International, Inc.
Estimated value: under $12

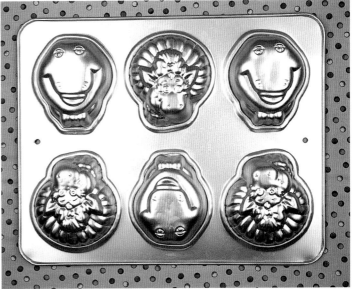

Barney™ and Baby Bop™ Mini
Wilton Industries, multiple cavity, licensed, Lyons Partnership, L.P.
Yearbooks 1995 through 1996, 2105-x-6620
$9.99 (1995); $10.99 (1996)
On pan: 2105-6620, 1994, Wilton, Indonesia, The Lyons Group
Estimated value: under $12

Left: *Barney*
Wilton Industries, full size, licensed, Lyons Partnership, L.P.
Yearbooks 1995 through 1998, 2105-x-6713
$9.99 (1995–1998)
On pan: 2105-6713, 1993, Wilton, Indonesia, The Lyons Group
Estimated value: under $12

Right: *Barney*
Wilton Industries, full size, licensed, Lyons Partnership, L.P.
Yearbooks 1999 through 2002, 2105-x-3450
$10.99 (1999–2002)
On pan: 2105-3450, 1998, Wilton, Indonesia, The Lyons Group, Inc.
Estimated value: under $12

The graphics on this box are great, but the box itself is in only fair condition.
Mint condition boxes of this age are rare.
Wonder Woman™
Wilton Industries, full size, licensed, DC Comics, with lay-on
Yearbooks 1979 through 1984, 2105-x-2622
$7.50 (1979); $7.95 (1980); $8.50 (1981); $8.95 (1982–1984)
On pan: 502-7679, 1978, Wilton, Korea, DC Comics, Inc.
Estimated value: $12 to $25

Left: *Batman Beyond*™
Wilton Industries, full size, licensed, DC Comics
Yearbooks 2001 through 2003, 2105-x-9900
$10.99 (2001–2003)
On pan: 2105-9900, 2000, Wilton, China, DE Comics [sic]
List price: $11

Center: *Batman Emblem*
Wilton Industries, full size, licensed, DC Comics
On pan: 2105-9490, 1964, Wilton Enterprises, Korea, DC Comics [date applies

to copyright of emblem, not to pan]
Estimated value: under $12

Right: *Batman*
Wilton Industries, full size, licensed, DC Comics
Yearbooks 1991 through 2003, 2105-x-6501
$9.99 (1991–1998); $10.99 (1999–2003)
On pan: 2105-6501, 1989, Wilton Enterprises, China, DC Comics, Inc.
List price: $10

The Super Heroes pan came with hard plastic lay-ons for both Superman™ and Batman™. There is no chest insignia on the pan itself. The Superman pan had the insignia on the chest, and a Superman faceplate of lightweight flexible plastic. Extra sets of Super Heroes face and emblem were sold for $1.99 for either Superman or Batman. The later Superman faceplate was not sold separately. Note that both pans have the same stock number stamped on them.

Left: *Super Heroes*
Wilton Industries, full size, licensed, DC Comics, with lay-on
Yearbooks 1978 through 1993, 2105-x-8507 also called *Batman and Superman*
$6.99 (1978); $7.50 (1979); $7.95 (1980); $8.50 (1981); $8.95 (1982–1984); $8.99 (1985–1987); $9.99 (1988–1993)
On pan: 502-1212, 1977, Wilton Enterprises, Korea, DC Comics, Inc.
Courtesy of Denise Mayoff
Estimated value: under $12

Right: *Superman*
Wilton Industries, full size, licensed, DC Comics, with lay-on
Yearbooks 1993 through 1996, 2105-x-2555
$9.99 (1993–1996)
On pan: 502-1212, 1977, Wilton Enterprises, Korea, DC Comics, Inc.
Estimated value: under $12

***Spider-Man*™**
Wilton Industries, full size, licensed, Marvel
Yearbook 2003, 2105-x-5050
$10.99 (2003)
On pan: 2105-5050, 2002, Wilton Industries, China, Marvel & CPII
List price: $11

***Power Rangers/Mighty Morphin Power Rangers*™**
Wilton Industries, full size, licensed, Sabar
Yearbooks 1995 through 1998, 2105-x-5975, also in index as
Power Rangers
$9.99 (1995–1998)
On pan: 2105-5975, 1994, Wilton, Indonesia, Sabar
Estimated value: under $12

***He-Man Masters of the Universe*™**
Wilton Industries, full size, licensed, Mattel, Inc., with lay-on
Yearbooks 1986 through 1989, 503-x-3184, 2105-x-3184
$8.99 (1986–1989); extra faceplate $1.99
On pan: 2105-3184, 1983, Wilton Enterprises, Korea, Mattell, Inc.
Estimated value: under $12

Left: *Darth Vader*™
Wilton Industries, full size, licensed, LFL
Yearbooks 1981 through 1984, and 1986,
2105-x-1278
$8.50 (1981); $8.95 (1982–1984); $4.00 (1986,
"Super Sale!")
On pan: 502-1409, 1980, Wilton, Korea, LFL
Estimated value: $12 to $25

Right: *Boba Fett*™
Wilton Industries, full size, licensed, LFL
Yearbooks 1984 and 1986, 2105-x-1741
$8.95 (1984); $4.00 (1986, "Super Sale!")
On pan: 502-1852, 1983, Wilton, Korea,
Lucasfilm Ltd
On insert: 2105-1741
Estimated value: $26 to $40

Left: *R2-D2*™
Wilton Industries, full size, licensed,
LFL
Yearbooks 1981 through 1984,
2105-x-1294
$8.50 (1981); $8.95 (1982–1984)
On pan: 502-1425, 1980, Wilton,
Korea, LFL
Estimated value: $12 to $25

Right: *C-3PO*™
Wilton Industries, full size, licensed,
LFL
Yearbooks 1984 through 1986,
2105-x-1464
$8.95 (1984); $8.99 (1985); $4.00
(1986, "Super Sale!")
On pan: 502-2197, 1983, Wilton,
Korea, Lucasfilm Ltd
Estimated value: $12 to $25

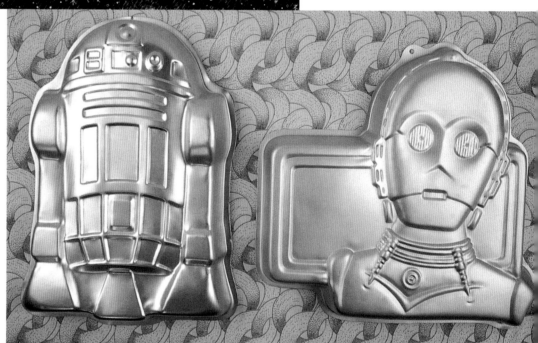

WWF*™ *Superstars
Wilton Industries, full size, licensed, Titan Sports, Inc.
Yearbooks 1993 through 1994, 2105-x-2552
$9.99 (1993–1994)
On pan: 2105-2552, no year, Wilton, Indonesia, no licensor
Estimated value: under $12

Left: *Fred Flintstone*™
Wilton Industries, full size, licensed, Hanna-Barbera
Yearbooks 1995 through 1996, 2105-x-1285, also
called *Flintstones Pan*
$9.99 (1995–1996)
On pan: 2105-1285, 1994, Wilton, Indonesia,
Hanna-Barbera Productions, Inc.
Estimated value: under $12

Right: *Fred Flintstone*
Wilton Industries, full size, licensed, Hanna-Barbera
Yearbooks 1977 through 1980, 2105-x-1863,
502-x-186
$4.95 (1977); $5.99 (1978); $5.95 (1979); $6.95
(1980)
On pan: 502-186, 1975, Wilton Enterprises, Korea,
Hanna-Barbera Productions, Inc.
Estimated value: under $12

Yogi Bear™
Wilton Industries, full size, licensed, Hanna-Barbera
Yearbooks 1977 through 1980, 502-x-178, 2105-x-1782
$4.95 (1977); $5.99 (1978); $5.95 (1979); $6.95 (1980)
On pan: 502-178, 1975, Wilton Enterprises, Korea, Hanna-
Barbera Productions, Inc.
Estimated value: $12 to $25

Left: *Scooby-Doo*™
Wilton Industries, full size, licensed, Hanna-
Barbera
Yearbooks 2000 through 2003,
2105-x-3206
$10.99 (2000–2003)
On pan: 2105-3206, 1999, Wilton,
Indonesia, Hanna-Barbera
List price: $11

Right: *Scooby-Doo*
Wilton Industries, full size, licensed, Hanna-
Barbera
Yearbooks 1977 through 1980, 502-x-224,
2105-x-2606
$4.95 (1977); $5.99 (1978); $5.95 (1979);
$6.95 (1980)
On pan: 502-224, 1975, Wilton Enterprises,
Korea, Hanna-Barbera Productions, Inc.
Estimated value: under $12

Rudolph The Red Nosed Reindeer™
Wilton Industries, full size, licensed, R. L. May Trust
Yearbooks 1982 through 1984, 2105-x-4722
$8.95 (1982–1983); $6.95 (1984, "Special Value!")
On pan: 502-3347, 1981, Wilton, Korea, R. L. May Trust
Estimated value: under $12

Thomas the Tank Engine™
Wilton Industries, full size, licensed, Gullane (Thomas) Limited
Yearbooks 1995 through 2003, 2105-x-1349
$9.99 (1995–1998); $10.99 (1999–2003)
On pan: 2105-1349, no year, Wilton, China, no licensor
List price: $11

Raggedy Ann™
Wilton Industries, full size, licensed, Bobbs-Merrill Co., Inc.
Yearbooks 1983 through 1985, 2105-x-4986
$8.95 (1983–1984); $8.99 (1985)
On pan: 502-3797, 1981, Wilton, Korea, The Bobbs-Merrill Co., Inc.
Estimated value: under $12

Left: *Smurfette*™
Wilton Industries, full size, licensed, Peyo
Yearbooks 1984 through 1986, 2105-x-5419
$8.95 (1984); $8.99 (1985–1986)
On pan: 502-4017, 1983, Wilton Enterprises, Korea,
Peyo, "Licensed by Wallace Berrie & Co. Inc., VAN
Nuys, CA"
Estimated value: under $12
Right: *Smurf*™
Wilton Industries, full size, licensed, Peyo
Yearbooks 1984 through 1986, 2105-x-5435
$8.95 (1984); $8.99 (1985–1986)
On pan: 502-4033, 1983, Wilton Enterprises, Korea,
Peyo, Licensed by Wallace Berrie & Co.
Estimated value: under $12

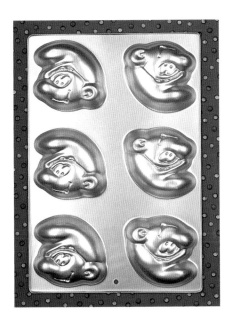

Mini Smurf
Wilton Industries, multiple cavity, licensed, Peyo
Yearbook 1986, 2105-x-2386
$7.99 (1986)
On pan: 2105-2386, 1984, Wilton, Korea, Peyo, "Licensed by Wallace Berrie & Company"
Estimated value: under $12

Bob the Builder™
Wilton Industries, full size, licensed, HIT/K Chapman
Yearbook 2003, 2105-x-5025
$10.99 (2003)
On pan: 2105-5025, 2002, Wilton Industries, China, HT/K Chapman
List price: $11

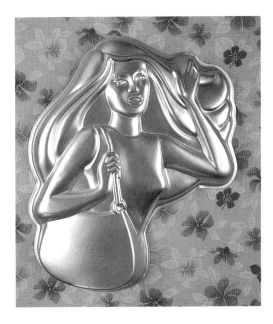

Barbie™
Wilton Industries, full size, licensed, Mattel, Inc., with lay-on
Yearbooks 1987 through 1989, 2105-x-2250
$8.99 (1987–1989), extra facemaker $1.99
On pan: 2105-2250, 1986, Wilton Enterprises, Korea, Mattel, Inc.
Estimated value: under $12

Left: *Barbie*
Wilton Industries, full size, licensed, Mattel, Inc., with lay-on
Yearbook 2003, 2105-x-8910
$10.99 (2003), extra facemaker $2.29
On pan: 2105-8910, 2002, Wilton Industries, China, Mattel
List price: $11
Right: *Barbie, Dreamtime Princess*
Wilton Industries, full size, licensed, Mattel, Inc., with lay-on
Yearbook 2002, 2105-x-8900
$10.99 (2002), extra facemaker $2.29
On pan: 2105-8900, 2000, Wilton, China, Mattel, Inc.
Estimated value: under $12

127

Beautiful Day Barbie
Wilton Industries, full size, licensed, Mattel, Inc., with lay-on
Yearbooks 1996 through 1998, 2105-x-3500
$10.99 (1996–1998)
On pan: 2105-3500, 1995, Wilton Enterprises, Indonesia, Mattel, Inc.
Estimated value: under $12

Flower Power™
Wilton Industries, full size, licensed, KI
Yearbooks 1999 through 2003, 2105-x-3055
$10.99 (1999–2003)
On pan: 2105-3055, 1998, Wilton, China, KI
List price: $11

Left: *Barbie*
Wilton Industries, full size, licensed, Mattel, Inc., with lay-on
Yearbooks 1999 through 2001, 2105-x-8900, 2105-x-3550, also called *Barbie: Dreamtime Princess*
$11.99 (1999–2000); $10.99 (2001); facemaker set and ethnic facemaker set also offered separately for $3.99
On pan: 2105-3550, 1998, Wilton, China, Mattel, Inc.
Estimated value: under $12

Right: *Barbie*
Wilton Industries, full size, licensed, Mattel, Inc., with lay-on
Yearbooks 1993 through 1996, 2105-x-2551
$9.99 (1993–1996)
On pan: 2105-2551, 1992, Wilton, Korea, Mattel, Inc.
Estimated value: under $12

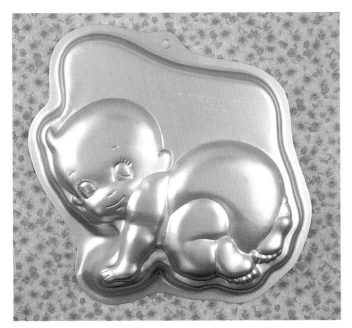

Special Delivery Baby™
Wilton Industries, full size, licensed, The Itsy Bitsy Entertainment Company
Yearbooks 2001 through 2003, 2105-x-2003
$10.99 (2001–2003)
On pan: 2105-2003, 2000, Wilton, China, The Itsy Bitsy Entertainment
Company
List price: $11

Playboy Bunny™
Wilton Industries, full size, licensed, Playboy Enterprises, Inc.
On pan: 502-2944, no year, Wilton, Korea, Playboy Enterprises, Inc.
Estimated value: $12 to $25

Left: *Poppin' Fresh*™
Wilton Industries, full size, licensed, The Pillsbury Company
Yearbooks 1975 through 1980, 502-x-704, also spelled *Poppin Fresh*
$4.95 (1975–1977); $5.50 (1978); $5.95 (1979); $6.95 (1980)
On pan: 502-704, 1974, Wilton Enterprises, Korea, The Pillsbury Company
Estimated value: $26 to $40
Right: *Pillsbury Poppin' Fresh Doughboy*
Unknown, individual serving, licensed, The Pillsbury Company
On pan: 3005-157, 1975, no company, Korea, The Pillsbury Company
Estimated value: $12 to $25

Not Pictured

Cinderella™
Wilton Industries, full size, stand-up, open mold, licensed, Disney
Similar to *Wonder Mold*, but asymmetrical, with back of skirt
deeper than front. Goldtone.
Yearbooks 1972 through 1974, 515-x-205, also called *Cinderella
Doll*
$4.95 (1972, blond doll pick, $1.00); $5.25 (1974, blond doll pick,
$1.25)
Estimated value: unknown

Chapter 7

Simple Shapes:
Plain and Fancy

Round is not a novelty shape, but the numerous variations on this basic shape are interesting in their own right.

Left: *Half Round*

The purpose of the half round is to enable a home baker to produce a round cake larger than the home oven will usually accommodate by baking it in two halves.

Unknown, double

On pan: no stock number, no year, no company, U. S. A., "18 x 3"

List price: $19

Center: *Miniature Wedding Tiers*

Parrish's Cake Decorating Supplies Inc., individual serving

On pan: no stock number, no year, Magic Line, U.S.A., "4x2"

On pan: no stock number, no year, Magic Line, U.S.A., "3x2"

On pan: no stamp on smallest pan

Courtesy of Nila Pudwill

 List price: $14

Right: A variety of rounds, 2" deep

Top of stack is *3 in. Round Singles!*

Wilton Industries, individual serving

Yearbooks 1998 through 2001, 2105-x-1113

$1.99 (1998–2000); $2.49 (2001)

On pan: no stamp

Estimated value: under $12

Round pans are available in sizes ranging from 3" to 20" from several manufacturers. (Pans larger than 16" in diameter do not fit in typical home ovens.) Pans have been sold in sets of two the same size, for layer cakes (with 8" and 9" being the most common sold this way), and in tiered sets in great profusion. Wilton has offered a set of three round pans that together hold a single cake mix, another that hold two mixes, as well as other sets of three or four pans. Pans by other companies are also sold individually and in tiered sets.

The rounded edges on these pans are suitable for use with a rolled fondant covering. Such pans are sold individually and in tiered sets, by several companies

Contour Baking Pan Set
Wilton Industries, mixed sizes in set
Yearbook 2000, 2105-x-6118
$39.99 (2000)
On pan: no stock number, no year, Wilton (script), U.S.A., each pan has size stamped on bottom: "7 x 3", "11 x 3", and "15 x 3"
Estimated value: under $40

This set of plastic pieces to place between cake tiers is an example of accessories offered throughout the years to provide an unusual presentation for basic cake shapes.

Carousel Separator Set
Wilton Industries, size not applicable
Yearbooks 2000 through 2003, 2103-x-1139
$11.99 (2000–2003); description says set/8, but lists 6 pieces
On clear separator plate only: 301-6016, 1979, Wilton, Hong Kong
List price: $12

4-Tier Cake Pan Set
Mirro, mixed sizes in set, box says 1 1/2 mixes, c. 1950
On pan: 1169M, no year, Mirro, U.S.A., "9 x 1 1/2"
On pan: 1177-M, no year, Mirro, U.S.A., "7 1/4 x 1 1/2"
On pan: 1175-M, no year, Mirro, U.S.A., "5 1/2 x 1 1/2"
On pan: 1173-M, no year, Mirro, U.S.A., "3 1/4 x 1 1/2"
Estimated value: under $12, more with box

Left: *Double Tier Round*
Wilton Industries, full size
Yearbooks 1987 through 1997, 2105-x-1400
$7.99 (1987–1988); $8.99 (1989–1990); $9.99 (1991–1997)
On pan: 2105-1400, 1986, Wilton, Korea
Estimated value: under $12

Right: *Triple-tier round*
Unknown, full size
On pan: no stamp
Estimated value: under $12

These pans are intended to be used with plain round pans of corresponding sizes, to produce a two-layer
cake with the top layer beveled.

Bevel Pan Set
Wilton Industries, mixed sizes in set
Yearbooks sporadically 1974 through 2002, 517-x-1200, 2105-x-6116, 2105-x-1200
$14 (1974–1975); $8.95 (1977); $8.99 (1978); 25.95 (1984); $25.99 (1985–1992); $39.99 (2000–2002); in 1977 each size was sold separately as well as in the set; in 2000 only the 10" pan was offered separately
On pan: no stock number, no year, Wilton (in outline script), USA, size also stamped on each pan
Estimated value: under $40

Twelve removable bottoms were offered for this Basic Ring pan.
Left: *Basic Ring* (for Sculptured Tops)
Wilton Industries, full size
Yearbooks 1976 through 1982, and 1984, 502-x-259
$3.95 (1976, 1977, and 1979); $3.99 (1978); $4.95 (1980–1981); $1.00 (1984, in Super Sale! section)
On pan: 502-259, 1974, Wilton (script), Korea
Estimated value: under $12
Right: *Insert for Ring Pan, Swirl*
Wilton Industries, full size
Yearbooks 1977 through 1980, 503-x-423
$2.95 (1977 and 1979); $2.99 (1978); $3.50 (1980); through 1979, any 4 inserts, $9.95; 1980, any 4 inserts, $11.95
On pan: 503-423, 1976, Wilton (script), Korea
Estimated value: under $12

Top Left: *Traditional Round Angel Food*
Comet, full size
On pan: no stock number, no year, Comet, U.S.A.
Estimated value: under $12
Top Center: *Angel Food Singles!*
Wilton Industries, individual serving
Yearbooks 1998 through 2003, 2105-x-1104
$2.49 (1998–2000); $2.99 (2001–2003)
On pan: no stamp
List price: $3
Top Right: *Angelaire Angel Food Cake Pan*
United Aircraft Products Inc., Dayton, Ohio, full size
On pan: no stock number, no year, United Aircraft Products Inc., Dayton, Ohio,
Estimated value: under $12

Bottom Left: *Mini Angel Food Pan*
Wilton Industries, multiple cavity
Yearbooks 1996 through 1999, 2105-x-9312
$14.99 (1996–1999)
On pan: 2105-9312, no year, Wilton, Indonesia
Courtesy of Nila Pudwill
Estimated value: under $12
Bottom Right: *Classic Angel Food Pan*
Wilton Industries, small
Yearbook 2003, 2105-x-9311
$11.99 (2003)
On pan: 2105-9311, 1993, Wilton, Indonesia "7" ANGEL FOOD"
Courtesy of Nila Pudwill
List price: $12

Top Left: *Fancy Ring Singles!*
Wilton Industries, individual serving
Yearbooks 1998 through 2003, 2105-x-1102
$2.49 (1998–2000); $2.99 (2001–2003)
On pan: no stamp
List price: $3

Bottom Left: *Fancy Ring*
Wilton Industries, full size
Yearbooks 1985 through 2003, 2105-x-5008
$7.99 (1985–1986); $8.99 (1987–1988); $9.99 (1989–2003)
On pan: 2105-5008, 1995, Wilton, Indonesia, (on top of center tube)
List price: $10

Right: *Petite Fancy Ring*
Wilton Industries, multiple cavity
Yearbooks 1987 through 2003, 2105-x-2097, also called *Mini Fluted Mold Pan*
$13.99 (1987–1988); $14.99 (1989); $15.99 (1990); $16.99 (1991–1993);
$17.99 (1994); $16.99 (1995); $17.99 (1996–2003, "New" in 2003)
On pan: 2105-2097, no year, Wilton, China
List price: $18

Left: *Shortcakes 'N' Treats*
Wilton Industries, multiple cavity
Yearbooks 1984 through 1996, 2105-x-5966, also spelled
Shortcakes 'N Treats
$5.95 (1984); $6.50 (1985–1986); $6.99 (1987–1993); $7.49
(1994); $7.99 (1995–1996)
On pan: 508-1376, no year, Wilton, Korea
Estimated value: under $12

Top Right: *Individual Swirled Mold with Indentation*
Unknown, individual serving
On pan: no stamp
Estimated value: under $12

Bottom Right: *Shortcake Singles!*
Wilton Industries, individual serving
Yearbooks 1998 through 2000, 2105-x-1108
$1.69 (1998); $1.99 (1999–2000)
On pan: no stamp
Estimated value: under $12

Top Left: *Turk's Head Mold*
Unknown (made in Portugal), full size
On pan: no stamp, paper label "Portugal"
List price: $8

Top Center: *Classic Tube Pan*
Wilton Industries, full size
Yearbooks 1986 through 1988, 2105-x-2174
$7.99 (1986–1988)
On pan: no stamp
Courtesy of Nila Pudwill

Estimated value: under $12

Top Right: *Tall Crown Mold, coppertone*
Unknown, full size
On pan: no stock number, no year, no company name, no country, "8 CUPS"
Estimated value: under $12

Bottom Left: *Coppertone Fancy Fluted Deep Ring*
Unknown, full size
On pan: no stamp
Estimated value: under $12

Bottom Right: *Fluted Ring*
Unknown (made in Portugal), full size
On pan: no stamp, paper label "Portugal"
Courtesy of Nila Pudwill
List price: $8

Top Left: *Ring Twist*
AHC, small
Yearbooks 1964, 309
$1.00 (1964)
On pan: no stock number, 1963, A.H.C. St. Louis, MO., Hong Kong, "4 CUPS"
Courtesy of Nila Pudwill
Estimated value: under $12

Top Center: *4 in. Ring Singles!*
Wilton Industries, individual serving
Yearbooks 1998 through 1999, 2105-x-1111
$1.99 (1998–1999)
On pan: no stamp
Estimated value: under $12

Top Right: *Decorated Ring*
Unknown, full size
On pan: no stock number, no company name, Hong Kong
Courtesy of Nila Pudwill
Estimated value: under $12

Middle Left: *Individual Ring Molds, coppertone*
Unknown, individual serving

On pan: no stamp
Estimated value: under $12

Middle Right: *Individual Fluted Ring Molds, coppertone*
Unknown, individual serving
On pan: no stamp
Estimated value: under $12

Bottom Left: *Swirl Ring*
Unknown (made in Portugal), full size
On pan: no stamp, paper label "Portugal"
Courtesy of Nila Pudwill
List price: $8

Bottom Center: *Coppertone Ring Mold*
Wilton Industries, full size
On pan: no stamp
Estimated value: under $12

Bottom Right: *Ring Mold, coppertone rope pattern*
Mirro, full size
On pan: no stock number, no year, MIRRO, "6 CUP, 1 1/2 QT."
Estimated value: under $12

Top Left: *Acorn on Round With Fluted Sides*
Unknown, full size
On pan: no stamp
Courtesy of Nila Pudwill
Estimated value: under $12

Top Right: *Coronet*
Wilton Industries, small
Yearbook 1964, 317
$1.00 (1964)
On pan: no stock number, no year, no country, "4 CUPS"
Courtesy of Nila Pudwill
Estimated value: under $12

Bottom Left: *Sculptured Mold (Coppertone)*
Wilton Industries, double
Yearbook 1974, 502-x-402
$5.25 (1974)
On pan: 502-402, no year, no company name, Korea
Estimated value: under $12

Bottom Right: *Round Sculpted Mold*
Mirro, full size
On pan: no stamp
Courtesy of Nila Pudwill
Estimated value: under $12

Left: Three-Tiered Mold
Unknown, full size
On pan: no stock number, no year, no company name, "6 CUPS"
Estimated value: under $12

Top Center: Coppertone Tall Tyrolean Mold
Nordic Ware, full size, also sold by Wilton
Yearbooks 1964 through 1971, 258, NA-258
Nordic Ware booklet 11-71, c. 1970, stock number 31001, Tall Tyrolean Mold, Copper anodized
$2.98 (1964–1969); $2.49 (c. 1970)
On pan: no stamp
Estimated value: under $12

Top Right: Swirled Cone
Mirro, small
On pan: no stock number, no year, no company name, no country, "6 CUPS," paper Mirro label
Courtesy of Nila Pudwill
Estimated value: under $12

Bottom Left: Tiara
Wilton Industries, full size
Yearbook 1964, 629
$1.49 (1964)
On pan: no stock number, no year, no company name, Hong Kong
Courtesy of Nila Pudwill
Estimated value: under $12

Bottom Right: Princess
Wilton Industries, small
Yearbook 1964, 323
$1.00 (1964)
On pan: no stock number, no year, no company name,, Hong Kong
Courtesy of Nila Pudwill
Estimated value: under $12

Top Left: Coppertone Fluted Mold
Unknown, small
On pan: no stamp
Estimated value: under $12

Top Center: Individual Fluted Molds
Unknown, individual serving
On pan: no stamp
Estimated value: under $12

Top Right: Small Fluted Mold
Unknown, full size
On pan: no stock number, no year, no company name, Hong Kong
Courtesy of Nila Pudwill
Estimated value: under $12

Center Right: Individual Swirled Mold
Unknown, individual serving
On pan: no stamp
Estimated value: under $12

Bottom Left: Swirled Fluted mold
Unknown, small
On pan: no stamp
Estimated value: under $12

Bottom Center: Decorated Domed Mold
Unknown, small
On pan: no stamp
Courtesy of Nila Pudwill
Estimated value: under $12

Bottom Right: Fluted Mold
Mirro, small
On pan: no stock number, no year, Mirro, USA
Estimated value: under $12

Top Left: *Magic Mold Baking Pan*
Parrish's Cake Decorating Supplies Inc., full size, stand-up, open mold
On pan: no stamp, stock Number on leaflet MM-68
List price: $17

Top Right: *Wonder Mold/Classic Wonder Mold*
Wilton Industries, full size, stand-up, open mold
Yearbooks 1969 through 2003, PR-68, PR 68, 501-x-3687, 2105-x-565, 501-x-3687, also called *Big Wonder Mold Kit, Magic Mold Pan, Large Wonder Mold and Doll Pick Kit, Large Wonder Mold Kit*, pan is shown as goldtone through 1987
$5.95 (1969, 1970, 1974, 1975, price for pan only, doll picks $.40, 3/$1.00); $5.75 (1972); $6.50 (1976); $6.95 (1977); $7.50 (1978); $7.95 (1979); $8.95 (1980); $9.95 (1981–1984); $10.99 (1985–1989); $11.99 (1990–1996); $12.99 (1997); $14.99 (1998–2000); $15.99 (2001–2003); except as noted, prices are for pan and one doll pick; pan was also sold without pick through 1991; little girl pick was introduced in 1976; new teen pick and blonde pick were introduced in

2003
On pan (on stand): 502-682, 1994, Wilton, Indonesia
List price: $16

Bottom Right: *Mini Wonder /Petite Doll*
Wilton Industries, multiple cavity, stand-up, open mold
Yearbooks 1972 through 2003, 508-x-302, 2105-x-3020, also called *Mini Wonder Mold, Petite Doll Pan Set, Small Wonder Mold Pan, Small Wonder Molds, Petite Doll Cake Pan*
$3.50 (1972); $3.95 (1974); $4.50 (1975); $4.75 (1976); $4.95 (1977); $5.50 (1978); $5.95 (1979); $6.95 (1980); $7.25 (1981); $7.95 (1982–1984); $7.99 (1985); $8.49 (1986); $8.99 (1987–1990); $9.99 (1991–2003); for many years the pan was available alone or as a kit with 4 doll picks; prices shown are for pan; pan has not been sold as a kit since 1990
On pan: 508-302, no year, Wilton, China
List price: $10

Petal-Shaped Pans, 4 tiered
Wilton Industries, mixed sizes in set
Yearbooks 1972 through 2003, 502-x-2138, 501-x-2138, 2105-x-2134, also called *4 PC. Petal Pan Set, 4-Pan Set, Petal Pan Set, Petal-Shaped Wedding tier set, Set of 4 Petal Pans*
$8.95 (1972); $9.95 (1974); $10.95 (1975); $12.95 (1976); $13.95 (1977); $14.99 (1978); $18.95 (1979); $21.50 (1980); $22.95 (1981–1984); $24.99 (1985–1988); $ (1989–1991); $26.99 (1992–1995); $27.99 (1996); $29.99 (1997–2003); in addition to the tiered set, Wilton offered the 9" and 12" pans individually, and a set of two 9" petal pans; all four sizes were offered individually in 1986
On pan: 502-2138, 1971, Wilton (script), Korea, same stamp on all 4 pans
Courtesy of Cheryl Thompson
List price: $30

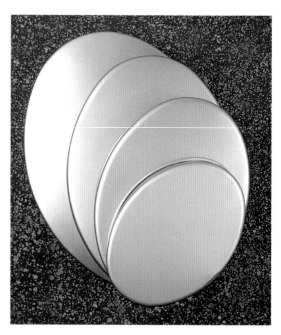

Oval Pan Set
Wilton Industries, full size
Yearbooks 1989 through 2003, 2105-x-2130
$19.99 (1989); $23.99 (1993); $27.99 (1997–2000); $29.99 (2001–2003)
On pan: 502-3130, no year, Wilton, China, "Performance Pans," each pan stamped with dimensions
List price: $30

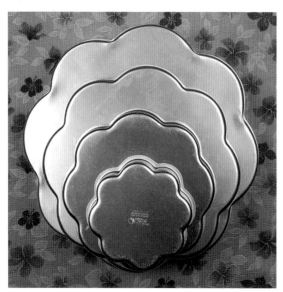

Top: *Oval Pans* **(sold as part of Course II Cake Decorating Kit)**
Wilton Industries, full size
On pan: 502-2131, 1997, Wilton, China
Estimated value: under $12

Bottom: *Ovals,* **two 9" pans**
Wilton Industries, full size
Yearbooks 1970 through 1993, W90, 502-x-909, 2105-x-1553, also called *Oval Pan Set, Pair Oval Pans*
$3.00 (1970); $3.25 (1972); $350 (1974); $4.25 (1975) $4.35 (1976); $4.50 (1977); $4.99 (1978); $5.50 (1979); $6.50 (1980); $7.25 (1981); $7.95 (1982–1983); $5.95 (1984, "Special Value!"); $5.99 (1985); $6.49 (1986); $7.99 (1987–1988); $8.99 (1989–1990); $9.99 (1991–1993)
On pan: no stock number, no year, Wilton (script, star), Japan
Estimated value: under $12

The Flower Cart is an example of an accessory set that turns a plain shape (in this case, oval) into a novel presentation. The plastic accessories were sold as a set with or without the pans.

Left: *Flower Cart Kit*
Wilton Industries, full size, stand-up, accessorize or stack
Yearbooks 1966 through 1969, W-86W, W-86, also called *Florentine Flower Cart, White*
$4.95 (1966–1969)
On pan: 502-909, no year, Wilton, Korean
On pan: no stock number, no year, Wilton (script, star), Japan, "Shapely Pans"
Estimated value: $26 to $40

Right: *Flower Cart Kit*
Wilton Industries, full size, stand-up, accessorize or stack
Yearbooks 1966 through 1978, W-86G, W86G, 501-x-8610, also called *Florentine Flower Cart, Gold*
$5.95 (1966–1969); $7.95 (1970); $9.50 (1972); $11.95 (1974); $12.95 (1975); $13.95 (1976–1977); $14.99 (1978)
On pan: 502-909, no year, Wilton, Korean
On pan: no stock number, no year, Wilton (script, star), Japan, "Shapely Pans"
Estimated value: over $40

Left and Right: *Coppertone Oval Seasons Molds*
Unknown, small
On pan: no stock number, no year, no company name, each pan stamped with season name and "3 CUPS"
Courtesy of Nila Pudwill
Estimated value: under $12

Center: *Oval with Fleur-de-Lis*
Unknown, small
On pan: no stamp
Estimated value: under $12

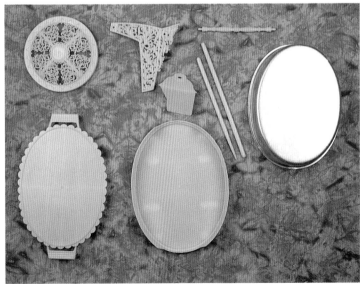

This photo shows each of the pieces in the Flower Cart kit above.

This clever pan has removable cubes that can be arranged to vary the shape of the cake.
Educated Cake Pan
Burvelle, full size
On pan: no stock number, no year, Burvelle Enterprises Inc., U. S. A.
Estimated value: $12 to $25

Square Angel Food Pan
Wear-Ever, full size
On pan: 2740, no year, WEAR-EVER, U.S.A, "9 x 9 x 4"
Estimated value: under $12

Left: *Contessa*
Wilton Industries, small
Yearbook 1964, 321
$1.00 (1964)
On pan: no stock number, no year, no company name, Hong Kong
Courtesy of Nila Pudwill
Estimated value: under $12
Right: *Square mold with top design*
Unknown, full size
On pan: no stamp
Estimated value: under $12

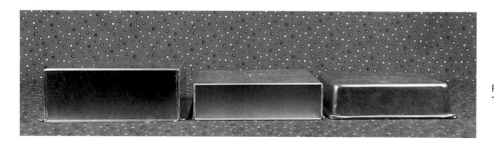

Pans vary in depth as well as in length and width. These are all 8" square pans.

The small size of these square pans is unusual; the plastic accessory kit provides a novel presentation.

Daisy Cart
Wilton Industries, full size
Yearbooks 1972 through 1978, 501-x-505
$5.00 (1972); $5.95 (1974); $7.50 (1975–1978); $7.95 (1976); $6.95 (1977); these prices are for kit; pans and plastic pieces were also sold separately
On pan: 502-2162, 1971, Wilton, Korea
Estimated value: $26 to $40

The *Daisy Cart Kit* consisted of four sets of the items pictured.

The loaf shape is not generally considered a novelty pan, but the variations on a loaf theme are interesting and many collectors include at least some loafs within their collections.

Top Left: *Standard loaf* with slightly sloped sides
Unknown, full size
On pan: no stock number, no year, no company name, no country, "9 5/8 x 5 1/2 x 2 3/4"
Estimated value: under $12

Top Center: *Petite Loaf*
Wilton Industries, multiple cavity
Yearbooks 1995 through 2003, 2105-x-8466, also called *9 Cavity Petite Loaf*
$9.99 (1995–2003)
On pan: 2105-8466, 1994, Wilton, Indonesia
List price: $10

Top Right: *Little Loafers*
Wilton Industries, individual serving
Yearbooks 1964 through 1986, AS-108, 512-x-1089, 2621-1
$1.00 (1964–1966); $1.50 (1969); $1.75 (1970); $2.00 (1972); $3.25 (1974–1975); $3.50 (1976); $3.95 (1977); $3.99 (1978); $4.50 (1979); $5.50 (1980); $5.95 (1981–1984); $5.99 (1985); $6.49 (1986)
On pan: 512-1089, 1972, Wilton (script), Korea
Estimated value: $12 to $25

Bottom, Far Left: *Long Loaf*
Wilton Industries, double size
Yearbooks 1974 through 2003, 512-x-1208, 2105-x-1588
$5.25 (1974); $5.50 (1975); $5.75 (1976); $5.95 (1977); $5.99 (1978); $6.95 (1979); $7.95 (1980); $8.50 (1981); $8.95 (1982–1984); $8.99 (1985–1986); $9.99 (1987–1994); $10.99 (1995–1996); $11.99 (1997–2000); $12.99 (2001–2003)

On pan: 512-1208, no year, Wilton, China
List price: $13

Middle Left: *Standard capacity loaf, long and narrow*
Mirro, full size
On pan: 5196M, no year, Mirro, U.S.A., "10 1/4 x 3 5/8 x 2 5/8"
Estimated value: under $12

Center: *Ribbed loaf, straight ends, long*
Unknown, full size
On pan: no stamp
Courtesy of Nila Pudwill
Estimated value: under $12

Bottom, Far Right: *Mini Loaf Pan Set*
Wilton Industries, multiple cavity
Yearbooks 1992 through 2003, 2105-x-9791, also called *6 Cavity Mini Loaf Pan*
$9.99 (1992–2003)
On pan: 2105-9791, 1991, Wilton, Indonesia
List price: $10

Bottom Left: *Ribbed loaf, straight ends, short*
Unknown, small
On pan: no stamp on
Courtesy of Nila Pudwill
Estimated value: under $12

Bottom Center: *Loaf Mold*
Unknown, full size
Yearbooks 1959 through 1970, HM-10, HM10
$1.00 (1959–1966); $1.75 (1969); $4 (1970)
Estimated value: under $12

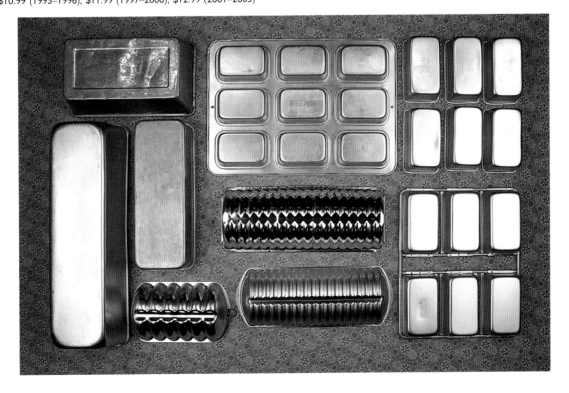

Hexagon Set
Wilton Industries, full size
Yearbooks 1976 through 2003, 502-x-356, 2105-x-3572, also called *4 Pc. Hexagon Pan Set*
$15.95 (1976–1977); $18.50 (1978); $18.95 (1979); $21.50 (1980); $22.95 (1981–1984); $24.99 (1985–1988); $26.99 (1989–1993); $28.99 (1994–1995); $29.99 (1996); $30.99 (1997–2003); each pan also sold separately in 1986; the 9" and 12" pans sold separately in some later years
On pan: 502-356, 1974, Wilton (script), Korea
Courtesy of Denise Mayoff
List price: $31

Left: *Jewel Mold (Coppertone)*
Wilton Industries, full size (probably not Wilton exclusive)
Yearbook 1969, MO-742
$1.95 (1969)
On pan: no stock number, no year, no company name, no country, "8 CUPS"
Estimated value: under $12
Right: *Jewel Mold*
Wilton Industries, individual serving (probably not Wilton exclusive)
Yearbooks 1969 through 1970, MO-2863
$1.25 (1969–1970); four set of four pans, $3.98
On pan: no stamp
Estimated value: under $12

Hexagon Cake Pan
Wilton Industries, full size
Yearbooks 1974 through 1980, 502-x-305, also called *Hexagon Ring Pan*
$3.25 (1974); $3.75 (1975); $3.95 (1976); $4.95 (1977); $5.50 (1978); $5.95 (1979); $6.95 (1980)
On pan: 502-305, 1973, Wilton (script), Korea
Estimated value: under $12

Mini Star
Wilton Industries, multiple cavity
Yearbooks 1996 through 2003, 2105-x-1235
$10.99 (1996–2003)
On pan: 2105-1235, 1995, Wilton Enterprises, Indonesia
List price: $11

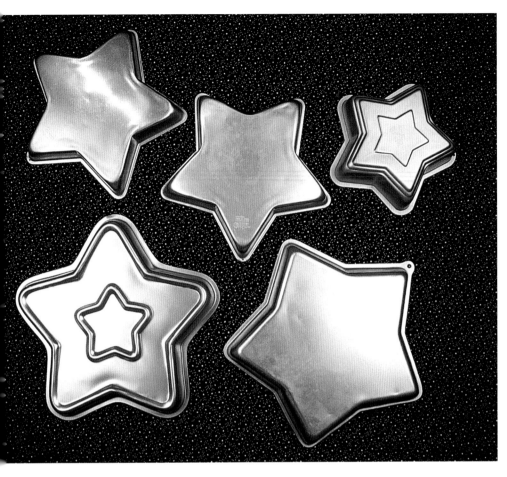

Top Left: *Star Pans*
Wilton Industries, full size (in two layers)
Yearbooks 1972 through 1982, 502-x-2154,
2105-x-2150
$3.25 (1972); $4.95 (1974); $5.75 (1975);
$5.95 (1976); $6.50 (1977–1979); $7.50
(1980); $8.25 (1981); $8.95 (1982)
On pan: 502-2154, 1971, Wilton (script),
Korea
Estimated value: under $12

Top Right: *Star, 5-pointed, deep mold*
Mirro, full size
On pan: 718AM, no year, Mirro, U. S. A.
Estimated value: under $12

Bottom Left: *Star, fancifill*
Wilton Industries, full size
Yearbooks 1981 through 1983, 2105-x-1413,
also called *Fancifill Star*
$7.25 (1981); $7.95 (1982–1983)
On pan: 502-1468, 1980, Wilton, Korea
Estimated value: under $12

Bottom Right: *Star*
Wilton Industries, full size
Yearbooks 1989 through 2003, 2105-x-2512
$8.99 (1989–2000); $9.99 (1991–2003)
On pan: 2105-2512, 1987, Wilton, China
List price: $10

Left: *Shooting Star*
Wilton Industries, full size
Yearbooks 1990 through 1991,
2105-x-804
$8.99 (1990); $9.99 (1991)
On pan: 2105-804, 1989, Wilton,
Korea
Estimated value: under $12

Top Center: *Star Singles!*
Wilton Industries, individual
serving
Yearbooks 1998 through 2000,
2105-x-9801, 2105-x-1127
$1.99 (1998–2000), also offered
as part of a set of 4 colored non-
stick pans, for $14.99
On pan: no stamp
Estimated value: under $12

Top Right: *Coppertone star
mold*
Unknown, individual serving
On pan: no stamp
Estimated value: under $12

Bottom Right: *Star*
Kungsors Pressprodukter AB
(Sweden), full size
On pan: no stamp, paper label:
Manufactured in Sweden by
Kungsors Pressprodukter AB for
JARK GROUP, INC., Houston
Texas
Estimated value: under $12

Left: *Large Shell Mold, coppertone*
Wear-Ever, full size
On pan: 29080, no year, WEAR-EVER, "6 cups"
Estimated value: under $12
Center: *Seashells*
Wilton Industries, individual serving (probably not Wilton exclusive)
Yearbooks 1969 through 1970, MO-2861
$1.25 (1969–1970) for package of 4, 4 packages for $3.98
On pan: no stamp
Courtesy of Nila Pudwill
Estimated value: under $12
Right: *Coppertone Seashell*
Unknown, full size
On pan: no stamp, "6 CUPS"
Estimated value: under $12

Left: *Mini Shell*
Wilton Industries, multiple cavity
Yearbooks 1994 through 2003, 2105-x-4396
$9.99 (1994–1995); $10.99 (1996–2003)
On pan: 2105-4396, no year, Wilton, Indonesia
List price: $11
Center: *Shell Singles!*
Wilton Industries, individual serving
Yearbooks 1998 through 2000, 2105-x-1106
$1.69 (1998); $1.99 (1999–2000)
On pan: no stamp
Estimated value: under $12
Right: *Shell*
Wilton Industries, full size
Yearbooks 1990 through 2002, 2105-x-8250
$8.99 (1990); $9.99 (1991–2002)
On pan: 2105-8250, 1989, Wilton, Korea
Estimated value: under $12

The small and individual number pans are shown with a full-size pan, for scale. They are described in the pictures that follow.
Left: *Number One*
Wilton Industries, full size
Yearbooks 1981 through 1985, 2105-x-7918
$7.25 (1981); $7.95 (1982–1983); $6.95 (1984, "Special Value!"); $6.99 (1985)
On pan: 502-1905, 1979, Wilton, Korea
Estimated value: under $12

Number Cake Pan 1
Wilton Industries, small
Yearbooks 1977 through 1980, 508-x-116, also called *Number "1", No. 1*
$2.50 (1977, any 2 number pans, $4.50); $2.99 (1978, any 2 number pans, $5.50); $2.95 (1979, any 2 number pans, $5.50); $3.50 (1980)
On pan: 508-116, 1976, Wilton (script), Korea
Estimated value: under $12
All data for Number Cake Pan 1 except for the stock number applies to the other pans in this series
Number Cake Pan 2, 508-x-124
Number Cake Pan 3, 508-x-132
Number Cake Pan 4, 508-x-140
Number Cake Pan 5, 508-x-158
Number Cake Pan 6, 508-x-167
Number Cake Pan 7, 508-x-175 [not shown]
Number Cake Pan 8, 508-x-183
Number Cake Pan 0, 508-x-108

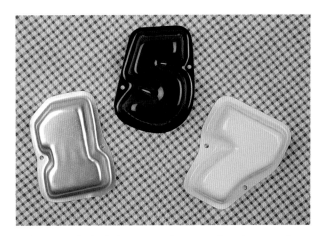

In this series of individual serving number pans, all numbers came in the colored enamel version, but only the number one came in plain aluminum.

Left: *Aluminum #1 Singles!*
Wilton Industries, individual serving
Yearbooks 1999 through 2000, 2105-x-1114
$1.99 (1999–2000)
On pan: no stamp
Estimated value: under $12

Center: *Color Enamel #5 Singles!*
Wilton Industries, individual serving
Yearbooks 1998 through 1999, 2105-x-1165
$2.99 (1998–1999)
On pan: no stamp
Estimated value: under $12

Right: *Color Enamel #7 Singles!*
Wilton Industries, individual serving
Yearbooks 1998 through 1999, 2105-x-1167
$2.99 (1998–1999)
On pan: no stamp
Estimated value: under $12

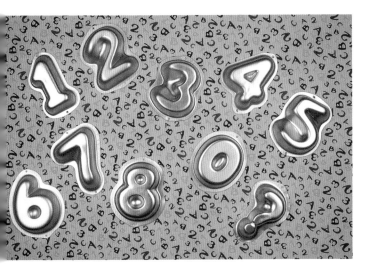

Numbers Set
Wilton Industries, individual serving
Yearbooks 1994 through 1997, 2105-x-9336, also called *10 PC Numbers Pan Set*
$19.99 (1994–1997)
On pan: no stamp
Estimated value: $26 to $40

Not Pictured

Angel Food
Wilton Industries, full size
Yearbooks 1985 through 1986, 2105-x-2525
$10.99 (1985–1986)
Estimated value: under $12

Charlotte
Tall ring mold with fluted sides
Wilton Industries, full size
Yearbook 1964, 625
$1.49 (1964)
Estimated value: unknown

Charlotte Mold
Plain round deep mold
Wilton Industries, full size
Yearbooks 1985 through 1986, 2105-x-1270
$5.99 (1985–1986)
Estimated value: unknown

Circus Wagon Kit
Wilton Industries, full size, stand-up, accessorize or stack
Yearbooks 1970 through 1977, W827, 501-x-8270, also called *Circus Cart*
$8.95 (1970); $9.95 (1972); $12.95 (1974); $14.95 (1975–1977); $15.95 (1976); prices shown are for kit, pans from $3.00 to $4.50 and plastic accessories only from $3.25
Estimated value: $26 to $40

Color Enamel Exclamation Singles!
Wilton Industries, individual serving
Yearbooks 1998 through 1999, 2105-x-1170
$2.99 (1998–1999)
Estimated value: unknown

Color Enamel Question Mark Singles!
Wilton Industries, individual serving
Yearbooks 1998 through 1999, 2105-x-1169
$2.99 (1998–1999)
Estimated value: unknown

Coppertone Jumbo Fluted Mold
Wilton Industries, full size
Yearbooks 1964 through 1969, NA-203A, 203A
$2.98 (1964–1969)
Estimated value: under $12

Coppertone Swirl Mold
Wilton Industries, full size
Yearbooks 1964 through 1969, NA-260, 260
$2.98 (1964–1969)
Estimated value: under $12

Question Mark
Wilton Industries, full size
Yearbooks 1988 through 1991, 2105-x-1840
$7.99 (1988); $8.99 (1989–1990); $9.99 (1991)
On pan: 2105-1840, 1987, Wilton, Korea
Estimated value: under $12

Duchess
Tall crown mold, three tiers, 6 cups
Wilton Industries, full size
Yearbook 1964, 633
$1.49 (1964)
Estimated value: under $12

Imperial
Three-tiers, bottom plain, top two fluted, 6 cups
Wilton Industries, full size
Yearbook 1964, 627
$1.49 (1964)
Estimated value: under $12

Insert for Ring Pan, Round
Wilton Industries, full size
Yearbooks 1977 through 1980, 503-x-474
$1.95 (1977–1979); $1.99 (1978); $2.50 (1980)
Estimated value: under $12

Kugelhopf Pan
Wilton Industries, full size
Yearbooks 1986 through 1987, 2105-x-2593
$6.99 (1986–1987)
Estimated value: under $12

Little Angels
Six angel food pans
Wilton Industries, individual serving
Yearbooks 1964 through 1970, AS-141, 5421-1
$1.00 (1964–1966); $1.50 (1969); $2.00 (1970)
Estimated value: under $12

Loaf Singles!
Wilton Industries, individual serving
Yearbooks 1998 through 2003, 2105-x-1107
$1.69 (1998); $1.99 (1999–2000); $2.49 (2001–2003)
On pan: no stamp
List Price: $2.50

Mini Loaf
Wilton Industries, multiple cavity (8)
Yearbooks 1986 through 1990, 2105-x-3844
$10.99 (1986); $12.99 (1987–1988); $14.99 (1990)
Estimated value: under $12

Multi-size square pan
Removable partitions allow for pan to make several different size cakes
Alan Silverwood of England, full size
Estimated value: unknown

Petal Angel Food
Wilton Industries, full size
Yearbooks 1999 through 2000, 2105-x-6510
$13.99 (1999–2000)
Estimated value: unknown

Petal Pans
Wilton Industries, full size (in two layers)
Yearbooks 1972 through 1983, 502-x-2146, 2105-x-2142
$3.00 (1972); $3.75 (1974); $4.75 (1975); $4.95 (1976–1977); $5.50 (1978); $6.50 (1979); $7.50 (1980); $8.95 (1982–1983)

Ribbed Loaf
Wilton Industries, full size
Yearbook 1986, 2105-x-2585
$4.99 (1986)
Estimated value: under $12

Ring Mold 10.5"
Wilton Industries, full size
Yearbooks 1974 through 2003, 512-x-2001
$3.50 (1974); $4.50 (1975); $4.75 (1976); $4.95 (1977); $5.99 (1978); $6.50 (1979); $6.95 (1980); $7.95 (1981–1984); $7.99 (1985–1996); $9.99 (1997 and 2003); $8.99 (1998–2000)
List Price: $10

Ring Mold 8"
Wilton Industries, full size
Yearbooks 1985 through 1995, 2105-x-190
$5.99 (1985–1988); $6.49 (1990–1992); $6.99 (1994–1995)
Estimated value: under $12

Sculptured Mold
Fancy tall ring, 10" by 3-1/2" deep, recommended for skirt of large doll cakes
Wilton Industries, full size
Yearbooks 1959 through 1970, no stock number, HM-72
$2.00 (1959–1966); $3.25 (1970)
Estimated value: unknown

Square Tier Kit
Wilton Industries, full size
Small square pans with plastic stand consisting of pole with cake platforms on arms
Yearbooks 1972 through 1979, 501-x-203, also called *Square Mini-Tier*
$5.95 (1972); $7.75 (1974); $8.50 (1975 and 1977); $8.75 (1976); $9.50 (1978); $10.95 (1979); prices are for kit; pans alone sold for $3.50 to $6.50; stand alone sold for $3.00 to $5.95
Estimated value: unknown

Three Tiered Angel Food Cake Pan
Metal not identified; described as holding "a full package of mix"
Wilton Industries, full size
Yearbooks 1959 through 1970, BL-202, 202
$2.45 (1959–1966); $4.50 (1969–1970)
Estimated value: $12 to $25

Turk's Head Mold
Tall swirled mold, recommended as skirt for doll cake
Wilton Industries, full size
Yearbooks 1959 through 1978, HM-9, HM9, 512-x-90
$1.25 (1959–1966); $2.00 (1969); $2.50 (1970); $3.50 (1972); $3.95 (1974); $4.95 (1975); $5.25 (1976); $5.95 (1977); $6.50 (1978)
Estimated value: under $12

Victoria
Crown mold, 6 cups
Wilton Industries, full size
Yearbook 1964, 631
$1.98 (1964)
Estimated value: under $12

Part III
Road Map

Index of Pans by Names and Keywords

101 Dalmatians
    101 Dalmatians Singles!, 106
    101 Dalmatians, 106
13-Star Flag, 81
18-Wheeler Truck, 54
3 in. Round Singles!, 130
3-D Cruiser, 53
3-D Cuddly Bear/Panda, 41
4 in. Ring Singles!, 134
4 Leaf Clover Mold with Teflon interior, 61
4 Leaf Clover Mold, Copper anodized, 61
4-Tier Cake Pan Set, 131
Acorn on Round With Fluted Sides, 134
Adorable Lamb Pan, 27
airplane, *Porky Pig*, 110
Alf, 114
Aluminum #1 Singles!, 143
American Eagle Mold, 83
angel
    Angel mold, 90
    Angel Singles!, 90
    Cupid Pan, 76
    Cupid's Delight, 76
    Joyful Angel, 90
angel food
    Angel Food, 144
    Angel Food Singles!, 132
    Angelaire Angel Food Cake Pan, 132
    Classic Angel Food Pan, 132
    Heart Angel Food, 99
    Heart Angel Food Singles!, 99
    Little Angels, 144
    Mini Angel Food Pan, 132
    Petal Angel Food, 144
    Square Angel Food Pan, 138
    Standard Round Angel Food, 132
    Three Tiered Angel Food Cake Pan, 144
Angelaire Angel Food Cake Pan, 132
Angelica, RugRats, 121
Ani-Mold Set, 39
Ariel, Little Mermaid, 104
ark, *Noah's Ark*, 39
astronaut, *Spaceman Pan*, 43
award
    Blue Ribbon, 68
    Insert for Ring Pan, blue ribbon, 68
    Trophy, 68
baby
    Baby Bootie Singles!, 57
    Baby Doll, 46
    Cabbage Patch Kids, 117
    Cabbage Patch Preemie, 117
    Cabbage Patch Stand-up, 117
    Cute Baby, 42
    Darling Dolly, 1-2-3, 46
    RugRats, 121
    Special Delivery Baby, 129
Baby Bootie Singles!, 57
Baby Doll, 46
baker
    Pillsbury Poppin' Fresh Doughboy, 129
    Poppin' Fresh, 129
ball
    Baseball Glove, 58
    Baseball Singles!, 58

Basketball Singles!, 74
Bowling a Strike, 60
Charlie Brown, 112
First and Ten Football pan, 60
Football, 60
Football Singles!, 60
Golf Ball Singles!, 59
Mini Ball, 58
Soccer Ball, 59
Soccer Singles!, 59
Sports Ball Pan Set, 58
Tee It Up, 59
Ballerina Bear, 40
Ballet Slippers, 67
balloon
    Big Bird, 107
    Clancy The Clown, 47
    Circus Clown, 47
    Millennium Special 2000, 65
    Mini Balloon, 65
    Smurfette, 126
    Up 'N Away Balloon, 57
Bambi, Mini Disney Bambi, 103
band leader, *Mickey Mouse*, 101
Barbie
    Barbie, 127, 128
    Barbie, Beautiful Day, 128
    Barbie, Dreamtime Princess, 127
barn, *Small house or barn*, 52
Barney
    Barney, 122
    Barney and Baby Bop Mini, 121
Bart Simpson, 114
baseball
    Baseball Glove, 58
    Baseball Singles!, 58
    Charlie Brown, 112
    Home Run Hitter, 58
Baseball Glove, 58
Basic Ring (for Sculptured Tops), 132
basket
    Bunny in a Basket, 24
    Easter Basket Pan, 79
    Fruit Basket Mold, 73
    Scarecrow, 84
    Special Delivery Bunny, 24
basketball, *Basketball Singles!*, 74
bat, *Bat Singles!*, 86
Batman
    Batman, 122
    Super Heroes, 123
    Batman Beyond, 122
    Batman Emblem, 122
Be Mine, 76
bear
    3-D Cuddly Bear/Panda, 41
    Ani-Mold Set, 39
    Ballerina Bear, 40
    Bear-y Christmas, 41
    Care Bears, 119
    Care Bears Stand-up, 119
    Cuddly Bear, 40
    Huggable Teddy Bear, 40
    Mini Bear, 41
    Panda/Mini Stand-Up Bear, 41

Paw Print Singles!, 40
Petite Huggable Bear, 41
Pooh #1, 104
Pooh Face, 104
Pooh Singles!, 104
Pooh Stand-up, 103
Pooh with Honey Pot, small, golden, 103
Santa Bear Pan, 41
Teddy (Mini Toy Cakes), 40
Teddy Bear Singles!, 40
Teddy Bear StandUp, 41
Teddy Bear with Block, 40
Teddy Bear, 1-2-3, 40
Winnie the Pooh, 103, 104
Yogi Bear, 125
Bear-y Christmas, 41
beer mug, *Good Cheer Mug*, 71
Bell
    Bell, 98
    Bell with Bow, 98
    Coppertone Bell Mold, 99
    Coppertone Twin Parti Bell Mold, 99
    Double Bell, 99
    Liberty Bell Mold, 83
    Mini Bell, 98
    Twin Parti Bell, orange coating, 97
Bert, Ernie and Bert, 108
Bevel Pan Set, 132
Big Bird
    Big Bird, 107
    Sesame Street Mini Pan, 108
    Big Bird, 1-2-3, 107
    Big Bird face, 106
    Big Bird Full Figure, 107
    Big Bird Happy Birthday, 1-2-3, 107
    Big Bird Pan, 107
    Big Bird small pan, 106
    Big Bird with Banner, 107
Big Fish, 36
Biker Mice from Mars, 115
bird (see also Big Bird)
    American Eagle Mold, 83
    Bird 'N Banner, 32
    Cheerful Chick, 30
    Chick Singles!, 30
    Chick-In-Egg, 30
    Coppertone Turkey Mold, 33
    Good News Stork, 33
    Goose/Country Goose, 32
    Graduate Owl, 33
    Just Hatched Chick, 30
    Little Boy Chick, 32
    Little Ducky, 31
    Little Girl Chick, 41
    Lovebirds, 32
    Mister Owl, 33
    Proud Rooster, 31
    Rubber Ducky, 31
    Stork, 33
    Sylvester and Tweety Mini, 111
    Tom Turkey, 41
    Turkey, 33
    Tweety, 110, 111
    Tweety Bird Mini, 111
Bird 'N Banner, 32

Bite-Size Bunny, 27
Bite-Size Gingerbread Boy, 49
Blossom, Powerpuff Girls, 118
Blossom Pan, 69
Blossom Pans, 74
Blue Ribbon, 68
Blue's Clues, 121
boat
    Cruise Ship, 57
    Noah's Ark, 39
    Sailboat, 57
Bob the Builder, 127
Bob the Tomato, Veggie Tales, 120
Boba Fett, 124
body
    Foot Singles!, 50
    Hand Singles!, 50
    Hot Lips, 50
    T-Nee-Bikini, 51
Boo Ghost, 86
book
    Book, 63
    Graduate Owl, 33
    Tweety, 110
    Two-Mix Book Pan, 64
boot, *Western Boot*, 50
bootie, *Baby Bootie Singles!*, 57
bounty hunter, *Boba Fett*, 124
bowling
    Bowling a Strike, 60
    Bowling Pin Set, 60
    Bowling Pin Singles!, 60
boy
    Bart Simpson, 114
    Charlie Brown, 112
    Dutch Boy Mold, 57
    Ernie, 108
    Ernie and Bert, 108
    Graduate, 68
    Harry Potter, 111
    Home Run Hitter, 58
    Li'l Cowboy, 43
    Lil' Pirate, 43
    Robby Hobbie, 116
    RugRats, 121
Brave Heart Lion, 119
Bubbles, Powerpuff Girls, 118
bug
    Flik Bug's Life, 105
    Mini Disney Jiminy Cricket, 103
Bugs Bunny
    Bugs, 109
    Bugs Bunny, 109, 110
    Bugs Bunny Singles!, 110
building
    Classic House Pan, 52
    Enchanted Castle, 51
    Gingerbread House, 52
    Haunted House, 52
    Holiday House/Stand-Up House, 51
    House, 52
    Small house or barn, 52
Bumblelion, 106
bunny (see also Bugs Bunny)
    Bite-Size Bunny, 27

Bunny Singles!, 26
Bunny Cake Mold, 25
Bunny Face, 1-2-3, 26
Bunny in a Basket, 24
Bunny Mold for 3-D Cake, 25
Coppertone Holiday Mold Set, 99
Cottontail Bunny, 24
Easter Bunny, 23
Easter Bunny Mold, 25
Funny Bunny nonstick, 26
Funny Rabbit, 26
Holiday Bunny, 25
Insert for Ring Pan, rabbit, 26
Mini Bunny, 27
Peek-A-Boo Bunny, 23
Playboy Bunny, 129
Quick as a Bunny, 1-2-3, 24
Sitting Rabbit, 26
Small Animal Molds: Squirrel, Duck, Pony, Rabbit, 39
Special Delivery Bunny, 24
Sunny Bunny, 24
Buttercup, *Powerpuff Girls*, 118
butterfly
    Butterfly, 34
    Butterfly Fancifill, 34
    Butterfly Molds, 34
C-3PO, 124
Cabbage Patch Kids
    Cabbage Patch Kids, 117
    Cabbage Patch Preemie, 117
    Cabbage Patch Stand-up, 117
cake
    Cookie Monster, 108
    Donald Duck, 102
    Garfield, 114
    Precious Moments, 117
camel, *Ani-Mold Set*, 39
candle, *Noel Candle*, 89
Candlelit Tree Pan Set, 96
candy, *Gumball Machine*, 71
candy cane
    Treats 4 You!, 97
    Candy Cane Singles!, 94
    Candy Cane Pan, 94
    Ginger Bread Mold, 49
car
    3-D Cruiser, 53
    Car (Mini Toy Cakes), 55
    Comical Car, 53
    Race Car, 55
    Race Car/Super Race Car, 55
    Sports Car, 53
    Sports Utility Vehicle, 54
    Sporty Car, 53
    Trail Rider, 54
    Van, 54
cards
    Club on Round, 63
    Grand Slam, 62
Care Bears
    Brave Heart Lion, 119
    Care Bears, 119
    Care Bears Stand-up, 119
Carousel Horse, 30
Carousel Separator Set, 131
cart
    Flower Cart Kit, 137
casino, *Slot Machine*, 62
castle, *Enchanted Castle*, 51
cat
    Cat, 22
    Cat Singles!, 21
    Cutie Cat, 1-2-3 (?), 21
    Garfield, 114
    Garfield Stand-up, 114
    Garfield the Cat, 1-2-3, 114
    Kitten, 21
    Kitty Cat Pan, 21
    Lovable Animal, 37
    Mini Garfield, 114
    Scary Cat, 21
    Sylvester and Tweety Mini, 111
Cathy, 113
Chanukah, *Happy Chanukah*, 88
Charlie Brown, 112
Charlotte, 144
Charlotte Mold, 144
Cheerful Chick, 30
cheerleader, *Dotty Dog*, 120
cherry, *Heart with Cherry*, 77
Chick Singles!, 30

chicken
    Cheerful Chick, 30
    Chick Singles!, 30
    Chick-In-Egg, 30
    Hen or Rooster Mold, 31
    Just Hatched Chick, 30
    Little Boy Chick, 32
    Little Girl Chick, 41
    Lovebirds, 32
    Proud Rooster, 31
Chick-In-Egg, 30
chocolate mold
    Dutch Boy Mold, 57
    Easter Bunny Mold, 25
    Elephant Chocolate Mold, 37
    Little Girl Chick, 41
    Lovebirds, 32
    Merry Monkey Mold, 41
    Panda/Mini Stand-Up Bear, 41
    Policeman Mold, 57
Choo Choo Train, 56
Christmas Stocking, 90
Christmas tree
    Christmas Tree, 97
    Candlelit Tree Pan Set, 96
    Christmas Tree Little Cakes, 95
    Christmas Tree Mold, 99
    Christmas Tree Mold (coppertone), 95
    Christmas Tree Mold, green coated, 97
    Christmas Tree, 1-2-3/Step-by-Step, 97
    Decorated Christmas Tree, 97
    Holiday Tree, 96
    Mini Christmas Tree, 95
    Petite Christmas Tree, 95
    Stand-up Tree Pan set, 96
    Three-Layer Tree, 96
    Treats 4 You!, 97
    Tree Cake and Mold Set, 94
    Tree Singles!, 95
    Treeliteful/Christmas Tree, 95
    Trees, 95
Chuckie, RugRats, 121
Cinderella, 129
Circus Clown, 47
Circus Clown, 1-2-3, 46, 48
Circus Wagon Kit, 144
Clancy The Clown, 47
Classic Angel Food Pan, 132
Classic House Pan, 52
Classic Tube Pan, 133
clock, *Good Time Clock*, 65
clothing
    Baby Bootie Singles!, 57
    Ballet Slippers, 67
    Christmas Stocking, 90
    Football Helmet, 61
    Holiday Stocking, 90
    Stocking Singles!, 90
    SuperStar Shoe, 59
    T-Shirt, 50
    Western Boot, 50
clover
    4 Leaf Clover Mold with Teflon interior, 61
    4 Leaf Clover Mold, Copper anodized, 61
    Insert for Ring Pan, Lucky Clover, 61
    Mini Shamrock, 79
    Shamrock, 80
    Shamrock minis, 79
    Shamrock Singles!, 80
    Shamrock, Coppertone, 80
clown
    Circus Clown, 47
    Circus Clown, 1-2-3, 46, 48
    Clancy The Clown, 47
    Clown, 47
    Cute Clown, 48
    Happy Clown, 46
    Jolly Clown 46
    Juggling Clown, 48
    Mini Clown, 47
club
    Grand Slam, 62
    Club on Round, 63
coin, *Silver Dollar Molds*, 83
Color Enamel #0 Singles!, 143
Color Enamel #1 Singles!, 143
Color Enamel #2 Singles!, 143
Color Enamel #3 Singles!, 143
Color Enamel #4 Singles!, 143
Color Enamel #5 Singles!, 143
Color Enamel #6/9 Singles!, 143
Color Enamel #7 Singles!, 143

Color Enamel #8 Singles!, 143
Color Enamel Exclamation Singles!, 144
Color Enamel Question Mark Singles!, 144
Colored Snowflake Molds, 89
Comical Car, 53
Computer, 63
Congratulations, 64
construction, *Bob the Builder*, 127
Contessa, 138
Contour Baking Pan Set, 131
Cookie Monster
    Cookie Monster, 108
    Cookie Monster, 108
    Cookie Monster small pan, 108
    Sesame Street Mini Pan, 108
Coppertone Bell Mold, 99
Coppertone Cornucopia, 72
Coppertone Fancy Fluted Deep Ring, 133
Coppertone Fish Mold, 35
Coppertone Fluted Mold, 135
Coppertone Fruit Salad Mold, 74
Coppertone Holiday Mold Set, 99
Coppertone Jumbo Fluted Mold, 144
Coppertone Leaf, 70
Coppertone Oval Seasons Molds, 137
Coppertone Ring Mold, 134
Coppertone Seashell, 142
Coppertone star mold, 141
Coppertone Swirl Mold, 144
Coppertone Tall Tyrolean Mold, 135
Coppertone Turkey Mold, 33
Coppertone Twin Parti Bell Mold, 99
corn
    Ear of Corn, 74
    Harvest Coppertone Mold, 71
cornucopia
    Coppertone Cornucopia, 72
    Cornucopia Mold, 72
    Cornucopia, 6 cup coppertone, 72
    Cornucopia, yellow enameled, 72
Coronet, 134
Cottontail Bunny, 24
cow, *Cuddles the Cow*, 29
cowboy
    Li'l Cowboy, 43
    Western Boot, 50
    Yosemite Sam, 112
cross
    Cross/Bevelled Cross, 79
    Cross Singles!, 79
    Cross, 2 mix, 99
Cruise Ship, 57
cub, *Lovable Animal*, 37
cucumber, *Veggie Tales*, 120
Cuddles the Cow, 29
Cuddly Bear, 40
Cupid Pan, 76
Cupid's Delight, 76
Cupid's Heart, 76
Curved Fish, 35
Cute Baby, 42
Cute Clown, 48
Cute Witch, 87
Cutie Cat, 1-2-3 (?), 21
daisy
    Flower Power, 128
    Flower Singles!, 69
Daisy Cart Cake, 139
dalmatian
    101 Dalmatians, 106
    101 Dalmatians Singles!, 106
    Dalmatian Pup, 23
dance
    Ballerina Bear, 40
    Ballet Slippers, 67
Darling Dolly, 1-2-3, 46
Darth Vader, 124
Decorated Christmas Tree, 97
Decorated Domed Mold, 135
Decorated Egg, 81
Decorated Ring, 134
Decorative Pumpkin, 85
deer
    Mini Disney Bambi, 103
    Rudolph The Red Nosed Reindeer, 126
    Rudy Reindeer, 93
Deluxe Coppertone Fruit Ring Mold, 74
diamond, *Grand Slam*, 62
dinosaur
    Barney, 122
    Barney and Baby Bop Mini, 121
    Dinosaur, 1-2-3, 39

    Friendly (?) Dinosaur, 1-2-3, 39
    Megasaurus, 38
    Mini Dinosaur, 39
    Partysaurus, 38
dog
    101 Dalmatians, 106
    101 Dalmatians Singles!, 106
    Blue's Clues, 121
    Dalmatian Pup, 23
    Dotty Dog, 120
    Goofy, 102
    Little Dog Mold, 41
    Lovable Animal, 37
    Mini Disney Goofy, 102
    Mini Disney Pluto, 102
    Playful Pup, 23
    Playful Puppy, 22
    Pluto, 102
    Precious Puppy, 1-2-3, 22
    Puppy Dog, 22
    Scooby-Doo, 125
    Sitting Dog with Bow, 22
    Snoopy, 112
doll
    Baby Doll, 46
    Barbie, 127, 128
    Barbie, Beautiful Day, 128
    Barbie, Dreamtime Princess, 127
    Cabbage Patch Kids, 117
    Cabbage Patch Preemie, 117
    Cabbage Patch Stand-up, 117
    Cinderella, 129
    Cute Baby, 42
    Darling Dolly, 1-2-3, 46
    Little Dolly, 46
    Magic Mold Baking Pan, 136
    Mini Wonder/Petite Doll Pan, 136
    Rag Doll (Mini Toy Cakes), 44
    Rag Doll Pan, 45
    Raggedy Ann, 126
    Storybook Doll, 44, 45
    Wonder Mold/Classic Wonder Mold, 136
dome
    Cinderella, 129
    Magic Mold Baking Pan, 136
    Mini Wonder/Petite Doll Pan, 136
    Wonder Mold/Classic Wonder Mold, 136
Donald Duck
    Donald Duck, 102
    Mini Disney Donald Duck, 102
Dotty Dog, 120
Double Bell, 99
Double Heart Fancifill, 77
Double Heart with Embossing, 77
Double Tier Heart, 75
Double Tier Round, 131
Doughboy
    Pillsbury Poppin' Fresh Doughboy, 129
    Poppin' Fresh, 129
dove
    Bird 'N Banner, 32
    Lovebirds, 32
dragon, *Mystical Dragon*, 38
droid
    C-3PO, 124
    R2-D2, 124
Duchess, 144
drum
    Bugs Bunny, 110
    Toy Soldier, 44
duck (see also Donald Duck)
    Little Ducky, 31
    Rubber Ducky, 31
    Small Animal Molds: Squirrel, Duck, Pony, Rabbit, 39
Dumbo, Mini Disney Dumbo, 103
Dutch Boy Mold, 57
eagle, *American Eagle Mold*, 83
Ear of Corn, 74
Easter basket
    Bunny in a Basket, 24
    Easter Basket Pan, 79
    Easter Bunny, 23
    Special Delivery Bunny, 24
Easter Bunny Mold, 25
Easter egg (see egg)
Easter Eggs, 81
Educated Cake Pan, 138
egg
    Chick-In-Egg, 30
    Decorated Egg, 81
    Easter Basket Pan, 79

Easter Bunny, 23
Easter Eggs, 81
Egg Pan Set, 80
Egg Singles!, 81
Happy Easter Egg, 81
Holiday Bunny, 25
Just Hatched Chick, 30
Mini Egg, 80
Peek-A-Boo Bunny, 23
Petite Egg, 80
Egg Pan Set, 80
Egg Singles!, 81
Eisenhower, Silver Dollar Molds, 83
elephant
    Ani-Mold Set, 39
    Eleroo, 106
    Mini Disney Dumbo, 103
    Elephant Chocolate Mold, 37
    Elephant Pan, 37
Eleroo, 106
Elmo
    Elmo, 109
    Elmo, 109
    Elmo Singles!, 109
emblem
    American Eagle Mold, 83
    Batman Emblem, 122
    Cross/Bevelled Cross, 79
    Cross Singles!, 79
    Cross, 2 mix, 99
    Playboy Bunny, 129
Embossed Heart, 77
Enchanted Castle, 51
Ernie, 108
Ernie and Bert, 108
Esmeralda, 105
exclamation mark, Color Enamel Exclamation Singles!, 144
fairy (see angel)
Fanciful Heart Singles!, 76
Fancy Heart Singles!, 76
Fancy Ring, 133
Fancy Ring Singles!, 133
farm,
    Tractor, 54
    Small house or barn, 52
firetruck, Little Fire Truck/Firetruck, 54
First and Ten Football pan, 60
fish
    Big Fish, 36
    Coppertone Fish Mold, 35
    Curved Fish, 35
    Fish, 35, 35
    Flying Fish, 36
    Lobster, 35
flag
    13-Star Flag, 81
    Flag Singles!, 82
    Patriotic Flag, 81
    Stars & Stripes, 82
    US Flag, 82
Flik Bug's Life, 105
Flintstones, Fred Flintstone, 125
flower
    Blossom Pan, 69
    Blossom Pans, 74
    Cuddly Bear, 40
    Daisy Cart Cake, 139
    Flower Cart Kit, 137
    Flower Pot, 70
    Flower Singles!, 69
    Morning Glory, 70
    Petal Angel Food, 144
    Petal Pan Fancifill, 69
    Petal Pans, 144
    Petal-Shaped Pans, 4 tiered, 136
    Poinsettia, 93
    Rose Mold Ring, Light Coppertone, 69
    Rose Mold Ring, Silvertone, 69
    Rose Mold, round, fluted sides, 74
    Sunflower, 70
    Viennese Swirl, 69
    Viennese Swirl Singles!, 69
Flower Cart Kit
    Flower Cart Kit, 137
Flower Pot, 70
Flower Power, 128
Flower Singles!, 69
Fluted Mold, 135
Fluted Ring, 133
Flying Fish, 36
food
    Coppertone Fruit Salad Mold, 74

Deluxe Coppertone Fruit Ring Mold, 74
Ear of Corn, 74
Fruit Basket Mold, 73
Fruit Oval Mold, 72
Fruit Round Mold, 72
Grape Cluster, 74
Gumball Machine, 71
Hamburger, 71
Harvest Coppertone Mold, 71
Harvest Crown, 72
Heart with Cherry, 77
Ice Cream Cone, 71
Individual Fruit Mold Set, 72
Large Fruit Ring Mold, 74
Melon, 74
Melon on Fluted Base, 73
Mini Molds, 74
Pineapple Mold, Teflon interior, Lemon or
    Orange exterior, 73
Pumpkin Singles!, 71
Traditional Melon-Shaped Mold, 73
foot
    Baby Bootie Singles!, 57
    Foot Singles!, 50
    SuperStar Shoe, 59
    Western Boot, 50
football
    First and Ten Football pan, 60
    Football, 60
    Football Helmet, 61
    Football Hero, 61
    Football Singles!, 60
    Mini Football Helmet, 61
footprint, Foot Singles!, 50
four leaf clover
    4 Leaf Clover Mold with Teflon interior, 61
    4 Leaf Clover Mold, Copper anodized, 61
    Insert for Ring Pan, Lucky Clover, 61
Fred Flintstone, 125
Free-Wheelin' Truck, 54
Friendly (?) Dinosaur, 1-2-3, 39
Frog, 36
fruit
    Coppertone Fruit Salad Mold, 74
    Deluxe Coppertone Fruit Ring Mold, 74
    Fruit Basket Mold, 73
    Fruit Oval Mold, 72
    Fruit Round Mold, 72
    Grape Cluster, 74
    Harvest Coppertone Mold, 71
    Harvest Crown, 71
    Heart with Cherry, 78
    Individual Fruit Mold Set, 72
    Large Fruit Ring Mold, 74
    Melon, 74
    Melon on Fluted Base, 73
    Mini Molds, 74
    Pineapple, 74
    Pineapple Mold, 73
    Pineapple, avocado green, 73
    Pineapple, coppertone, 73
    Pineapple, harvest gold, 73
    Pumpkin Singles!, 71
    Traditional Melon-Shaped Mold, 73
Fruit Basket Mold, 73
Fruit Oval Mold, 72
Fruit Round Mold, 72
Fun Train, 1-2-3, 56
Funny Bunny nonstick, 26
Funny Rabbit, 26
G. I. Joe, 116
gambling, Slot Machine, 62
Garfield
    Garfield, 114
    Garfield Stand-up, 114
    Garfield the Cat, 1-2-3, 114
    Mini Garfield, 114
Gentle Lamb, 28, 29
Get Along Gang
    Dotty Dog, 120
    Montgomery Good News Moose, 120
ghost
    Boo Ghost, 86
    Ghost Singles!, 86
    Ghostly Greeting, 85
    Ghosts, 86
    Haunted Pumpkin, 85
    Mini Ghost, 86
    Playful Ghost, 1-2-3, 86
    Scary Ghost, 86
gift
    Barney, 122

Big Bird Full Figure, 107
Cathy, 113
Donald Duck, 102
Elmo, 109
Ernie, 108
Old World Santa, 93
Pink Panther, 113
Santa Bear, 41
Santa with Gift, 94
Santa's Sleigh, 93
Santa's Treasures, 94
Smurf, 126
Ginger Bread Mold, 49
Gingerbread Boy, 48
Gingerbread Boy on Round, 48
Gingerbread House, 52
Gingerbread Man, 48
Gingerbread Pair, 49
gingerbread person
    Bite-Size Gingerbread Boy, 49
    Ginger Bread Mold, 49
    Gingerbread Boy, 48
    Gingerbread Boy on Round, 48
    Gingerbread Man, 48
    Gingerbread Pair, 49
    Mini Gingerbread Boy, 49
giraffe, Mini Jungle Animals, 38
girl
    Holly Hobbie, 116
    Little Dolly, 46
    Powerpuff Girls, 118
    Precious Moments, 117
    Rag Doll (Mini Toy Cakes), 44
    Rag Doll Pan, 45
    Raggedy Ann, 126
    Rainbow Brite, 118
    RugRats, 121
    Storybook Doll, 44, 45
    Strawberry Shortcake, 118
golf
    Golf Bag, 59
    Golf Ball Singles!, 59
    Tee It Up, 59
Golf Bag, 59
Golf Ball Singles!, 59
Good Cheer Mug, 71
Good News Stork, 33
Good Time Clock, 65
Goofy
    Goofy, 102
    Mini Disney Goofy, 102
Goose/Country Goose, 32
graduation
    Graduate, 68
    Graduate Owl, 33
    Topping Off Success, 68
    Mister Owl, 33
Grand Slam, 62
Grape Cluster, 74
grave marker, Over the Hill Tombstone, 86
guitar, Guitar, 66
Gumball Machine, 71
Half Round, 130
Halloween
    Bat Singles!, 86
    Boo Ghost, 86
    Classical House, 52
    Cute Witch, 87
    Ghost Singles!, 86
    Ghostly Greeting, 85
    Ghosts, 86
    Haunted House, 52
    Haunted Pumpkin, 85
    High Flyin' Witch, 87
    Insert for Ring Pan, Pumpkin, 85
    Jack-O-Lantern, 85
    Jack-O-Lantern Singles!, 86
    Jack-O-Lantern Stand-Up, 84
    Mini Ghost, 86
    Mini Pumpkin, 84
    Monster Party Pan, 87
    Party Pumpkin, 1-2-3, 85
    Petite Jack-O-Lantern, 84
    Playful Ghost, 1-2-3, 86
    Pumpkin (Domed), 85
    Scary Cat, 21
    Scary Ghost, 86
    Smiling Skull, 87
    Whimsical Witch, 88
    Wicked Witch, 88
Hamburger, 71
Hand Singles!, 50

Handsome Guy, 42
Hanukkah, Happy Chanukah, 88
Happiness Heart pans, 75
Happy Birthday
    Happy Birthday, 64
    Insert for Ring Pan, Birthday, 64
    Rainbow Birthday Cake Pan, 65
Happy Chanukah, 88
Happy Clown, 46
Happy Easter Egg, 81
Happy Hippo, 37
Harry Potter, 111
Harvest Coppertone Mold, 71
Harvest Crown, 72
hat, Topping Off Success, 68
hatching chick
    Chick-In-Egg, 30
    Just Hatched Chick, 30
Haunted House, 52
Haunted Pumpkin, 85
heart
    Be Mine, 76
    Cupid Pan, 76
    Cupid's Delight, 76
    Cupid's Heart, 76
    Double Heart Fancifill, 77
    Double Heart with Embossing, 77
    Double Tier Heart, 75
    Embossed Heart, 77
    Fanciful Heart Singles!, 76
    Fancy Heart Singles!, 76
    Grand Slam, 62
    Happiness Heart pans, 75
    Heart Mini-Tier, 75
    Heart mold, deep with arrow, 78
    Heart mold, small embossed coppertone 77
    Heart On Round, 63
    Heart Quartet, 78
    Heart Ring, 78
    Heart Set, 75
    Heart with Cherry, 77
    Hearts Entwined, 76
    I Love You, 78
    Individual Heart Mold, 76
    Insert for Ring Pan, heart, 77
    Lacy Heart, 77
    Mini Embossed Heart, 78
    Mini Heart, 78
    Petite Heart, 78
    Puffed Heart, 76
    Sweetheart Mold with Teflon Interior
        (Lemon or Orange exterior), 99
    Sweetheart/Fancy Heart Mold, 77
Heart Angel Food
    Heart Angel Food, 99
    Heart Angel Food, 99
    Heart Angel Food Singles!, 99
Heart Mini-Tier, 75
Heart mold, deep with arrow, 78
Heart mold, small embossed coppertone, 77
Heart On Round, 63
Heart Quartet, 78
Heart Ring, 78
Heart Set, 75
Heart with Cherry, 77
Hearts Entwined, 76
He-Man Masters of the Universe, 123
Hen or Rooster Mold, 31
Hercules, 105
hero
    Football Hero, 61
    He-Man Masters of the Universe, 123
    Hercules, 105
    Power Rangers/Mighty Morphin Power
        Rangers, 123
    Powerpuff Girls, 118
    Spider-Man, 123
    Super Heroes, 123
    Superman, 123
    Wonder Woman, 122
hexagon
    Hexagon Cake Pan, 140
    Hexagon Set, 140
    Jewel Mold, 140
    Jewel Mold (Coppertone), 140
High Flyin' Witch, 87
hippopotamus, Happy Hippo, 37
hobby horse, Rocking Horse, 30
Hockey Player, 60
Holiday Bunny, 25
Holiday House/Stand-Up House, 51
Holiday Stocking, 90

Holiday Tree, 96
Holly Hobbie, 116
Home Run Hitter, 58
horn of plenty
    Coppertone Cornucopia, 72
    Cornucopia Mold, 72
    Cornucopia, 6 cup coppertone, 72
    Cornucopia, yellow enameled, 72
horse
    Carousel Horse, 30
    Carousel Separator Set, 131
    Insert for Ring Pan, Horse, 29
    Precious Pony, 29
    Rocking Horse, 30
    Small Animal Molds: Squirrel, Duck, Pony,
        Rabbit, 39
horseshoe
    Horseshoe, 62
    Insert for Ring Pan, horseshoe, 62
    Horseshoe, 2 mix, 62
hot air balloon, Up 'N Away Balloon, 57
Hot Lips, 50
house
    Classic House Pan, 52
    Gingerbread House, 52
    Haunted House, 52
    Holiday House/Stand-Up House, 51
    House, 52
    Small house or barn, 52
Huggable Teddy Bear, 40
Hunchback of Notre Dame, Esmeralda, 105
I Love You, 78
Ice Cream Cone, 71
Imperial, 144
Indian princess, Pocahontas, 105
Individual Fluted Molds, 135
Individual Fluted Ring Molds, coppertone, 134
Individual Fruit Mold Set, 72
Individual Heart Mold, 76
Individual Ring Molds, coppertone, 134
Individual Swirled Mold, 135
Individual Swirled Mold with Indent, 133
insect
    Flik Bug's Life, 105
    Mini Disney Jiminy Cricket, 103
Insert for Ring Pan
    Insert for Ring Pan, Pumpkin, 85
    Insert for Ring Pan, Birthday, 64
    Insert for Ring Pan, blue ribbon, 68
    Insert for Ring Pan, heart, 77
    Insert for Ring Pan, Horse, 29
    Insert for Ring Pan, horseshoe, 62
    Insert for Ring Pan, Lucky Clover, 61
    Insert for Ring Pan, rabbit, 26
    Insert for Ring Pan, round, 144
    Insert for Ring Pan, Santa, 91
    Insert for Ring Pan, Shower, 67
    Insert for Ring Pan, Swirl, 132
jack-o-lantern
    Decorative Pumpkin, 85
    Ghostly Greeting, 85
    Haunted Pumpkin, 85
    Insert for Ring Pan, Pumpkin, 85
    Jack-O-Lantern, 85
    Jack-O-Lantern Singles!, 86
    Jack-O-Lantern Stand-Up, 84
    Mini Pumpkin, 84
    Party Pumpkin, 1-2-3, 85
    Petite Jack-O-Lantern, 84
    Pumpkin (Domed), 85
jeep, Trail Rider, 54
Jewel Mold
    Jewel Mold, 140
    Jewel Mold (Coppertone), 140
Jiminy Cricket, Mini Disney Jiminy Cricket, 103
Jolly Clown, 46
Joyful Angel, 90
Juggling Clown, 48
juke box, Rockin' Juke Box, 67
jump rope, Raggedy Ann, 126
Jungle Lion, 38
Just Hatched Chick, 30
kitten (see cat)
Kitty Cat Pan, 21
Kugelhopf Pan, 144
Lacy Heart, 77
lady, Pretty Lady, 42 (see also woman)
lamb
    Adorable Lamb Pan, 27
    Coppertone Holiday Mold Set, 99
    Gentle Lamb, 28, 29
    Lamb Chop, 117

Little Lamb, 41
Little Lamb/Stand-Up Lamb, 27
Lovable Lamb, 29
Mini Lamb, 27
Lamb Chop, 117
Large Fruit Ring Mold, 74
Large Shell Mold, coppertone, 142
Larry the Cucumber, Veggie Tales, 120
leaf
    4 Leaf Clover Mold with Teflon interior, 61
    4 Leaf Clover Mold, Copper anodized, 61
    Acorn on Round With Fluted Sides, 134
    Coppertone Leaf, 70
    Coppertone Oval Seasons Molds, 137
    Insert for Ring Pan, Lucky Clover, 61
    Maple Leaf Singles!, 70
    Mini Shamrock, 79
    Shamrock, 80
    Shamrock minis, 79
    Shamrock Singles!, 80
    Shamrock, Coppertone, 80
    Wreath, 91
liberty, Statue of Liberty, 83
Liberty Bell Mold, 83
Li'l Cowboy, 43
Lil' Pirate, 43
lion
    Ani-Mold Set, 39
    Brave Heart Lion, 119
    Bumblelion, 106
    Jungle Lion, 38
    Lovable Animal, 37
    Mini Jungle Animals, 38
lips, Hot Lips, 50
Little Angels, 144
Little Boy Chick, 32
Little Dog Mold, 41
Little Dolly, 46
Little Ducky, 31
Little Fire Truck/Firetruck, 54
Little Girl Chick, 41
Little Lamb, 41
Little Lamb/Stand-Up Lamb, 27
Little Loafers, 139
Little Locomotive, 56
Little Mermaid, 104
Little Mouse, 36
Little Train, 56
loaf
    Little Loafers, 139
    Loaf Mold, 139
    Loaf Singles!, 144
    Long Loaf, 139
    Mini Loaf, 144
    Mini Loaf Pan Set, 139
    Petite Loaf, 139
    Ribbed Loaf, 144
    Ribbed loaf, staight ends, long, 139
    Ribbed loaf, staight ends, short, 139
    Standard capacity loaf, long and narrow, 139
    Standard loaf with slightly sloped sides, 139
Lobster, 35
Lone-Star State, 83
Long Loaf, 139
Lovable Animal, 37
Lovable Lamb, 29
Lovebirds, 32
loving cup, Trophy, 68
Magic Mold Baking Pan, 136
man
    Batman, 122
    Batman Beyond, 122
    Batman Emblem, 122
    Bob the Builder, 127
    Boba Fett, 124
    Darth Vader, 124
    Dutch Boy Mold, 57
    Football Hero, 61
    G. I. Joe, 116
    Handsome Guy, 42
    He-Man Masters of the Universe, 123
    Hercules, 105
    Hockey Player, 60
    Policeman Mold, 57
    Popeye, 112
    Power Rangers/Mighty Morphin Power
Rangers, 123
    Spider-Man, 123
    Super Heroes, 123
    Super Mario Brothers, 120
    Troll, 44
    Wizard, 45

WWF Superstars, 124
Yosemite Sam, 112
Ziggy, 113
map
    Lone-Star State, 83
    USA, 82
Maple Leaf Singles!, 70
mars
    Biker Mice from Mars, 115
    Marvin the Martian, 115
Marvin the Martian, 115
medal
    Blue Ribbon, 68
    Insert for Ring Pan, blue ribbon, 68
Megasaurus, 38
Melon, 74
Melon on Fluted Base, 73
mermaid
    Little Mermaid, 104
    Merry Mermaid, 43
Merry Mermaid, 43
Merry Monkey Mold, 41
merry-go-round
    Carousel Horse, 30
    Carousel Separator Set, 131
message
    Boo Ghost, 86
    Congratulations, 64
    Ghostly Greeting, 85
    Happy Birthday, 64
    Happy Chanukah, 88
    Insert for Ring Pan, Birthday, 64
    Noel Candle, 89
    Over the Hill Tombstone, 86
    Rainbow Birthday Cake Pan, 65
Mickey Face, 101
Mickey Mouse
    Mickey Mouse, 100, 101
    Mickey Singles!, 101
    Mini Disney Mickey, 101
    Mini Mickey Mouse, 101
Mighty Morphin Power Rangers, Power Rangers/
    Mighty Morphin Power Rangers, 123
Millennium Special 2000, 65
Mini Angel Food Pan, 132
Mini Ball, 58
Mini Balloon, 65
Mini Bear, 41
Mini Bell, 98
Mini Big Bird, 106
Mini Bunny, 27
Mini Christmas Tree, 95
Mini Clown, 47
Mini Dinosaur, 39
Mini Disney Bambi, 103
Mini Disney Donald Duck, 102
Mini Disney Dumbo, 103
Mini Disney Goofy, 102
Mini Disney Jiminy Cricket, 103
Mini Disney Mickey, 101
Mini Disney Pinocchio, 103
Mini Disney Pluto, 102
Mini Egg, 80
Mini Embossed Heart, 78
Mini Football Helmet, 61
Mini Garfield, 114
Mini Ghost, 86
Mini Gingerbread Boy, 49
Mini Heart, 78
Mini Jungle Animals, 38
Mini Lamb, 27
Mini Loaf, 144
Mini Loaf Pan Set, 139
Mini Locomotive, 55
Mini Mickey Mouse, 101
Mini Molds, 74
Mini Pumpkin, 84
Mini Santa, 91
Mini Shamrock, 79
Mini Shell, 142
Mini Smurf, 127
Mini Snowman, 89
Mini Star, 140
Mini Umbrella, 67
Mini Wonder/Petite Doll Pan, 136
Miniature Wedding Tiers, 130
Minnie Mouse, 100
Mister Owl, 33
money
    Lil' Pirate, 43
    Silver Dollar Molds, 83

monkey, Merry Monkey Mold, 99
monster
    Cookie Monster, 108
    Cookie Monster small pan, 108
    Megasaurus, 38
    Mystical Dragon, 38
    Sesame Street Mini Pan, 108
    Monster Party Pan, 87
Monster Party Pan, 87
Montgomery Good News Moose, 120
moose, Montgomery Good News Moose, 120
Morning Glory, Morning Glory, 70
Motorcycle, 55
mouse
    Biker Mice from Mars, 115
    Little Mouse, 36
    Mickey Mouse, 100, 101
    Mickey Singles!, 101
    Mini Disney Mickey, 101
    Mini Mickey Mouse, 101
    Minnie Mouse, 100
mouth, Hot Lips, 50
mug, Good Cheer Mug, 71
Multi-size square pan, 144
music
    Ballerina Bear, 40
    Ballet Slippers, 67
    Bugs Bunny, 110
    Guitar, 66
    Mickey Mouse, 101
    Piano, 66
    Pink Panther, 113
    Rockin' Juke Box, 67
    Toy Soldier, 44
Mystical Dragon, 38
national symbols
    13-Star Flag, 81
    American Eagle Mold, 83
    Flag Singles!, 82
    Liberty Bell Mold, 83
    Lone-Star State, 83
    Patriotic Flag, 81
    Silver Dollar Molds, 83
    Stars & Stripes, 82
    Statue of Liberty, 83
    US Flag, 82
    USA, 82
nest, Big Bird Pan, 107
Noah's Ark, 39
Noel Candle, 89
number
    Aluminum #1 Singles!, 143
    Color Enamel #0 Singles!, 143
    Color Enamel #1 Singles!, 143
    Color Enamel #2 Singles!, 143
    Color Enamel #3 Singles!, 143
    Color Enamel #4 Singles!, 143
    Color Enamel #5 Singles!, 143
    Color Enamel #6/9 Singles!, 143
    Color Enamel #7 Singles!, 143
    Color Enamel #8 Singles!, 143
    Color Enamel Exclamation Singles!, 144
    Color Enamel Question Mark Singles!, 144
    Millennium Special 2000, 65
    Number Cake Pan 0, 143
    Number Cake Pan 1, 143
    Number Cake Pan 2, 143
    Number Cake Pan 3, 143
    Number Cake Pan 4, 143
    Number Cake Pan 5, 143
    Number Cake Pan 6, 143
    Number Cake Pan 7, 143
    Number Cake Pan 8, 143
    Number One, 142
    Numbers Set, 143
    Pooh #1, 104
Number Cake Pan 0, 143
Number Cake Pan 1, 143
Number Cake Pan 2, 143
Number Cake Pan 3, 143
Number Cake Pan 4, 143
Number Cake Pan 5, 143
Number Cake Pan 6, 143
Number Cake Pan 7, 143
Number Cake Pan 8, 143
Number One, 143
Numbers Set, 143
oak, Acorn on Round With Fluted Sides, 134
Old World Santa, 93
Oscar the Grouch, 108
oval

Oval pan set, 136
Oval Pans, 137
Oval with Fleur-de-Lis, 137
Ovals, 2 9" pans, 137
Over the Hill Tombstone, 86
owl
  Graduate Owl, 33
  Mister Owl, 33
P. C. Popple, 119
panda
  3-D Cuddly Bear/Panda, 41
  Panda/Mini Stand-Up Bear, 41
panther, Pink Panther, 113
Party Popple, 119
Party Pumpkin, 1-2-3, 85
Partysaurus, 38
Patriotic Flag, 81
Paw Print Singles!, 40
Peanuts
  Charlie Brown, 112
  Snoopy, 112
Peek-A-Boo Bunny, 23
pencil, Mickey Mouse, 100
Petal Angel Food, 144
Petal Pan Fancifill, 69
Petal Pans, 144
Petal-Shaped Pans, 4 tiered, 136
Petite Christmas Tree, 95
Petite Egg, 80
Petite Fancy Ring, 133
Petite Heart, 78
Petite Huggable Bear, 41
Petite Jack-O-Lantern, 84
Petite Loaf, 139
Piano, 66
pig, Porky Pig, 110
Pikachu, Pokémon, 120
Pillsbury
  Poppin' Fresh, 129
  Pillsbury Poppin' Fresh Doughboy, 129
pin
  Bowling Pin Set, 60
  Bowling Pin Singles!, 60
Pineapple, 74
Pineapple Mold, 73
Pineapple Mold, Teflon interior, Lemon or
  Orange exterior, 73
Pineapple, avocado green, 73
Pineapple, coppertone, 73
Pineapple, harvest gold, 73
Pink Panther, Pink Panther, 113
Pinocchio, Mini Disney Pinocchio, 103
pirate, Lil' Pirate, 43
Playboy Bunny, 129
Playful Ghost, 1-2-3, 86
Playful Pup, 23
Playful Puppy, 22
playing card suite
  Club on Round, 63
  Grand Slam, 62
  Heart On Round, 63
Pluto
  Mini Disney Pluto, 102
  Pluto, 102
Po, Teletubbies, 121
Pocahontas, 105
Poinsettia, 93
Pokémon, 120
Policeman Mold, 57
pony
  Precious Pony, 29
  Small Animal Molds: Squirrel, Duck, Pony,
    Rabbit, 39
Pooh (see Winnie the Pooh)
Popeye, 112
Poppin' Fresh
  Pillsbury Poppin' Fresh Doughboy, 129
  Poppin' Fresh, 129
Popple
  P. C. Popple, 119
  Party Popple, 119
  Popples, 1-2-3, 119
Porky Pig, 110
pot
  Flower Pot, 70
  Monster Party Pan, 87
  Pooh Stand-up, 103
  Pooh with Honey Pot, small, golden, 103
  Winnie the Pooh, 104
Power Rangers/Mighty Morphin Power Rangers, 123
Powerpuff Girls, 118
Precious Moments, 117

Precious Pony, 29
Precious Puppy, 1-2-3, 22
present (see gift)
president, Silver Dollar Molds, 83
Pretty Lady, 42
princess
  Barbie, Dreamtime Princess, 127
  Pocahontas, 105
  Princess, 135
  Swan Princess, 118
prize (see award)
Proud Rooster, 31
Puffed Heart, 76
pumpkin
  Decorative Pumpkin, 85
  Harvest Coppertone Mold, 71
  Haunted Pumpkin, 85
  Insert for Ring Pan, Pumpkin, 85
  Jack-O-Lantern, 85
  Jack-O-Lantern Singles!, 86
  Jack-O-Lantern Stand-Up, 84
  Party Pumpkin, 1-2-3, 85
  Petite Jack-O-Lantern, 84
  Pumpkin Singles!, 71
  Pumpkin (Domed), 85
punctuation mark
  Enamel Exclamation Singles!, 144
  Color Enamel Question Mark Singles!, 144
  Question Mark, 144
puppet, Mini Disney Pinocchio, 103
puppy (see dog)
Puppy Dog, 22
question mark
  Color Enamel Question Mark Singles!, 144
  Question Mark, 144
Quick as a Bunny, 1-2-3, 24
R2-D2, 124
rabbit (see bunny)
Race Car, 55
Race Car/Super Race Car, 55
Rag Doll (Mini Toy Cakes), 44
Rag Doll Pan, 45
Raggedy Ann, 126
Rainbow Birthday Cake Pan, 65
Rainbow Brite, 118
reindeer
  Rudolph The Red Nosed Reindeer, 126
  Rudy Reindeer, 93
Ribbed Loaf, 144
Ribbed loaf, straight ends, long, 139
Ribbed loaf, straight ends, short, 139
ribbon
  Blue Ribbon, 68
  Insert for Ring Pan, blue ribbon, 68
ring
  4 in. Ring Singles!, 134
  Basic Ring (for Sculptured Tops), 132
  Charlotte, 144
  Classic Tube Pan, 133
  Coppertone Fancy Fluted Deep Ring, 133
  Coppertone Ring Mold, 134
  Coppertone Swirl Mold, 144
  Decorated Ring, 134
  Deluxe Coppertone Fruit Ring Mold, 74
  Fancy Ring, 133
  Fancy Ring Singles!, 133
  Fluted Ring, 133
  Individual Fluted Ring Molds, coppertone, 134
  Individual Ring Molds, coppertone, 134
  Kugelhopf Pan, 144
  Large Fruit Ring Mold, 74
  Petite Fancy Ring, 133
  Ring Mold 10.5", 144
  Ring mold 8", 144
  Ring Mold, coppertone rope pattern, 134
  Ring Twist, 134
  Rose Mold Ring, Light Coppertone, 69
  Rose Mold Ring, Silvertone, 69
  Sculptured Mold, 144
  Swirl Ring, 134
  Tall Crown Mold, coppertone, 133
robot
  C-3PO, 124
  R2-D2, 124
rocket, Spaceship, 57
Rockin' Juke Box, 67
Rocking Horse, 30
root beer mug, Good Cheer Mug, 71
Rose Mold Ring, Light Coppertone, 69
Rose Mold Ring, Silvertone, 69
Rose Mold, round, fluted sides, 74

round
  3 in. Round Singles!, 130
  4-Tier Cake Pan Set, 131
  Bevel Pan Set, 132
  Charlotte Mold, 144
  Contour Baking Pan Set, 131
  Coppertone Fluted Mold, 135
  Coppertone Jumbo Fluted Mold, 144
  Coppertone Tall Tyrolean Mold, 135
  Coronet, 134
  Decorated Domed Mold, 135
  Double Tier Round, 131
  Duchess, 144
  Fluted Mold, 135
  Fruit Round Mold, 72
  Half Round, 130
  Harvest Crown, 72
  Imperial, 144
  Individual Fluted Molds, 135
  Individual Swirled Mold, 135
  Individual Swirled Mold with Indent, 133
  Insert for Ring Pan, round, 144
  Insert for Ring Pan, Swirl, 132
  Miniature Wedding Tiers, 130
  Princess, 135
  Round Sculpted Mold, 134
  Round Tier Set, 130
  Sculptured Mold (Coppertone), 134
  Shortcake Singles!, 133
  Shortcakes 'N' Treats, 133
  Small Fluted Mold, 135
  Swirled Cone, 135
  Swirled Fluted mold, 135
  Three-Tiered Mold, 135
  Tiara, 135
  Triple-tier round, 131
  Turks Head, 133
  Turk's Head Mold, 144
  Victoria, 144
  Viennese Swirl, 69
  Viennese Swirl Singles!, 69
Rubber Ducky, 31
Rudolph The Red Nosed Reindeer, 126
Rudy Reindeer, 93
RugRats, 121
Sailboat, 57
sailor, Popeye, 112
Santa Claus
  Bear-y Christmas, 41
  Christmas Stocking, 90
  Coppertone Holiday Mold Set, 99
  Insert for Ring Pan, Santa, 91
  Mini Santa, 91
  Old World Santa, 93
  Santa, 91, 92
  Santa Bear Pan, 41
  Santa Checking List, 93
  Santa Face, 91
  Santa in Chimney Stand-Up Cake Mold, 91
  Santa Stand Up, 92
  Santa with Gift, 94
  Santa's List, 93
  Santa's Sleigh, 93
  Santa's Treasures, 94
  Smiling Santa, 91
saxaphone, Pink Panther, 113
scallop
  Petal Angel Food, 144
  Petal Pan Fancifill, 69
  Petal Pans, 144
  Petal-Shaped Pans, 4 tiered, 136
Scarecrow, 84
Scary Cat, 21
Scary Ghost, 86
Scooby-Doo, 125
Sculptured Mold, 144
Sculptured Mold (Coppertone), 134
seal, Ani-Mold Set, 39
seashell (see shell)
season, Coppertone Oval Seasons Molds, 137
Sesame Street
  Big Bird, 107
  Big Bird, 1-2-3, 107
  Big Bird face, 106
  Big Bird Full Figure, 107
  Big Bird Happy Birthday, 1-2-3, 107
  Big Bird Pan, 107
  Big Bird small pan, 106
  Big Bird with Banner, 107
  Cookie Monster, 108
  Cookie Monster small pan, 108
  Elmo, 109

  Elmo Singles!, 109
  Ernie, 108
  Ernie and Bert, 108
  mini Big Bird, 106
  Sesame Street Mini Pan, 108
  Oscar the Grouch, 108
  The Count, 109
shamrock
  Mini Shamrock, 79
  Shamrock, 80
  Shamrock minis, 79
  Shamrock Singles!, 80
  Shamrock, Coppertone, 80
sheep (see lamb)
sheet
  Educated Cake Pan, 138
  Multi-size square pan, 144
shell
  Coppertone Seashell, 142
  Large Shell Mold, coppertone, 142
  Mini Shell, 142
  Seashells, 142
  Shell, 142
  Shell Singles!, 142
ship
  Cruise Ship, 57
  Noah's Ark, 39
shoe
  Ballet Slippers, 67
  SuperStar Shoe, 59
  Western Boot, 50
Shooting Star, 141
Shortcake Singles!, 133
Shortcakes 'N' Treats, 133
shower
  Insert for Ring Pan, Shower, 67
  Mini Umbrella, 67
  Shower Umbrella, 67
Silver Dollar Molds, 83
Simpsons, Bart Simpson, 114
Sitting Dog with Bow, 22
Sitting Rabbit, 26
skating,
  Hockey Player, 60
  Montgomery Good News Moose, 120
skeleton, Smiling Skull, 87
skipping rope, Raggedy Ann, 126
skull, Smiling Skull, 87
sled, Santa's Sleigh, 93
sleigh, Santa's Sleigh, 93
slipper, Ballet Slippers, 67
Slot Machine, 62
Small Animal Molds: Squirrel, Duck, Pony, Rabbit, 39
Small Fluted Mold, 135
Small house or barn, 52
Smiling Santa, 91
Smiling Skull, 87
Smurf
  Mini Smurf, 127
  Smurf, 126
  Smurfette, 126
Snoopy, 112
snowflake
  Colored Snowflake Molds, 89
  Coppertone Oval Seasons Molds, 137
  Jewel Mold, 140
  Jewel Mold (Coppertone), 140
  Snowflake, 89
  Snowflake Singles!, 89
snowman
  Mini Snowman, 89
  Snowman, 88, 89
  Snowman Singles!, 89
  Snowman Stand-up, 90
Soccer Ball, 59
Soccer Singles!, 59
sock, Baby Bootie Singles!, 57
soldier
  G. I. Joe, 116
  Toy Soldier, 44
space (see also Star Wars)
  Alf, 114
  Biker Mice from Mars, 115
  Marvin the Martian, 115
  Spaceman Pan, 43
  Spaceship, 57
Spaceman Pan, 43
Spaceship, 57
spade, Grand Slam, 62
Special Delivery Baby, 129
Special Delivery Bunny, 24
Spider-Man, 123

Sports Ball Pan Set, 58
Sports Car, 53
sports clothing
   Football Helmet, 61
   Mini Football Helmet, 61
   SuperStar Shoe, 59
   T-Shirt, 50
sports equipment
   Baseball Glove, 58
   Bowling Pin Set, 60
   Bowling Pin Singles!, 60
   Football Helmet, 61
   Golf Bag, 59
   Mini Football Helmet, 61
   Tee It Up, 59
sports player
   Charlie Brown, 112
   Football Hero, 61
   Hockey Player, 60
   Home Run Hitter, 58
   WWF Superstars, 124
Sports Utility Vehicle, 54
Sporty Car, 53
square
   Contessa, 138
   Daisy Cart Cake, 139
   Educated Cake Pan, 138
   Multi-size square pan, 144
   Square Angel Food Pan, 138
   Square mold with top design, 138
   Square Tier Kit, 144
squirrel, Small Animal Molds: Squirrel,
   Duck, Pony, Rabbit, 39
St. Patrick's Day
   Mini Shamrock, 79
   Shamrock, 80
   Shamrock minis, 79
   Shamrock Singles!, 80
   Shamrock, Coppertone, 80
Standard capacity loaf, long and narrow, 139
Standard loaf with slightly sloped sides, 139
Standard Round Angel Food, 132
Stand-up Tree Pan set, 96
star
   Bear-y Christmas, 41
   Coppertone star mold, 141
   Mini Star, 141
   Rainbow Brite, 118
   Shooting Star, 141
   Star, 140, 141
   Star, 5-pointed, deep mold, 141
   Star, fancifill, 141
   Star Pans, 141
   Star Singles!, 141
   Treats 4 You!, 97
Star Wars
   Boba Fett, 124
   C-3PO, 124
   Darth Vader, 124
   R2-D2, 124
Star, 5-pointed, deep mold, 141
Star, fancifill, 141
Stars & Stripes, 82
Statue of Liberty, 83
stocking
   Christmas Stocking, 90
   Holiday Stocking, 90
   Stocking Singles!, 90
   Treats 4 You!, 97
stork
   Good News Stork, 33
   Stork, 33
Storybook Doll, 44, 45
Strawberry Shortcake, 118

sun, Coppertone Oval Seasons Molds, 137
Sunflower, 70
Sunny Bunny, 24
Super Heroes, 123
Super Mario Brothers, 120
Superman
   Super Heroes, 123
   Superman, 123
SuperStar Shoe, 59
SUV, Sports Utility Vehicle, 54
swan, Goose/Country Goose, 32
Swan Princess, 118
Sweetheart Mold with Teflon Interior (Lemon or
   Orange exterior), 99
Sweetheart/Fancy Heart Mold, 77
Swirl Ring, 134
Swirled Cone, 135
Swirled Fluted mold, 135
Sylvester and Tweety Mini, 111
Tall Crown Mold, coppertone, 133
Tasmanian Devil, 111
Taz, Tasmanian Devil, 111
teddy bear (see bear)
Teddy (Mini Toy Cakes), 40
Teddy Bear Singles!, 40
Teddy Bear StandUp, 41
Teddy Bear with Block, 40
Teddy Bear, 1-2-3, 40
Tee It Up, 59
Teenage Mutant Ninja Turtles
   Teenage Mutant Ninja Turtles, 115
   Teenage Mutant Ninja Turtles Face, Mini, 115
Teletubbies, 121
Texas, Lone-Star State, 83
Thanksgiving basket
   Coppertone Cornucopia, 72
   Cornucopia Mold, 72
   Cornucopia, 6 cup coppertone, 72
   Cornucopia, yellow enameled, 72
Thanksgiving turkey
   Coppertone Turkey Mold, 33
   Tom Turkey, 41
   Turkey, 33
The Count, 109
Thomas the Tank Engine, 126
Three Tiered Angel Food Cake Pan, 144
Three-Layer Tree, 96
Three-Tiered Mold, 135
Tiara, 135
tiger
   Lovable Animal, 37
   Tigger, 104
   Tigger Singles!, 104
Tigger, 104
Tigger Singles!, 104
Tinky Winky, Teletubbies, 121
T-Nee-Bikini, 51
toddler, Teletubbies, 121
Tom Turkey, 41
tomato, Veggie Tales, 120
tombstone, Over the Hill Tombstone, 86
Tommy, RugRats, 121
Topping Off Success, 68
Toy Soldier, 44
Tractor, 54
Traditional Melon-Shaped Mold, 73
Trail Rider, 54
train
   Choo Choo Train, 56
   Fun Train, 1-2-3, 56
   Little Locomotive, 56
   Little Train, 56
   Mini Locomotive, 55
   Thomas the Tank Engine, 126

Train (Mini Toy Cakes), 56
trash can, Oscar the Grouch, 108
Treats 4 You!, 97
tree (see Christmas tree)
Tree Cake and Mold Set, 94
Tree Singles!, 95
Treeliteful/Christmas Tree, 95
Trees, 95
Triple-tier round, 131
Troll, 44
Trophy, 68
truck
   18-Wheeler Truck, 54
   Free-Wheelin' Truck, 54
   Little Fire Truck/Firetruck, 54
T-Shirt, 50
turkey
   Coppertone Turkey Mold, 33
   Tom Turkey, 41
   Turkey, 33
Turks Head, 133
Turk's Head Mold, 144
turtle
   Teenage Mutant Ninja Turtles, 115
   Teenage Mutant Ninja Turtles Face, Mini, 115
Tweety, Sylvester and Tweety Mini, 111
Tweety, 110, 111
Tweety Bird Mini, 111
Twin Parti Bell, orange coating, 97
Two-Mix Book Pan, 64
umbrella
   Cheerful Chick, 30
   Insert for Ring Pan, Shower, 67
   Mini Umbrella, 67
   Shower Umbrella, 67
Up 'N Away Balloon, 57
US Flag, 82
USA, 82
valentine
   Be Mine, 76
   Cupid Pan, 76
   Cupid's Delight, 76
   Cupid's Heart, 76
   Double Heart Fancifill, 77
   Double Heart with Embossing, 77
   Double Tier Heart, 75
   Embossed Heart, 77
   Fanciful Heart Singles!, 76
   Fancy Heart Singles!, 76
   Happiness Heart pans, 75
   Heart Angel Food, 99
   Heart Angel Food Singles!, 99
   Heart Mini-Tier, 75
   Heart mold, deep with arrow, 78
   Heart mold, small embossed coppertone, 77
   Heart On Round, 63
   Heart Quartet, 78
   Heart Ring, 78
   Heart Set, 75
   Heart with Cherry, 77
   Hearts Entwined, 76
   I Love You, 78
   Individual Heart Mold, 76
   Insert for Ring Pan, heart, 77
   Lacy Heart, 77
   Mini Embossed Heart, 78
   Mini Heart, 78
   Petite Heart, 78
   Puffed Heart, 76
   Sweetheart/Fancy Heart Mold, 77
vampire
   Monster Party Pan, 87
   The Count, 109
van, Sports Utility Vehicle, 54

Van, 54
Veggie Tales, 120
vehicle
   18-Wheeler Truck, 54
   3-D Cruiser, 53
   Car (Mini Toy Cakes), 55
   Comical Car, 53
   Free-Wheelin' Truck, 54
   Little Fire Truck/Firetruck, 54
   Motorcycle, 55
   Race Car, 55
   Race Car/Super Race Car, 55
   Sports Car, 53
   Sports Utility Vehicle, 54
   Sporty Car, 53
   Trail Rider, 54
   Van, 54
Victoria, 144
video game, Super Mario Brothers, 120
Viennese Swirl, 69
Viennese Swirl Singles!, 69
wagon
   Circus Wagon Kit, 144
   Daisy Cart Cake, 139
   Flower Cart Kit, 137
western
   Li'l Cowboy, 43
   Lone-Star State, 83
   Yosemite Sam, 112
Western Boot, 50
Whimsical Witch, 88
Wicked Witch, 88
Winnie the Pooh
   Pooh #1, 104
   Pooh Face, 104
   Pooh Singles!, 104
   Pooh Stand-up, 103
   Pooh with Honey Pot, small, golden, 103
   Tigger, 104
   Tigger Singles!, 104
   Winnie the Pooh, 103, 104
witch
   Cute Witch, 87
   High Flyin' Witch, 87
   Monster Party Pan, 87
   Whimsical Witch, 88
   Wicked Witch, 88
Wizard, 45
wolf, Ani-Mold Set, 39
woman
   Barbie, 127, 128
   Barbie, Beautiful Day, 128
   Barbie, Dreamtime Princess, 127
   Cathy, 113
   Cinderella, 129
   Esmeralda, 105
   Pretty Lady, 42
   Swan Princess, 118
   T-Nee-Bikini, 51
   Wonder Woman, 122
Wonder Mold/Classic Wonder Mold, 136
Wonder Woman, 122
words on pan (see message)
Wreath, 91
wrestler, WWF Superstars, 124
Wuzzles
   Bumblelion, 106
   Eleroo, 106
WWF Superstars, 124
Yogi Bear, 125
Yosemite Sam, 112
Ziggy, 113
Zodiac Astrological Copper Mold, 65

Index of Pans by Stock Numbers

These codes appear in catalogs, yearbooks, and stamped on pans. Many pans have been associated with several different codes, and there may be other codes not shown here that have been used in some production runs or in some publications.

A code with an embedded "-x-" is from a Wilton yearbook, and the "x" replaces the issue code.

105-3200, Bugs Bunny, 110
1169M, 4-Tier Cake Pan Set, 131
1173-M, 4-Tier Cake Pan Set, 131
1175-M, 4-Tier Cake Pan Set, 131
1177-M, 4-Tier Cake Pan Set, 131
1190M, Tree Cake and Mold Set, 94
16234, Little Boy Chick, 32
201, Lamb Mold, 28
202, Three Tiered Angel Food Cake, 144
2024, Coppertone Holiday Mold Set, 99
203A, Coppertone Jumbo Fluted Mold, 144
205, Bell Pans, 98
2103-x-1139, Carousel Separator Set, 131
2105-0018, 18-Wheeler Truck, 54
2105-1009, Kitty Cat Pan, 21
2105-1031, Boo Ghost, 86
2105-1073, Happy Birthday, 64
2105-11044, Mini Heart, 78
2105-1224, Rudy Reindeer, 93
2105-1225, Jolly Santa, 92
2105-1234, Baseball Glove, 58
2105-1235, Mini Star, 140
2105-1236, Tasmanian Devil, 111
2105-1237, Over the Hill Tombstone, 86
2105-1238, Western Boot, 50
2105-1275, Mini Lamb, 27
2105-1280, Partysaurus, 38
2105-1285, Fred Flintstone, 125
2105-1317, Charlie Brown, 112
2105-1349, Thomas the Tank Engine, 126
2105-1350, Race Car, 55
2105-1394, Snowman Stand-up, 90
2105-1400, Double Tier Round, 131
2105-1414, Heart Quartet, 78
2105-1510, Holiday Tree, 96
2105-1518, Funny Bunny nonstick, 26
2105-1519, Computer, 63
2105-1520, Old World Santa, 93
2105-172, Puffed Heart, 76
2105-173, Cupid Pan, 76
2105-174, Decorated Egg, 81
2105-1741, Boba Fett, 124
2105-1750, Mystical Dragon, 38
2105-1760, Mini Ball, 58
2105-1779, Mini Christmas Tree, 95
2105-1793, Care Bears, 119
2105-1800, Graduate, 68
2105-181, Haunted House, 52
2105-183, Stars & Stripes, 82
2105-1836, Golf Bag, 59
2105-1840, Question Mark, 144
2105-1850, Patriotic Flag, 81
2105-1875, Bumblelion, 106
2105-1950, Eleroo, 106
2105-1968, Montgomery Good News Moose, 120
2105-1984, Cabbage Patch Kids, 117
2105-1988, Cabbage Patch Stand-up, 117
2105-1990, Cabbage Patch Preemie, 117
2105-2001, Scarecrow, 84

2105-2003, Special Delivery Baby, 129
2105-2015, Cottontail Bunny, 24
2105-2017, Millennium Special 2000, 65
2105-2020, Home Run Hitter, 58
2105-2021, Ballerina Bear, 40
2105-2022, Pretty Lady, 42
2105-2023, Handsome Guy, 42
2105-2024, Mini Balloon, 65
2105-2025, Motorcycle, 55
2105-2026, Noah's Ark, 39
2105-2028, Megasaurus, 38
2105-2029, Little Ducky, 31
2105-2030, Flower Pot, 70
2105-2031, Enchanted Castle, 51
2105-2032, Tee It Up, 59
2105-2033, Slot Machine, 62
2105-2034, Sports Utility Vehicle, 54
2105-2035, Hot Lips, 50
2105-2036, Cheerful Chick, 30
2105-2037, Bunny in a Basket, 24
2105-2038, Topping Off Success, 68
2105-2039, Monster Party Pan, 87
2105-2040, Holiday Stocking, 90
2105-2043, 3-D Cruiser, 53
2105-2044, Soccer Ball, 59
2105-2047, Snowman Stand-up, 90
2105-2048, Storybook Doll, 45
2105-2056, Candy Cane Pan, 94
2105-2056, Party Popple, 119
2105-2057, Smiling Skull, 87
2105-2060, Just Hatched Chick, 30
2105-2060, P. C. Popple, 119
2105-2061, Little Fire Truck/Firetruck, 54
2105-2063, Tractor, 54
2105-2064, Playful Pup, 23
2105-2065, Ballet Slippers, 67
2105-2067, Snowflake, 89
2105-2068, Whimsical Witch, 88
2105-2070, Holiday House/Stand-Up House, 51
2105-2072, Gingerbread Boy, 48
2105-2094, Rubber Ducky, 31
2105-2095, Jungle Lion, 38
2105-2096, Mini Jungle Animals, 38
2105-2097, Petite Fancy Ring, 133
2105-2118, Mini Egg, 80
2105-2120, Bite-Size Bunny, 27
2105-215, I Love You, 78
2105-2250, Barbie, 127
2105-2293, Shower Umbrella, 67
2105-2325, Teddy Bear StandUp, 41
2105-2350, Care Bears Stand-up, 119
2105-2356, Chick-In-Egg, 30
2105-2380, Little Mouse, 36
2105-2384, mini Big Bird, 106
2105-2386, Mini Smurf, 127
2105-2388, Rocking Horse, 30
2105-2430, Puppy Dog, 22
2105-2432, Petite Heart, 78
2105-2435, Sunny Bunny, 24
2105-2447, Garfield, 114
2105-2499, Goose /Country Goose, 32
2105-2512, Star, 141
2105-2514, Lovable Lamb, 29
2105-2515, Gentle Lamb, 28
2105-2521, Two-Mix Book Pan, 64
2105-2530, Horseshoe, 2 mix, 62
2105-2550, Mini Garfield, 114
2105-2551, Barbie, 128
2105-2552, WWF Superstars, 124
2105-2553, Bugs Bunny, 109
2105-2705, Alf, 114
2105-2711, Biker Mice from Mars, 115
2105-2763, Big Fish, 36
2105-2858, Gumball Machine, 71
2105-2875, Cuddles the Cow, 29

2105-2908, Blue Ribbon, 68
2105-2914, Precious Pony, 29
2105-2950, G. I. Joe, 116
2105-2989, Super Mario Brothers, 120
2105-3000, Winnie the Pooh, 104
2105-3001, Tigger, 104
2105-3002, Pooh Stand-up, 103
2105-3003, Pooh #1, 104
2105-3004, Pooh Face, 104
2105-3050, RugRats, 121
2105-3055, Flower Power, 128
2105-3060, Blue's Clues, 121
2105-3065, Teletubbies, 121
2105-3068, Jack-O-Lantern, 85
2105-3070, Haunted Pumpkin, 85
2105-3075, Teenage Mutant Ninja Turtles, 115
2105-3147, Garfield Stand-up, 114
2105-3150, Jack-O-Lantern Stand-Up, 84
2105-3184, He-Man Masters of the Universe, 123
2105-3197, Brave Heart Lion, 119
2105-3201, Tweety, 111
2105-3202, Marvin the Martian, 115
2105-3203, Flik Bug's Life, 105
2105-3204, Bugs, 109
2105-3205, Tweety, 111
2105-3206, Scooby-Doo, 125
2105-3219, Heart Ring, 78
2105-3235, Santa's Sleigh, 93
2105-3250, 101 Dalmatians, 106
2105-3254, Horseshoe, 62
2105-3300, Hercules, 105
2105-3306, Hamburger, 71
2105-3310, Smiling Santa, 91
2105-3312, Poinsettia, 93
2105-3313, Gingerbread Boy, 48
2105-3314, Bear-y Christmas, 41
2105-3323, Santa Checking List, 93
2105-3400, Little Mermaid, 104
2105-3450, Barney, 122
2105-3461, Elmo, 109
2105-3500, Barbie, Beautiful Day, 128
2105-3523, Congratulations, 64
2105-3550, Barbie, 128
2105-3600, Mini Mickey Mouse, 101
2105-3601, Mickey Mouse, 100
2105-3602, Minnie Mouse, 100
2105-3603, Mickey Face, 101
2105-3636, Ice Cream Cone, 71
2105-3654, Big Bird with Banner, 107
2105-3655, Petite Huggable Bear, 41
2105-37, Pokémon, 115
2105-3700, Pocahontas, 105
2105-3800, Esmeralda, 105
2105-3845, Mini Ghost, 86
2105-3951, Swan Princess, 118
2105-3975, Dotty Dog, 120
2105-425, Treeliteful/Christmas Tree, 95
2105-4298, Elmo, 109
2105-4308, Mini Football Helmet, 61
2105-4358, Mickey Mouse, 100
2105-4395, Peek-A-Boo Bunny, 23
2105-4396, Mini Shell, 142
2105-4426, Mini Bunny, 27
2105-4432, Santa Bear Pan, 41
2105-4436, Teenage Mutant Ninja Turtles, 115
2105-4497, Mini Bear, 41
2105-4590, Wicked Witch, 88
2105-4610, Football Hero, 61
2105-472, Mini Snowman, 89
2105-4793, Egg Pan Set, 80
2105-4794, Petite Egg, 80
2105-4798, Rainbow Brite, 118
2105-4911, Cupid's Heart, 76
2105-4943, Huggable Teddy Bear, 40
2105-5000, Harry Potter, 111

2105-5008, Fancy Ring, 133
2105-5025, Bob the Builder, 127
2105-5050, Spider-Man, 123
2105-5207, Scary Cat, 21
2105-5621, Mini Clown, 47
2105-570, Guitar, 66
2105-572, Juggling Clown, 48
2105-573, Baby Doll, 46
2105-5975, Power Rangers/Mighty Morphin, 123
2105-606, Heart Set, 75
2105-6500, Little Train, 56
2105-6501, Batman, 122
2105-6503, Mini Gingerbread Boy, 49
2105-6504, First and Ten Football pan, 60
2105-6505, Bowling a Strike, 60
2105-6507, Carousel Horse, 30
2105-6508, Race Car/Super Race Car, 55
2105-6620, Barney and Baby Bop Mini, 121
2105-6710, Merry Mermaid, 43
2105-6711, Cute Clown, 48
2105-6712, Troll, 44
2105-6713, Barney, 122
2105-724, Hockey Player, 60
2105-801, Scarecrow, 84
2105-802, Happy Clown, 46
2105-803, Snowman, 88
2105-804, Shooting Star, 141
2105-805, Big Bird Pan, 107
2105-8250, Shell, 142
2105-8251, USA, 82
2105-8252, Viennese Swirl, 69
2105-8253, Bugs Bunny, 110
2105-8254, Mini Bell, 98
2105-8255, Mini Embossed Heart, 78
2105-8256, Mini Umbrella, 67
2105-8257, Teddy Bear with Block, 40
2105-8423, Sporty Car, 53
2105-8461, Cute Baby, 42
2105-8462, Petite Jack-O-Lantern, 84
2105-8463, Petite Christmas Tree, 95
2105-8466, Petite Loaf, 139
2105-8468, Lamb Chop, 117
2105-8471, Sylvester and Tweety Mini, 111
2105-8472, Sesame Street Mini Pan, 108
2105-8473, Teenage Mutant Ninja Turtles, 115
2105-8900, Barbie, Dreamtime Princess, 127
2105-8910, Barbie, 127
2105-9001, Special Delivery Bunny, 24
2105-9002, Bart Simpson, 114
2105-9110, Little Fire Truck/Firetruck, 54
2105-9111, Good Time Clock, 65
2105-926, Bite-Size Gingerbread Boy, 49
2105-9311, Classic Angel Food Pan, 132
2105-9312, Mini Angel Food Pan, 132
2105-9330, Cute Witch, 87
2105-9331, Mini Dinosaur, 39
2105-9332, Mini Locomotive, 55
2105-9333, Lil' Pirate, 43
2105-9334, Dalmatian Pup, 23
2105-9340, Embossed Heart, 77
2105-9365, Precious Moments, 117
2105-9401, Circus Clown, 1-2-3, 48
2105-9402, Teddy Bear, 1-2-3, 40
2105-9404, Little Dolly, 46
2105-9406, Popples, 1-2-3, 119
2105-9407, Big Bird Happy Birthday, 1-2-3, 107
2105-9408, Quick as a Bunny, 1-2-3, 24
2105-9409, Friendly (?) Dinosaur, 1-2-3, 39
2105-9410, Christmas Tree, 1-2-3/Step-by-Step, 97
2105-9424, Cutie Cat, 1-2-3 (?), 21
2105-9427, Playful Ghost, 1-2-3, 86
2105-9433, Bunny Face, 1-2-3, 26
2105-9433, Fun Train, 1-2-3, 56
2105-9434, Precious Puppy, 1-2-3, 22
2105-9436, Darling Dolly, 1-2-3, 46

2105-9474, Circus Clown, 1-2-3, 46
2105-9475, Dinosaur, 1-2-3, 39
2105-9476, Big Bird, 1-2-3, 107
2105-9490, Batman Emblem, 122
2105-9496, Christmas Tree Little Cakes, 95
2105-972, Book Pan, 64
2105-9791, Mini Loaf Pan Set, 139
2105-9900, Batman Beyond, 122
2105-9902, Powerpuff Girls, 118
2105-9904, Veggie Tales, 120
2105-x-0018, 18-Wheeler Truck, 54
2105-x-0805, Big Bird Pan, 107
2105-x-0926, Bite-Size Gingerbread Boy, 49
2105-x-1009, Kitty Cat Pan, 21
2105-x-1031, Boo Ghost, 86
2105-x-1073, Happy Birthday, 64
2105-x-1102, Fancy Ring Singles!, 133
2105-x-1104, Angel Food Singles!, 132
2105-x-1044, Mini Heart, 78
2105-x-1105, Fancy Heart Singles!, 76
2105-x-1106, Shell Singles!, 142
2105-x-1107, Loaf Singles!, 144
2105-x-1108, Shortcake Singles!, 133
2105-x-1109, Teddy Bear Singles!, 40
2105-x-1110, Viennese Swirl Singles!, 69
2105-x-1111, 4 in. Ring Singles!, 134
2105-x-1113, 3 in. Round Singles!, 130
2105-x-1114, Aluminum #1 Singles!, 143
2105-x-1115, Hand Singles!, 50
2105-x-1116, Foot Singles!, 50
2105-x-1117, Cat Singles!, 21
2105-x-1118, Paw Print Singles!, 40
2105-x-1119, Flower Singles!, 69
2105-x-1120, Jack-O-Lantern Singles!, 86
2105-x-1121, Ghost Singles!, 86
2105-x-1122, Bat Singles!, 86
2105-x-1123, Cat Singles!, 21
2105-x-1124, Tree Singles!, 95
2105-x-1125, Snowman Singles!, 89
2105-x-1126, Stocking Singles!, 90
2105-x-1127, Star Singles!, 141
2105-x-1128, Candy Cane Singles!, 94
2105-x-1129, Bell Singles!, 99
2105-x-1130, Snowflake Singles!, 89
2105-x-1131, Angel Singles!, 90
2105-x-1132, Flag Singles!, 82
2105-x-1133, 101 Dalmatians Singles!, 106
2105-x-1134, Bugs Bunny Singles!, 110
2105-x-1135, Pooh Singles!, 104
2105-x-1136, Mickey Singles!, 101
2105-x-1137, Fanciful Heart Singles!, 76
2105-x-1138, Heart Angel Food Singles!, 99
2105-x-1140, Shamrock Singles!, 80
2105-x-1141, Egg Singles!, 81
2105-x-1142, Bunny Singles!, 26
2105-x-1143, Chick Singles!, 30
2105-x-1144, Baby Bootie Singles!, 57
2105-x-1145, Tigger Singles!, 104
2105-x-1146, Cross Singles!, 79
2105-x-1160, Color Enamel #0 Singles!, 143
2105-x-1161, Color Enamel #1 Singles!, 143
2105-x-1162, Color Enamel #2 Singles!, 143
2105-x-1163, Color Enamel #3 Singles!, 143
2105-x-1164, Color Enamel #4 Singles!, 143
2105-x-1165, Color Enamel #5 Singles!, 143
2105-x-1166, Color Enamel #6/9 Singles!, 143
2105-x-1167, Color Enamel #7 Singles!, 143
2105-x-1168, Color Enamel #8 Singles!, 143
2105-x-1169, Color Enamel Question Mark, 144
2105-x-1170, Color Enamel Exclamation, 144
2105-x-1172, Baseball Singles!, 58
2105-x-1173, Basketball Singles!, 74
2105-x-1174, Bowling Pin Singles!, 60
2105-x-1175, Football Singles!, 60
2105-x-1176, Golf Ball Singles!, 59
2105-x-1177, Soccer Singles!, 59
2105-x-1197, Free-Wheelin' Truck, 54
2105-x-1200, Bevel Pan Set, 132
2105-x-1219, Butterfly Fancifill, 34
2105-x-1224, Rudy Reindeer, 93
2105-x-1225, Jolly Santa, 92
2105-x-123, Big Bird Full Figure, 107
2105-x-1234, Baseball Glove, 58
2105-x-1235, Mini Star, 140
2105-x-1236, Tasmanian Devil, 111
2105-x-1237, Over the Hill Tombstone, 86
2105-x-1238, Western Boot, 50
2105-x-1270, Charlotte Mold, 144
2105-x-1275, Mini Lamb, 27
2105-x-1278, Darth Vader, 124
2105-x-1280, Partysaurus, 38
2105-x-1285, Fred Flintstone, 125

2105-x-1294, R2-D2, 124
2105-x-1317, Charlie Brown, 112
2105-x-1319, Snoopy, 112
2105-x-1349, Thomas the Tank Engine, 126
2105-x-1350, Race Car, 55
2105-x-1383, Tweety, 110
2105-x-1394, Snowman Stand-up, 90
2105-x-1400, Double Tier Round, 131
2105-x-1413, Star, fancifill, 141
2105-x-1414, Heart Quartet, 78
2105-x-1464, C-3PO, 124
2105-x-1499, Mini Pumpkin, 84
2105-x-1502, Wreath, 91
2105-x-1510, Holiday Tree, 96
2105-x-1518, Funny Bunny nonstick, 26
2105-x-1519, Computer, 63
2105-x-1537, Double Bell, 99
2105-x-1553, Ovals, 2 9" pans, 137
2105-x-1588, Long Loaf, 139
2105-x-1618, Snowman, 88
2105-x-1699, Double Tier Heart, 75
2105-x-172, Puffed Heart, 76
2105-x-1720, Mystical Dragon, 38
2105-x-173, Cupid Pan, 76
2105-x-174, Decorated Egg, 81
2105-x-1741, Boba Fett, 124
2105-x-175, Cottontail Bunny, 24
2105-x-1750, Mystical Dragon, 38
2105-x-1760, Mini Ball, 58
2105-x-1779, Mini Christmas Tree, 95
2105-x-1782, Yogi Bear, 125
2105-x-1793, Care Bears, 119
2105-x-180, Rudy Reindeer, 93
2105-x-181, Haunted House, 52
2105-x-183, Stars & Stripes, 82
2105-x-1836, Golf Bag, 59
2105-x-1840, Question Mark, 144
2105-x-1863, Fred Flintstone, 125
2105-x-1875, Bumblelion, 106
2105-x-1898, Up 'N Away Balloon, 57
2105-x-190, Ring mold 8", 144
2105-x-1928, Spaceship, 57
2105-x-1944, Popeye, 112
2105-x-1950, Eleroo, 106
2105-x-1968, Montgomery Good News Moose, 120
2105-x-1984, Cabbage Patch Kids, 117
2105-x-1988, Cabbage Patch Stand-up, 117
2105-x-1990, Cabbage Patch Preemie, 117
2105-x-1995, Santa's List, 93
2105-x-2000, Maple Leaf Singles!, 70
2105-x-2001, Scarecrow, 84
2105-x-2002, Pumpkin Singles!, 71
2105-x-2003, Special Delivery Baby, 129
2105-x-2010, Little Lamb / Stand-Up Lamb, 27
2105-x-2015, Cottontail Bunny, 24
2105-x-2017, Millennium Special 2000, 65
2105-x-2020, Home Run Hitter, 58
2105-x-2021, Ballerina Bear, 40
2105-x-2022, Pretty Lady, 42
2105-x-2023, Handsome Guy, 42
2105-x-2024, Mini Balloon, 65
2105-x-2025, Motorcycle, 55
2105-x-2026, Noah's Ark, 39
2105-x-2028, Megasaurus, 38
2105-x-2029, Little Ducky, 31
2105-x-2030, Flower Pot, 70
2105-x-2031, Enchanted Castle, 51
2105-x-2032, Tee It Up, 59
2105-x-2033, Slot Machine, 62
2105-x-2034, Sports Utility Vehicle, 54
2105-x-2035, Hot Lips, 50
2105-x-2037, Bunny in a Basket, 24
2105-x-2037, Toy Soldier, 44
2105-x-2038, Topping Off Success, 68
2105-x-2039, Monster Party Pan, 87
2105-x-2040, Holiday Stocking, 90
2105-x-2041, Old World Santa, 93
2105-x-2043, 3-D Cruiser, 53
2105-x-2044, Soccer Ball, 59
2105-x-2047, Snowman Stand-up, 90
2105-x-2048, Storybook Doll, 45
2105-x-2056, Candy Cane Pan, 94
2105-x-2056, Party Popple, 119
2105-x-2057, Smiling Skull, 87
2105-x-2058, Christmas Tree, 1-2-3/Step-by-Step, 97
2105-x-2059, Just Hatched Chick, 30
2105-x-2060, P. C. Popple, 119
2105-x-2061, Little Fire Truck/Firetruck, 54
2105-x-2063, Tractor, 54
2105-x-2064, Playful Pup, 23
2105-x-2065, Ballet Slippers, 67

2105-x-2067, Snowflake, 89
2105-x-2068, Whimsical Witch, 88
2105-x-2070, Holiday House/Stand-Up House, 51
2105-x-2072, Gingerbread Boy, 48
2105-x-2094, Rubber Ducky, 31
2105-x-2095, Jungle Lion, 38
2105-x-2096, Mini Jungle Animals, 38
2105-x-2097, Petite Fancy Ring, 133
2105-x-2106, Cheerful Chick, 30
2105-x-2118, Mini Egg, 80
2105-x-2120, Bite-Size Bunny, 27
2105-x-2130, Oval pan set, 136
2105-x-2131, Heart Set, 75
2105-x-2134, Petal-Shaped Pans, 4 tiered, 136
2105-x-214, Puffed Heart, 76
2105-x-2142, Petal Pans, 144
2105-x-215, I Love You, 78
2105-x-2150, Star Pans, 141
2105-x-2174, Classic Tube Pan, 133
2105-x-220, Bell Pans, 98
2105-x-2223, Bunny Cake Mold, 25
2105-x-2250, Barbie, 127
2105-x-2282, Holiday House/Stand-Up House, 51
2105-x-2293, Shower Umbrella, 67
2105-x-2325, Teddy Bear StandUp, 41
2105-x-2347, T-Shirt, 50
2105-x-2350, Care Bears Stand-up, 119
2105-x-2356, Chick-In-Egg, 30
2105-x-2371, Porky Pig, 110
2105-x-2380, Little Mouse, 36
2105-x-2384, mini Big Bird, 106
2105-x-2386, Mini Smurf, 127
2105-x-2388, Rocking Horse, 30
2105-x-2428, Sports Car, 53
2105-x-2430, Puppy Dog, 22
2105-x-2432, Petite Heart, 78
2105-x-2435, Sunny Bunny, 24
2105-x-2444, SuperStar Shoe, 59
2105-x-2447, Garfield, 114
2105-x-2452, Frog, 36
2105-x-2479, Kitten, 21
2105-x-2495, Easter Bunny, 23
2105-x-2499, Goose /Country Goose, 32
2105-x-2505, Bird 'N Banner, 32
2105-x-2509, Cross /Bevelled Cross, 79
2105-x-2510, Cross, 2 mix, 99
2105-x-2512, Star, 141
2105-x-2514, Lovable Lamb, 29
2105-x-2515, Gentle Lamb, 28
2105-x-2517, Double Heart Fancifill, 77
2105-x-2521, Two-Mix Book Pan, 64
2105-x-2530, Horseshoe, 2 mix, 62
2105-x-2533, Insert for Ring Pan, Lucky Clover, 61
2105-x-255, Spaceman Pan, 43
2105-x-2550, Mini Garfield, 114
2105-x-2551, Barbie, 128
2105-x-2552, WWF Superstars, 124
2105-x-2553, Bugs Bunny, 109
2105-x-2555, Superman, 122
2105-x-2576, Pink Panther, 113
2105-x-2585, Ribbed Loaf, 144
2105-x-2593, Kugelhopf Pan, 144
2105-x-2606, Scooby-Doo, 125
2105-x-2622, Wonder Woman, 122
2105-x-2633, Wizard, 45
2105-x-2665, Oscar the Grouch, 108
2105-x-2673, The Count, 109
2105-x-2703, Donald Duck, 102
2105-x-2705, Alf, 114
2105-x-2711, Biker Mice from Mars, 115
2105-x-2738, Football Helmet, 61
2105-x-27544, Jolly Clown, 46
2105-x-2763, Big Fish, 36
2105-x-2797, Joyful Angel, 90
2105-x-2827, 13-Star Flag, 81
2105-x-2858, Gumball Machine, 71
2105-x-2861, Choo Choo Train, 55
2105-x-2875, Cuddles the Cow, 29
2105-x-2886, Insert for Ring Pan, Horse, 29
2105-x-2908, Blue Ribbon, 68
2105-x-2914, Precious Pony, 29
2105-x-2950, G. I. Joe, 116
2105-x-298, Cuddly Bear, 40
2105-x-299, Super Mario Brothers, 120
2105-x-3000, Winnie the Pooh, 104
2105-x-3001, Tigger, 104
2105-x-3002, Pooh Stand-up, 103
2105-x-3002, Sports Ball Pan Set, 58
2105-x-3003, Pooh #1, 104
2105-x-3004, Pooh Face, 104
2105-x-3020, Mini Wonder /Petite Doll Pan, 136
2105-x-3050, RugRats, 121

2105-x-3055, Flower Power, 128
2105-x-3060, Blue's Clues, 121
2105-x-3065, Teletubbies, 121
2105-x-3068, Jack-O-Lantern, 85
2105-x-3070, Haunted Pumpkin, 85
2105-x-3075, Teenage Mutant Ninja Turtles, 115
2105-x-3092, Petal Pan Fancifill, 69
2105-x-3114, Turkey, 33
2105-x-3147, Garfield Stand-up, 114
2105-x-3150, Jack-O-Lantern Stand-Up, 84
2105-x-3173, Ernie, 108
2105-x-3184, He-Man Masters of the Universe, 123
2105-x-3197, Brave Heart Lion, 119
2105-x-3200, Bugs Bunny, 110
2105-x-3201, Tweety, 111
2105-x-3202, Marvin the Martian, 115
2105-x-3203, Flik Bug's Life, 105
2105-x-3204, Bugs, 109
2105-x-3205, Tweety, 111
2105-x-3206, Scooby-Doo, 125
2105-x-3207, Yosemite Sam, 112
2105-x-3219, Heart Ring, 78
2105-x-3235, Santa's Sleigh, 93
2105-x-3250, 101 Dalmatians, 106
2105-x-3254, Horseshoe, 62
2105-x-3279, Cupid's Delight, 76
2105-x-328, Mickey Mouse, 101
2105-x-3300, Hercules, 105
2105-x-3306, Hamburger, 71
2105-x-3310, Smiling Santa, 91
2105-x-3311, Holiday House/Stand-Up House, 51
2105-x-3312, Poinsettia, 93
2105-x-3313, Gingerbread Boy, 48
2105-x-3314, Bear-y Christmas, 41
2105-x-3319, Santa, 92
2105-x-3323, Santa Checking List, 93
2105-x-3351, Bugs Bunny, 110
2105-x-336, Minnie Mouse, 100
2105-x-3400, Little Mermaid, 104
2105-x-344, Goofy, 102
2105-x-3450, Barney, 122
2105-x-3459, Mini Shamrock, 79
2105-x-3460, Elmo Singles!, 109
2105-x-3461, Elmo, 109
2105-x-3500, Barbie, Beautiful Day, 128
2105-x-352, Pluto, 102
2105-x-3523, Congratulations, 64
2105-x-3550, Barbie, 128
2105-x-3572, Hexagon Set, 140
2105-x-360, Donald Duck, 102
2105-x-3600, Mini Mickey Mouse, 101
2105-x-3601, Mickey Mouse, 100
2105-x-3602, Bell, 98
2105-x-3602, Minnie Mouse, 100
2105-x-3603, Mickey Face, 101
2105-x-3636, Ice Cream Cone, 71
2105-x-3653, Big Bird, 107
2105-x-3654, Big Bird with Banner, 107
2105-x-3655, Petite Huggable Bear, 41
2105-x-37, Pokémon, 120
2105-x-3700, Pocahontas, 105
2105-x-3749, Happy Easter Egg, 81
2105-x-379, Winnie the Pooh, 103
2105-x-3800, Esmeralda, 105
2105-x-3823, Circus Clown, 47
2105-x-3844, Mini Loaf, 144
2105-x-3845, Mini Ghost, 86
2105-x-395, Mickey Mouse, 100
2105-x-3951, Swan Princess, 118
2105-x-3975, Dotty Dog, 120
2105-x-4013, Ring Mold 10.5", 144
2105-x-409, Heart Mini-Tier, 75
2105-x-425, Treeliteful/Christmas Tree, 95
2105-x-4269, Gentle Lamb, 29
2105-x-4298, Elmo, 109
2105-x-4307, Insert for Ring Pan, horseshoe, 62
2105-x-4308, Mini Football Helmet, 61
2105-x-4331, Be Mine, 76
2105-x-4358, Mickey Mouse, 100
2105-x-4374, Easter Basket Pan, 79
2105-x-4395, Peek-A-Boo Bunny, 23
2105-x-4396, Mini Shell, 142
2105-x-4426, Mini Bunny, 27
2105-x-4432, Santa Bear Pan, 41
2105-x-4436, Teenage Mutant Ninja Turtles, 115
2105-x-4458, Strawberry Shortcake, 118
2105-x-4497, Mini Bear, 41
2105-x-4498, Little Locomotive, 56
2105-x-4528, Pink Panther, 113
2105-x-4556, Donald Duck, 102
2105-x-4587, Good News Stork, 33
2105-x-4590, Wicked Witch, 88

2105-x-4610, *Football Hero*, 61
2105-x-4641, *Cathy*, 113
2105-x-4668, *Insert for Ring Pan, blue ribbon*, 68
2105-x-4692, *Mini Santa*, 91
2105-x-4706, *Noel Candle*, 89
2105-x-472, *Mini Snowman*, 89
2105-x-4722, *Rudolph The Red Nosed Reindeer*, 126
2105-x-4757, *Li'l Cowboy*, 43
2105-x-4773, *High Flyin' Witch*, 87
2105-x-4793, *Egg Pan Set*, 80
2105-x-4794, *Petite Egg*, 80
2105-x-4798, *Rainbow Brite*, 118
2105-x-4821, *Insert for Ring Pan, heart*, 77
2105-x-4889, *Scary Ghost*, 86
2105-x-489, *Panda/Mini Stand-Up Bear*, 41
2105-x-4911, *Cupid's Heart*, 76
2105-x-4927, *Cookie Monster*, 108
2105-x-4943, *Huggable Teddy Bear*, 40
2105-x-4986, *Raggedy Ann*, 126
2105-x-5000, *Harry Potter*, 111
2105-x-5008, *Fancy Ring*, 133
2105-x-5025, *Bob the Builder*, 127
2105-x-5036, *Mister Owl*, 33
2105-x-5044, *Playful Puppy*, 22
2105-x-5050, *Spider-Man*, 123
2105-x-5053, *Ziggy*, 113
2105-x-5087, *Bugs Bunny*, 110
2105-x-5184, *Van*, 54
2105-x-5207, *Scary Cat*, 21
2105-x-5311, *Rockin' Juke Box*, 67
2105-x-5370, *Classic House Pan*, 52
2105-x-5409, *Butterfly*, 34
2105-x-5419, *Smurfette*, 126
2105-x-5435, *Smurf*, 126
2105-x-5496, *Good Cheer Mug*, 71
2105-x-5532, *Sailboat*, 57
2105-x-5559, *Insert for Ring Pan, Santa*, 91
2105-x-5583, *Trail Rider*, 54
2105-x-5621, *Mini Clown*, 47
2105-x-565, *Wonder Mold/Classic Wonder*, 136
2105-x-570, *Guitar*, 66
2105-x-5702, *Insert for Ring Pan, Shower*, 67
2105-x-572, *Juggling Clown*, 48
2105-x-573, *Baby Doll*, 46
2105-x-5737, *Insert for Ring Pan, Shower*, 67
2105-x-5885, *Holiday Bunny*, 25
2105-x-5966, *Shortcakes 'N' Treats*, 133
2105-x-5975, *Power Rangers/Mighty Morphin*, 123
2105-x-5982, *Insert for Ring Pan, Pumpkin*, 85
2105-x-6007, *Santa Stand Up*, 92
2105-x-603, *3-D Cuddly Bear/ Panda*, 41
2105-x-606, *Heart Set*, 75
2105-x-6116, *Bevel Pan Set*, 132
2105-x-6118, *Contour Baking Pan Set*, 131
2105-x-6121, *Insert for Ring Pan, Birthday*, 64
2105-x-638, *Cookie Monster*, 108
2105-x-646, *Big Bird face*, 106
2105-x-6500, *Little Train*, 56
2105-x-6501, *Batman*, 122
2105-x-6503, *Mini Gingerbread Boy*, 49
2105-x-6504, *First and Ten Football pan*, 60
2105-x-6505, *Bowling a Strike*, 60
2105-x-6506, *Sports Ball Pan Set*, 58
2105-x-6507, *Carousel Horse*, 30
2105-x-6508, *Race Car/Super Race Car*, 55
2105-x-6509, *Heart Angel Food*, 99
2105-x-6510, *Petal Angel Food*, 99
2105-x-6620, *Barney and Baby Bop Mini*, 121
2105-x-6710, *Merry Mermaid*, 43
2105-x-6711, *Cute Clown*, 48
2105-x-6712, *Troll*, 44
2105-x-6713, *Barney*, 122
2105-x-700, *Egg Pan Set*, 80
2105-x-719, *Candlelit Tree Pan Set*, 96
2105-x-724, *Hockey Player*, 60
2105-x-743, *Elephant Pan*, 37
2105-x-743, *Happy Hippo*, 37
2105-x-750, *Stand-up Tree Pan set*, 96
2105-x-778, *Holly Hobbie*, 116
2105-x-7918, *Number One*, 142
2105-x-7925, *Lone-Star State*, 83
2105-x-801, *Scarecrow*, 84
2105-x-802, *Happy Clown*, 46
2105-x-803, *Snowman*, 88
2105-x-804, *Shooting Star*, 141
2105-x-8250, *Shell*, 142
2105-x-8251, *USA*, 82
2105-x-8252, *Viennese Swirl*, 69
2105-x-8253, *Bugs Bunny*, 110
2105-x-8254, *Mini Bell*, 98
2105-x-8255, *Mini Embossed Heart*, 78
2105-x-8256, *Mini Umbrella*, 67
2105-x-8257, *Teddy Bear with Block*, 40
2105-x-8461, *Cute Baby*, 42
2105-x-8462, *Petite Jack-O-Lantern*, 84
2105-x-8463, *Petite Christmas Tree*, 95
2105-x-8466, *Petite Loaf*, 139
2105-x-8468, *Lamb Chop*, 117
2105-x-8471, *Sylvester and Tweety Mini*, 111
2105-x-8472, *Sesame Street Mini Pan*, 108
2105-x-8473, *Teenage Mutant Ninja Turtles*, 115
2105-x-8507, *Super Heroes*, 123
2105-x-8900, *Barbie, Dreamtime Princess*, 127
2105-x-8910, *Barbie*, 127
2105-x-9001, *Special Delivery Bunny*, 24
2105-x-9110, *Little Fire Truck/Firetruck*, 54
2105-x-9111, *Good Time Clock*, 65
2105-x-926, *Bite-Size Gingerbread Boy*, 49
2105-x-9311, *Classic Angel Food Pan*, 132
2105-x-9312, *Mini Angel Food Pan*, 132
2105-x-9330, *Cute Witch*, 87
2105-x-9331, *Mini Dinosaur*, 39
2105-x-9332, *Mini Locomotive*, 55
2105-x-9333, *Lil' Pirate*, 43
2105-x-9334, *Dalmatian Pup*, 23
2105-x-9336, *Numbers Set*, 143
2105-x-9338, *Santa's Treasures*, 94
2105-x-9339, *Heart Angel Food*, 99
2105-x-9340, *Embossed Heart*, 77
2105-x-9365, *Precious Moments*, 117
2105-x-9431, *Bart Simpson*, 114
2105-x-948, *Book*, 63
2105-x-956, *Happiness Heart pans*, 75
2105-x-964, *Storybook Doll Pan*, 44
2105-x-972, *Book Pan*, 64
2105-x-9791, *Mini Loaf Pan Set*, 139
2105-x-9800, *Bell Singles!*, 99
2105-x-9801, *Star Singles!*, 141
2105-x-9802, *Angel Singles!*, 90
2105-x-9900, *Batman Beyond*, 122
2105-x-9902, *Powerpuff Girls*, 118
2105-x-9904, *Veggie Tales*, 120
2105-x-999, *Ernie and Bert*, 108
2105-x-x-565, *Wonder Mold/Classic Wonder*, 136
210B-x-3654, *Big Bird with Banner*, 107
22105-x-387, *Insert for Ring Pan, Santa*, 91
22105-x-5559, *Insert for Ring Pan, Santa*, 91
244, *Coppertone Fish Mold*, 35
250, *Christmas Tree Mold (coppertone)*, 95
252, *Sweetheart/Fancy Heart Mold*, 77
253, *Deluxe Coppertone Fruit Ring*, 74
255, *Harvest Coppertone Mold*, 71
256, *Coppertone Twin Parti Bell Mold*, 99
257, *Rose Mold, round, fluted sides*, 74
258, *Coppertone Tall Tyrolean Mold*, 135
259, *Coppertone Fruit Salad Mold*, 74
260, *Coppertone Swirl Mold*, 144
2621-1, *Little Loafers*, 139
2740, *Square Angel Food Pan*, 138
29080, *Large Shell Mold, coppertone*, 142
294 1/2, *Heart mold, deep with arrow*, 78
2971, *Shamrock*, 80
2977, *Cornucopia, 6 cup coppertone*, 72
3005-157, *Pillsbury Poppin' Fresh Doughboy*, 129
3005-203, *Pooh with Honey Pot, small*, 103
3005-246, *Tweety Bird Mini*, 111
3005-262, *Bugs Bunny*, 109
3005-513, *Holly Hobbie*, 116
3005-602, *Big Bird small pan*, 106
3005-629, *Cookie Monster small pan*, 108
3005-696, *Mickey Mouse*, 101
30101, *Coppertone Fish Mold*, 35
301-6016, *Carousel Separator Set*, 131
30301, *Christmas Tree Mold (coppertone)*, 95
3033, *Christmas Tree Mold, green*, 97
30401, *Sweetheart/Fancy Heart Mold*, 78
3043, *Sweetheart Mold with Teflon*, 99
30501, *Deluxe Coppertone Fruit Ring*, 74
306, *Ani-Mold Set*, 39
30701, *Harvest Coppertone Mold*, 71
30801, *Coppertone Twin Parti Bell Mold*, 99
3083, *Twin Parti Bell, orange coating*, 97
309, *Ring Twist*, 134
30901, *Rose Mold, round, fluted sides*, 74
3093, *Rose Mold with Teflon Interior*, 74
31001, *Coppertone Tall Tyrolean Mold*, 135
311, *Pineapple Mold*, 73
31101, *Coppertone Fruit Salad Mold*, 74
3113, *Fruit Salad Mold with Teflon*, 74
312, *Individual Fruit Mold Set*, 72
313, *Fish*, 35
31301, *4 Leaf Clover Mold with Teflon*, 61
31301, *4 Leaf Clover Mold, Copper*, 61
31401, *Ginger Bread Mold*, 49
315, *Rose Mold Ring, Light Coppertone*, 69
317, *Coronet*, 134
319, *Cornucopia Mold*, 72
321, *Contessa*, 138
323, *Princess*, 135
41300, *Bunny Mold for 3-D Cake*, 25
41300, *Lamb Mold for 3-D Cake*, 28
41300, *Santa in Chimney Stand-Up Cake*, 91
501-8270, *Circus Wagon Kit*, 144
501-x-1005, *Goofy*, 102
501-x-203, *Square Tier Kit*, 144
501-x-2138, *Petal-Shaped Pans, 4 tiered*, 136
501-x-3687, *Wonder Mold/Classic Wonder*, 136
501-x-408, *Heart Mini-Tier*, 75
501-x-505, *Daisy Cart Cake*, 139
501-x-5078, *Donald Duck*, 102
501-x-6074, *Candlelit Tree Pan Set*, 96
501-x-8093, *Piano*, 66
501-x-8270, *Circus Wagon Kit*, 144
501-x-858, *Guitar*, 66
501-x-8610, *Flower Cart Kit*, 137
501-x-904, *Guitar*, 66
502-1107, *Treeliteful/Christmas Tree*, 95
502-1158, *Butterfly Fancifill*, 34
502-1212, *Super Heroes*, 123
502-1212, *Superman*, 123
502-1220, *Double Bell*, 99
502-1319, *Snoopy*, 112
502-135, *Lovable Animal*, 37
502-1387, *Rockin' Juke Box*, 67
502-1409, *Darth Vader*, 124
502-1425, *R2-D2*, 124
502-1468, *Star, fancifill*, 141
502-1484, *Wreath*, 91
502-1522, *Double Heart Fancifill*, 77
502-1565, *Free-Wheelin' Truck*, 54
502-1646, *Snowman*, 88
502-1719, *Popeye*, 112
502-1727, *Easter Basket Pan*, 79
502-178, *Yogi Bear*, 125
502-1816, *Frog*, 36
502-1852, *Boba Fett*, 124
502-186, *Fred Flintstone*, 125
502-1905, *Number One*, 142
502-1913, *Easter Bunny*, 23
502-194, *Holly Hobbie*, 116
502-1948, *Sports Car*, 53
502-1964, *SuperStar Shoe*, 59
502-1972, *Kitten*, 21
502-2014, *Lamb Mold*, 28
502-2014, *Little Lamb / Stand-Up Lamb*, 27
502-2065, *Big Bird Full Figure*, 107
502-208, *Rag Doll Pan*, 45
502-2098, *Spaceman Pan*, 43
502-2131, *Oval Pans*, 137
502-2138, *Petal-Shaped Pans, 4 tiered*, 136
502-2146, *Petal Pans*, 144
502-2154, *Star Pans*, 141
502-2162, *Daisy Cart Cake*, 139
502-2197, *C-3PO*, 124
502-2235, *Wizard*, 45
502-224, *Scooby-Doo*, 125
502-2243, *Bunny Cake Mold*, 25
502-2286, *Blue Ribbon*, 68
502-2308, *Santa*, 92
502-236, *Comical Car*, 53
502-2464, *Classic House Pan*, 52
502-2499, *Scary Ghost*, 86
502-2502, *Cross /Bevelled Cross*, 79
502-2505, *Bird 'N Banner*, 32
502-259, *Basic Ring (for Sculptured Tops)*, 132
502-2634, *Turkey*, 33
502-2695, *Double Tier Heart*, 75
502-2738, *Football Helmet*, 61
502-275, *Jolly Clown*, 46
502-2790, *Be Mine*, 76
502-283, *13-Star Flag*, 81
502-2908, *Yosemite Sam*, 112
502-2944, *Playboy Bunny*, 129
502-2987, *Mickey Mouse*, 100
502-305, *Hexagon Cake Pan*, 140
502-3053, *Heart Mini-Tier*, 75
502-313, *Holly Hobbie*, 116
502-3130, *Oval pan set*, 136
502-3169, *Up 'N Away Balloon*, 57
502-3193, *Circus Clown*, 47
502-321, *Robby Hobbie*, 116
502-3258, *Horseshoe*, 62
502-3304, *Noel Candle*, 89
502-3347, *Rudolph The Red Nosed Reindeer*, 126
502-3363, *Li'l Cowboy*, 43
502-3398, *High Flyin' Witch*, 87
502-3401, *Big Bird*, 107
502-3444, *Gentle Lamb*, 29
502-3452, *Holiday Bunny*, 25
502-3495, *Happy Easter Egg*, 81
502-3517, *Bugs Bunny*, 110
502-3533, *Porky Pig*, 110
502-356, *Hexagon Set*, 140
502-3584, *Spaceship*, 57
502-3614, *Ernie*, 108
502-3649, *Little Locomotive*, 56
502-3681, *Donald Duck*, 102
502-3738, *Cookie Monster*, 108
502-3754, *Huggable Teddy Bear*, 40
502-3797, *Raggedy Ann*, 126
502-3835, *Strawberry Shortcake*, 118
502-385, *Good News Stork*, 33
502-386, *Adorable Lamb Pan*, 27
502-3878, *Mini Santa*, 91
502-3894, *Cathy*, 113
502-3902, *Pink Panther*, 113
502-3937, *Holiday House/Stand-Up House*, 51
502-3965, *Good Cheer Mug*, 71
502-3983, *Sailboat*, 57
502-4017, *Smurfette*, 126
502-402, *Sculptured Mold (Coppertone)*, 134
502-4033, *Smurf*, 126
502-4050, *Trail Rider*, 54
502-4165, *Petal Pan Fancifill*, 69
502-4203, *Santa's List*, 93
502-4246, *Joyful Angel*, 90
502-4262, *Cupid's Delight*, 76
502-437, *Blossom Pan*, 69
502-4424, *Bowling Pin Set*, 60
502-4548, *Pink Panther*, 113
502-501, *3-D Cuddly Bear/ Panda*, 41
502-5161, *Toy Soldier*, 44
502-5409, *Butterfly*, 34
502-5617, *T-Shirt*, 50
502-6007, *Santa Stand Up*, 92
502-6007, *Santa's Treasures*, 94
502-607, *Candlelit Tree Pan Set*, 96
502-704, *Poppin' Fresh*, 129
502-712, *Happy Hippo*, 37
502-720, *Elephant Pan*, 37
502-7245, *Donald Duck*, 102
502-7407, *Big Bird face*, 106
502-7415, *Cookie Monster*, 108
502-7423, *Ernie and Bert*, 108
502-7431, *The Count*, 109
502-7458, *Cuddly Bear*, 40
502-7512, *Oscar the Grouch*, 108
502-7598, *Bugs Bunny*, 110
502-7628, *Ziggy*, 113
502-7636, *Playful Puppy*, 22
502-7644, *Mister Owl*, 33
502-7652, *Van*, 54
502-7679, *Wonder Woman*, 122
502-7687, *Tweety*, 110
502-852, *Choo Choo Train*, 56
502-887, *Piano*, 66
502-909, *Flower Cart Kit*, 137
502-933, *Guitar*, 66
502-940, *Book*, 63
502-9403, *Garfield the Cat, 1-2-3*, 114
502-9414, *Party Pumpkin, 1-2-3*, 85
502-951, *Happiness Heart pans*, 75
502-968, *Storybook Doll Pan*, 44
502-976, *Grand Slam*, 62
502-x-1107, *Treeliteful/Christmas Tree*, 95
502-x-135, *Lovable Animal*, 37
502-x-178, *Yogi Bear*, 125
502-x-186, *Fred Flintstone*, 125
502-x-194, *Holly Hobbie*, 116
502-x-2014, *Lamb Mold*, 28
502-x-2014, *Little Lamb / Stand-Up Lamb*, 27
502-x-2057, *Bell Pans*, 98
502-x-208, *Rag Doll Pan*, 45
502-x-2121, *Egg Pan Set*, 80
502-x-2138, *Petal-Shaped Pans, 4 tiered*, 136
502-x-2146, *Petal Pans*, 144
502-x-2154, *Star Pans*, 141
502-x-2227, *Bunny Cake Mold*, 25
502-x-224, *Scooby-Doo*, 125
502-x-236, *Comical Car*, 53
502-x-2502, *Cross /Bevelled Cross*, 79
502-x-259, *Basic Ring (for Sculptured Tops)*, 132
502-x-275, *Jolly Clown*, 46
502-x-283, *13-Star Flag*, 81
502-x-3002, *Sports Ball Pan Set*, 58
502-x-305, *Hexagon Cake Pan*, 140
502-x-313, *Holly Hobbie*, 116
502-x-321, *Robby Hobbie*, 116

502-x-3258, *Horseshoe*, 62
502-x-356, *Hexagon Set*, 140
502-x-386, *Adorable Lamb Pan*, 27
502-x-402, *Sculptured Mold (Coppertone)*, 134
502-x-437, *Blossom Pan*, 69
502-x-4424, *Bowling Pin Set*, 60
502-x-4513, *Pink Panther*, 113
502-x-501, *3-D Cuddly Bear/ Panda*, 41
502-x-704, *Poppin' Fresh*, 129
502-x-712, *Happy Hippo*, 37
502-x-720, *Elephant Pan*, 37
502-x-7474, *The Count*, 109
502-x-7539, *Cuddly Bear*, 40
502-x-7548, *Oscar the Grouch*, 108
502-x-7555, *Ernie and Bert*, 108
502-x-836, *Choo Choo Train*, 56
502-x-909, *Ovals, 2 9" pans*, 137
502-x-940, *Book*, 63
502-x-951, *Happiness Heart pans*, 75
502-x-956, *Happiness Heart pans*, 75
502-x-968, *Storybook Doll Pan*, 44
502-x-976, *Grand Slam*, 62
503-253, *Insert for Ring Pan, Lucky Clover*, 61
503-288, *Insert for Ring Pan, Horse*, 29
503-407, *Insert for Ring Pan, heart*, 77
503-415, *Insert for Ring Pan, blue ribbon*, 68
503-423, *Insert for Ring Pan, Swirl*, 132
503-458, *Insert for Ring Pan, horseshoe*, 62
503-466, *Insert for Ring Pan, rabbit*, 26
503-474, *Insert for Ring Pan, round*, 144
503-555, *Insert for Ring Pan, Santa*, 91
503-570, *Insert for Ring Pan, Shower*, 67
503-598, *Insert for Ring Pan, Pumpkin*, 85
503-611, *Insert for Ring Pan, Birthday*, 64
503-x-253, *Insert for Ring Pan, Lucky Clover*, 61
503-x-2533, *Insert for Ring Pan, Lucky Clover*, 61
503-x-288, *Insert for Ring Pan, Horse*, 29
503-x-3184, *He-Man Masters of the Universe*, 123
503-x-407, *Insert for Ring Pan, heart*, 77
503-x-415, *Insert for Ring Pan, blue ribbon*, 68
503-x-423, *Insert for Ring Pan, Swirl*, 132
503-x-458, *Insert for Ring Pan, horseshoe*, 62
503-x-466, *Insert for Ring Pan, rabbit*, 26
503-x-474, *Insert for Ring Pan, round*, 144
503-x-555, *Insert for Ring Pan, Santa*, 91
503-x-570, *Insert for Ring Pan, Shower*, 67
503-x-598, *Insert for Ring Pan, Pumpkin*, 85
503-x-611, *Insert for Ring Pan, Birthday*, 64
504-x-207, *Heart Set*, 75
508-1007, *Blossom Pans*, 74
508-1040, *Mini Pumpkin*, 84
508-108, *Number Cake Pan 0*, 143
508-116, *Number Cake Pan 1*, 143
508-124, *Number Cake Pan 2*, 143
508-132, *Number Cake Pan 3*, 143
508-1376, *Shortcakes 'N' Treats*, 133

508-140, *Number Cake Pan 4*, 143
508-1465, *Mini Shamrock*, 79
508-158, *Number Cake Pan 5*, 143
508-167, *Number Cake Pan 6*, 143
508-175, *Number Cake Pan 7*, 143
508-183, *Number Cake Pan 8*, 143
508-2119, *Mini Egg*, 80
508-302, *Mini Wonder /Petite Doll Pan*, 136
508-434, *Car (Mini Toy Cakes)*, 55
508-450, *Rag Doll (Mini Toy Cakes)*, 45
508-477, *Teddy (Mini Toy Cakes)*, 40
508-493, *Train (Mini Toy Cakes)*, 56
508W-493, *Train (Mini Toy Cakes)*, 56
508-x-1007, *Blossom Pans*, 74
508-x-108, *Number Cake Pan 0*, 143
508-x-1104, *Mini Heart*, 78
508-x-116, *Number Cake Pan 1*, 143
508-x-124, *Number Cake Pan 2*, 143
508-x-132, *Number Cake Pan 3*, 143
508-x-140, *Number Cake Pan 4*, 143
508-x-158, *Number Cake Pan 5*, 143
508-x-167, *Number Cake Pan 6*, 143
508-x-175, *Number Cake Pan 7*, 143
508-x-183, *Number Cake Pan 8*, 143
508-x-2119, *Mini Egg*, 80
508-x-302, *Mini Wonder /Petite Doll Pan*, 136
508-x-434, *Car (Mini Toy Cakes)*, 55
508-x-450, *Rag Doll (Mini Toy Cakes)*, 44
508-x-477, *Teddy (Mini Toy Cakes)*, 40
508-x-493, *Train (Mini Toy Cakes)*, 56
512-1089, *Little Loafers*, 139
512-1208, *Long Loaf*, 139
512-2001, *Ring Mold 10.5"*, 144
512-90, *Turk's Head Mold*, 144
512-x-1089, *Little Loafers*, 139
512-x-1208, *Long Loaf*, 139
512-x-2001, *Ring Mold 10.5"*, 144
512-x-90, *Turk's Head Mold*, 144
514-154, *Cinderella*, 129
515-1007, *Goofy*, 102
515-1104, *Mini Disney Goofy*, 102
515-1503, *Mini Disney Donald Duck*, 102
515-1805, *Mickey Mouse*, 100
515-205, *Cinderella*, 129
515-205, *Mini Disney Jiminy Cricket*, 103
515-302, *Mickey Mouse*, 101
515-329, *Mini Disney Mickey*, 101
515-401, *Winnie the Pooh*, 103
515-434, *Mini Disney Dumbo*, 103
515-469, *Mini Disney Bambi*, 103
515-507, *Donald Duck*, 102
515-515, *Mini Disney Donald Duck*, 102
515-604, *Pluto*, 102
515-612, *Mini Disney Pluto*, 102
515-701, *Mini Disney Pinocchio*, 103
515-809, *Minnie Mouse*, 100

515-x-1007, *Goofy*, 102
515-x-1104, *Mini Disney Goofy*, 102
515-x-205, *Cinderella*, 129
515-x-205, *Mini Disney Jiminy Cricket*, 103
515-x-221, *Mini Disney Jiminy Cricket*, 103
515-x-302, *Mickey Mouse*, 101
515-x-329, *Mini Disney Mickey*, 101
515-x-401, *Winnie the Pooh*, 103
515-x-434, *Mini Disney Dumbo*, 103
515-x-469, *Mini Disney Bambi*, 103
515-x-507, *Donald Duck*, 102
515-x-515, *Mini Disney Donald Duck*, 102
515-x-604, *Pluto*, 102
515-x-612, *Mini Disney Pluto*, 102
515-x-701, *Mini Disney Pinocchio*, 103
515-x-809, *Minnie Mouse*, 100
516-3004, *Little Lamb*, 41
516-3100, *Elephant Chocolate Mold*, 37
516-3203, *Flying Fish*, 36
516-3306, *Grape Cluster*, 74
516-3403, *Proud Rooster*, 31
516-3608, *Bell*, 98
516-3705, *Pineapple*, 74
516-803, *Mini Molds*, 74
516-x-3004, *Little Lamb*, 41
516-x-3100, *Elephant Chocolate Mold*, 37
516-x-3209, *Flying Fish*, 36
516-x-3306, *Grape Cluster*, 74
516-x-3403, *Proud Rooster*, 31
516-x-3500, *Lovebirds*, 32
516-x-3608, *Bell*, 98
516-x-3705, *Pineapple*, 74
516-x-803, *Mini Molds*, 74
517-x-1200, *Bevel Pan Set*, 132
518-209, *Dutch Boy Mold*, 57
518-284, *Easter Bunny Mold*, 25
518-306, *Little Boy Chick*, 32
518-322, *Little Girl Chick*, 41
518-349, *Little Dog Mold*, 41
518-365, *Policeman Mold*, 57
518-446, *Merry Monkey Mold*, 41
518-489, *Panda/Mini Stand-Up Bear*, 41
518-x-209, *Dutch Boy Mold*, 57
518-x-268, *Christmas Tree Mold*, 99
518-x-284, *Easter Bunny Mold*, 25
518-x-306, *Little Boy Chick*, 32
518-x-322, *Little Girl Chick*, 41
518-x-349, *Little Dog Mold*, 41
518-x-365, *Policeman Mold*, 57
518-x-446, *Merry Monkey Mold*, 41
518-x-489, *Panda/Mini Stand-Up Bear*, 41
5196M, *Standard capacity loaf, long and narrow*, 139
5421-1, *Little Angels*, 144
621, *Harvest Crown*, 72
623, *Melon*, 74
625, *Charlotte*, 144

627, *Imperial*, 144
629, *Tiara*, 135
631, *Victoria*, 144
633, *Duchess*, 144
718AM, *Star, 5-pointed, deep mold*, 141
725M, *Curved Fish*, 35
AS-108, *Little Loafers*, 139
AS-141, *Little Angels*, 144
BL-201, *Lamb Mold*, 28
BL-202, *Three Tiered Angel Food Cake*, 144
BL-205, *Bell Pans*, 98
CRT-1, *Computer*, 63
HM10, *Loaf Mold*, 139
HM-10, *Loaf Mold*, 139
HM-39, *Gingerbread Man*, 48
HM-72, *Sculptured Mold*, 144
HM9, *Turk's Head Mold*, 144
HM-9, *Turk's Head Mold*, 144
MO-2861, *Seashells*, 142
MO-2862, *Butterfly Molds*, 34
MO-2863, *Jewel Mold*, 140
MO-2864, *Morning Glory*, 70
MO-742, *Jewel Mold (Coppertone)*, 140
Mo-755, *Morning Glory*, 70
NA- 253, *Deluxe Coppertone Fruit Ring*, 74
NA-203A, *Coppertone Jumbo Fluted Mold*, 144
NA-244, *Coppertone Fish Mold*, 35
NA-250, *Christmas Tree Mold (coppertone)*, 95
NA-252, *Sweetheart/Fancy Heart Mold*, 77
NA-255, *Harvest Coppertone Mold*, 71
NA-256, *Coppertone Twin Parti Bell Mold*, 98
NA-257, *Rose Mold, round, fluted sides*, 74
NA-258, *Coppertone Tall Tyrolean Mold*, 135
NA-259, *Coppertone Fruit Salad Mold*, 74
NA-260, *Coppertone Swirl Mold*, 144
Patent D-221,577, *T-Nee-Bikini*, 51
PR 68, *Wonder Mold/Classic Wonder*, 136
PR-68, *Wonder Mold/Classic Wonder*, 136
TRP-1, *Trophy*, 68
W 95, *Happiness Heart pans*, 75
W809, *Piano*, 66
W-809, *Piano*, 66
W827, *Circus Wagon Kit*, 144
W-85, *Guitar*, 66
W-86, *Flower Cart Kit*, 137
W86G, *Flower Cart Kit*, 137
W-86G, *Flower Cart Kit*, 137
W-86W, *Flower Cart Kit*, 137
W87, *Piano*, 66
W-87, *Piano*, 66
W90, *Ovals, 2 9" pans*, 137
W-94, *Book*, 63
W-95, *Happiness Heart pans*, 75
W-96, *Storybook Doll Pan*, 44
W-97, *Grand Slam*, 62

Index of Licensed Pans by
Image Owner

Alien Productions
  Alf, 114
American Greetings Corp
  Brave Heart Lion, 119
  Dotty Dog, 120
  Holly Hobbie, 116
  Montgomery Good News Moose, 120
  Robby Hobbie, 116
  Strawberry Shortcake, 118
Big Idea Productions
  Veggie Tales, 120
Bobbs-Merrill Co., Inc.
  Raggedy Ann, 126
Brentwood Television Funnies, Inc.
  Biker Mice from Mars, 115
Cartoon Network
  Powerpuff Girls, 118
DC Comics
  Batman, 122
  Batman Beyond, 122
  Batman Emblem, 122
  Super Heroes, 123
  Superman, 123
  Wonder Woman, 122
Disney
  101 Dalmatians Singles!, 106
  101 Dalmatians, 106
  Bumblelion, 106
  Cinderella, 129
  Donald Duck, 102
  Eleroo, 106
  Esmeralda, 105
  Flik Bug's Life, 105
  Goofy, 102
  Hercules, 105
  Little Mermaid, 104
  Mickey Face, 101
  Mickey Mouse, 100, 101
  Mickey Singles!, 101
  Mini Disney Bambi, 103
  Mini Disney Donald Duck, 102
  Mini Disney Dumbo, 103
  Mini Disney Goofy, 102
  Mini Disney Jiminy Cricket, 103
  Mini Disney Mickey, 101
  Mini Disney Pinocchio, 103
  Mini Disney Pluto, 102
  Mini Mickey Mouse, 101
  Minnie Mouse, 100
  Pluto, 102
  Pocahontas, 105
  Pooh #1, 104
  Pooh Face, 104
  Pooh Singles!, 104
  Pooh Stand-up, 103
  Pooh with Honey Pot, small, golden, 103
  Tigger, 104
  Tigger Singles!, 104
  Tweety Bird Mini, 111
  Winnie the Pooh, 103, 104

Gullane (Thomas) Limited
  Thomas the Tank Engine, 126
Hallmark Cards, Inc.
  Rainbow Brite, 118
Hanna-Barbera
  Fred Flintstone, 125
  Scooby-Doo, 125
  Yogi Bear, 125
Hasbro Inc.
  G. I. Joe, 116
HIT/K Chapman
  Bob the Builder, 127
Jim Henson Productions, Inc.
  Elmo Singles!, 109
KI
  Flower Power, 128
King Features Syndicate, Inc.
  Popeye, 112
LFL
  Boba Fett, 124
  C-3PO, 124
  Darth Vader, 124
  R2-D2, 124
Lyons Partnership, L.P.
  Barney, 122
  Barney and Baby Bop Mini, 121
Marvel
  Spider-Man, 123
Mattel, Inc.
  Barbie, 127, 128
  Barbie, Beautiful Day, 128
  Barbie, Dreamtime Princess, 127
  He-Man Masters of the Universe, 123
Mirage Studio, USA
  Teenage Mutant Ninja Turtles, 115
  Teenage Mutant Ninja Turtles Face, Mini, 115
Nest Productions, Inc.
  Swan Princess, 118
Nintendo
  Pokémon, 120
  Super Mario Brothers, 120
Original Appalachian Artworks, Inc.
  Cabbage Patch Kids, 117
  Cabbage Patch Preemie, 117
  Cabbage Patch Stand-up, 117
Peyo
  Mini Smurf, 127
  Smurf, 126
  Smurfette, 126
Playboy Enterprises, Inc.
  Playboy Bunny, 129
Precious Moments
  Precious Moments, 117
R. L. May Trust
  Rudolph The Red Nosed Reindeer, 126
Ragdoll Productions (UK) Limited
  Teletubbies, 121
Sabar
  Power Rangers/Mighty Morphin Power Rangers, 123
Sesame Workshop

Big Bird, 107
Big Bird, 1-2-3, 107
Big Bird face, 106
Big Bird Full Figure, 107
Big Bird Happy Birthday, 1-2-3, 107
Big Bird Pan, 107
Big Bird small pan, 106
Big Bird with Banner, 107
Cookie Monster, 108
Cookie Monster small pan, 108
Elmo, 109
Ernie, 108
Ernie and Bert, 108
mini Big Bird, 106
Oscar the Grouch, 108
Sesame Street Mini Pan, 108
The Count, 109
Shari Lewis Enterprises, Inc.
  Lamb Chop, 117
The Itsy Bitsy Entertainment Company
  Special Delivery Baby, 129
The Pillsbury Company
  Pillsbury Poppin' Fresh Doughboy, 129
  Poppin' Fresh, 129
Those Characters From Cleveland, Inc.
  Care Bears, 119
  Care Bears Stand-up, 119
  P. C. Popple, 119
  Party Popple, 119
  Popples, 1-2-3, 119
Titan Sports, Inc.
  WWF Superstars, 124
Twentieth Century Fox Film Corporation
  Bart Simpson, 114
United Artists
  Pink Panther, 113
United Feature Syndicate, Inc.
  Charlie Brown, 112
  Garfield, 114
  Garfield Stand-up, 114
  Garfield the Cat, 1-2-3, 114
  Mini Garfield, 114
  Snoopy, 112
Universal Press Syndicate
  Cathy, 113
  Ziggy, 113
Viacom International Inc.
  Blue's Clues, 121
  RugRats, 121
Warner Bros.
  Bugs, 109
  Bugs Bunny, 109, 110
  Bugs Bunny Singles!, 110
  Harry Potter, 111
  Marvin the Martian, 115
  Porky Pig, 110
  Sylvester and Tweety Mini, 111
  Tasmanian Devil, 111
  Tweety, 110, 111
  Yosemite Sam, 112

Index of Pans by Manufacturer
(Excluding Wilton Pans)

AHC
American Eagle Mold, 83
Cornucopia, yellow enameled, 72
Liberty Bell Mold, 83
Pineapple Mold, 73
Pineapple, avocado green, 73
Pineapple, coppertone, 73
Pineapple, harvest gold, 73
Ring Twist, 134
Rose Mold Ring, Light Coppertone, 69
Statue of Liberty, 83
Alan Silverwood of England
Multi-size square pan, 144
Alumode
House, 52
Amscan
Clancy The Clown, 47
Decorative Pumpkin, 85
Easter Bunny, 23
Easter Eggs, 81
Football, 60
Ghostly Greeting, 85
Ghosts, 86
Graduate Owl, 33
Happy Chanukah, 88
Lacy Heart, 77
Rainbow Birthday Cake Pan, 65
Santa Face, 91
Santa with Gift, 94
Shamrock, 80
Shamrock minis, 79
Stork, 33
Tom Turkey, 41
Trees, 95
US Flag, 82
Bakery Crafts
Computer, 63
Trophy, 68
Blue Ribbon Bakeware Co., Downers Grove IL
Hearts Entwined, 76
Burvelle
Educated Cake Pan, 138
Comet
Traditional Round Angel Food, 132
Fancy Foods by Flo

T-Nee-Bikini, 51
Kungsors Pressprodukter AB (Sweden)
Star, 141
Marpol
Book, 63
Metalite (Canada)
Club on Round, 63
Gingerbread Boy on Round, 48
Heart On Round, 63
Meyco Imports
USA, 82
Mirro
4-Tier Cake Pan Set, 131
Coppertone Leaf, 70
Curved Fish, 35
Fluted Mold, 135
Fruit Basket Mold, 73
Hen or Rooster Mold, 31
Melon on Fluted Base, 73
Ring Mold, coppertone rope pattern, 134
Round Sculpted Mold, 134
Standard capacity loaf, long and narrow, 139
Star, 5-pointed, deep mold, 141
Swirled Cone, 135
Tree Cake and Mold Set, 94
Zodiac Astrological Copper Mold, 65
Nordic Ware
4 Leaf Clover Mold with Teflon interior, 61
4 Leaf Clover Mold, Copper anodized, 61
Bunny Mold for 3-D Cake, 25
Christmas Tree Mold (coppertone), 95
Christmas Tree Mold, lime coated, 97
Coppertone Fish Mold, 35
Coppertone Fruit Salad Mold, 74
Coppertone Tall Tyrolean Mold, 135
Coppertone Twin Parti Bell Mold, 99
Deluxe Coppertone Fruit Ring Mold, 74
Ginger Bread Mold, 49
Harvest Coppertone Mold, 71
Lamb Mold for 3-D Cake, 28
Rose Mold, round, fluted sides, 74
Santa in Chimney Stand-Up Cake Mold, 91
Sweetheart Mold with Teflon interior,
Orange or Lime exterior, 99
Sweetheart/Fancy Heart Mold, 77

Twin Parti Bell, orange coating, 97
Parrish's Cake Decorating Supplies Inc.
Magic Mold Baking Pan, 136
Miniature Wedding Tiers, 130
United Aircraft Products Inc., Dayton, Ohio
Angelaire Angel Food Cake Pan, 132
Unknown
Acorn on Round With Fluted Sides, 134
Angel mold, 90
Butterfly, 34
Colored Snowflake Molds, 89
Coppertone Bell Mold, 99
Coppertone Cornucopia Mold, 72
Coppertone Fancy Fluted Deep Ring, 133
Coppertone Fluted Mold, 135
Coppertone Oval Seasons Molds, 137
Coppertone Seashell, 142
Coppertone Star Mold, 141
Coppertone Turkey Mold, 33
Decorated Christmas Tree, 97
Decorated Domed Mold, 135
Decorated Ring, 134
Ear of Corn, 74
Fruit Oval Mold, 72
Fruit Round Mold, 72
Gingerbread Pair, 49
Half Round, 130
Heart mold, small embossed coppertone, 77
Horseshoe, 62
Individual Fluted Molds, 135
Individual Fluted Ring Molds, coppertone, 134
Individual Ring Molds, coppertone, 134
Individual Swirled Mold, 135
Individual Swirled Mold with Indentation, 133
Lamb Mold, 28
Large Fruit Ring Mold, 74
Loaf Mold, 139
Lobster, 35
Mickey Mouse, 101
Morning Glory, 70
Oval with Fleur-de-Lis, 137
Pillsbury Poppin' Fresh Doughboy, 129
Ribbed loaf, staight ends, long, 139
Ribbed loaf, staight ends, short, 139
Rose Mold Ring, Silvertone, 69

Santa, 92
Shamrock, 80
Shamrock, Coppertone, 80
Silver Dollar Molds, 83
Small Animal Molds: Squirrel, Duck, Pony,
Rabbit, 39
Small Fluted Mold, 135
Small house or barn, 52
Square mold with top design, 138
Standard loaf with slightly sloped sides, 139
Swirled Fluted mold, 135
Tall Crown Mold, coppertone, 133
Three-Layer Tree, 96
Three-Tiered Mold, 135
Traditional Melon-Shaped Mold, 73
Triple-tier round, 131
Unknown (made in Portugal)
Bell with Bow, 98
Butterfly, 34
Cat, 22
Christmas Stocking, 90
Christmas Tree, 97
Clown, 47
Cruise Ship, 57
Double Heart with Embossing, 77
Fluted Ring, 133
Funny Rabbit, 26
Gingerbread House, 52
Pumpkin (Domed), 85
Sitting Dog with Bow, 22
Sitting Rabbit, 26
Snowman, 88
Sunflower, 70
Swirl Ring, 134
Turks Head, 133
Wear-Ever
Cornucopia, 6 cup coppertone, 72
Heart mold, deep with arrow, 78
Large Shell Mold, coppertone, 142
Shamrock, 80
Square Angel Food Pan, 138
West Bend
Heart with Cherry, 77
Pineapple Mold, 73

Index of Stand-up Pans
by Mold Type

accessorize or stack
Circus Wagon Kit, 144
Flower Cart Kit, 137
Piano, 66
Three-Layer Tree, 96
clamp-together
3-D Cuddly Bear/ Panda, 41
Bell, 98
Cabbage Patch Stand-up, 117
Candlelit Tree Pan Set, 96
Care Bears Stand-up, 119
Christmas Tree Pan, 99
Easter Bunny Mold, 25
Elephant Chocolate Mold, 37
Garfield Stand-up, 114

Little Boy Chick, 32
Little Girl Chick, 41
Little Lamb, 41
Lovebirds, 32
Merry Monkey Mold, 41
Panda/Mini Stand-Up Bear, 41
Pineapple, 74
Pooh Stand-up, 103
Rag Doll Pan, 45
Stand-up Tree Pan set, 96
Teddy Bear StandUp, 41
join-after-baking
Bowling Pin Set, 60
Egg Pan Set, 80
Holiday Tree, 96

Santa Stand Up, 92
Snowman Stand-up, 90
Sports Ball Pan Set, 58
open mold
3-D Cruiser, 53
Cinderella, 129
Holiday House/Stand-Up House, 51
House, 52
Magic Mold Baking Pan, 136
Mini Wonder /Petite Doll Pan, 136
Small house or barn, 52
Wonder Mold/Classic Wonder Mold, 136
snap-together
Adorable Lamb Pan, 27
Bunny Cake Mold, 25

Bunny Mold for 3-D Cake, 25
Choo Choo Train, 56
Holiday Bunny, 25
Jack-O-Lantern Stand-Up, 84
Lamb Mold, 28
Little Lamb / Stand-Up Lamb, 27
Lovable Animal, 37
Rubber Ducky, 31
Santa, 92
Santa in Chimney Stand-Up Cake
Mold, 91
Snowman Stand-up, 90

Index of Pans by Earliest Date

This index provides an approximate chronology of when pans were first available. Dates shown are those stamped on the pan (excluding dates that refer to a copyright of a licensed image rather than the pan itself), or dates of publications where the pan appeared. If more than one date is available for a pan the earliest date is shown. Note that this chronology can only be approximate. A pan may have been on the market several years before it appeared in a catalog or other publication, for example.

It is possible to guess the approximate issue date of many pans based on their design and general style. I leave such conclusions up to the collector. The dates listed here have more tangible evidence.

1950s
4-Tier Cake Pan Set, 131
House, 52
Small house or barn, 52
Tree Cake and Mold Set, 94
1959
Bell Pans, 98
Gingerbread Man, 48
Lamb Mold, 28
Loaf Mold, 139
Sculptured Mold, 144
Three Tiered Angel Food Cake Pan, 144
Turk's Head Mold, 144
1960s
Individual Fluted Molds, 135
Individual Fluted Ring Molds, coppertone, 134
Tall Crown Mold, coppertone, 133
1961
Butterfly, 34
1963
Pineapple Mold, 73
Pineapple, avocado green, 73
Pineapple, coppertone, 73
Pineapple, harvest gold, 73
Ring Twist, 134
1964
Ani-Mold Set, 39
Book, 63
Charlotte, 144
Christmas Tree Mold (coppertone), 95
Contessa, 138
Coppertone Fish Mold, 35
Coppertone Fruit Salad Mold, 74
Coppertone Holiday Mold Set, 99
Coppertone Jumbo Fluted Mold, 144
Coppertone Swirl Mold, 144
Coppertone Tall Tyrolean Mold, 135
Coppertone Twin Parti Bell Mold, 99
Cornucopia Mold, 72
Coronet, 134
Deluxe Coppertone Fruit Ring Mold, 74
Duchess, 144
Fish, 35
Harvest Coppertone Mold, 71

Harvest Crown, 72
Horn of Plenty, 72
Imperial, 144
Individual Fruit Mold Set, 72
Little Angels, 144
Little Loafers, 139
Melon, 74
Princess, 135
Rose Mold Ring, Light Coppertone, 69
Rose Mold, round, fluted sides, 74
Sweetheart/Fancy Heart Mold, 77
Tiara, 135
Victoria, 144
1966
Flower Cart Kit, 137
Guitar, 66
Happiness Heart, 75
Piano, 66
1969
Butterfly Molds, 34
Jewel Mold, 140
Jewel Mold (Coppertone), 140
Morning Glory, 70
Piano, 66
Seashells, 142
Storybook Doll Pan, 44
Wonder Mold/Classic Wonder Mold, 136
1970
4 Leaf Clover Mold with Teflon interior, 61
4 Leaf Clover Mold, Copper anodized, 61
Christmas Tree Mold, green coated, 97
Circus Wagon Kit, 144
Fruit Basket Mold, 73
Ginger Bread Mold, 49
Lamb Mold for 3-D Cake, 28
Ovals, 2 9" pans, 137
Santa in Chimney Stand-Up Cake Mold, 92
Sweetheart Mold with Teflon Interior
(Lemon or Orange Exterior), 99
Twin Parti Bell, orange coating, 97
1971
Bell, 98
Bunny Mold for 3-D Cake, 25
Daisy Cart Cake, 139
Mini Egg, 80
Petal-Shaped Pans, 4 tiered, 136
Star Pans, 141
T-Nee-Bikini, 51
1972
Bowling Pin Set, 60
Bunny Cake Mold, 25
Cinderella, 129
Cross /Bevelled Cross, 79
Donald Duck, 102
Egg Pan Set, 80
Elephant Chocolate Mold, 37
Flying Fish, 36
Goofy, 102
Grand Slam, 62
Grape Cluster, 74
Heart Mini-Tier, 75
Horseshoe, 62
Lamb Mold, 28
Little Lamb, 41
Little Lamb/Stand-Up Lamb, 27
Lovebirds, 32
Mickey Mouse, 101
Mini Wonder /Petite Doll Pan, 136
Minnie Mouse, 100
Petal Pans, 144
Pineapple, 74
Pluto, 102
Proud Rooster, 31
Silver Dollar Molds, 83
Sports Ball Pan Set, 58

Square Tier Kit, 144
Treeliteful/Christmas Tree, 95
Winnie the Pooh, 103
1973
Candlelit Tree Pan Set, 96
Hexagon Cake Pan, 140
Rag Doll Pan, 45
1974
13-Star Flag, 81
3-D Cuddly Bear/ Panda, 41
Adorable Lamb Pan, 27
Basic Ring (for Sculptured Tops), 132
Bevel Pan Set, 132
Blossom Pans, 74
Choo Choo Train, 56
Christmas Tree Mold, 99
Dutch Boy Mold, 57
Easter Bunny Mold, 25
Elephant Pan, 37
Happy Hippo, 37
Hexagon Set, 140
Insert for Ring Pan, Horse, 29
Insert for Ring Pan, Lucky Clover, 61
Insert for Ring Pan, Santa, 91
Jolly Clown, 46
Little Boy Chick, 32
Little Dog Mold, 41
Little Girl Chick, 41
Long Loaf, 139
Lovable Animal, 37
Merry Monkey Mold, 41
Mini Heart, 78
Mini Molds, 74
Panda/Mini Stand-Up Bear, 41
Policeman Mold, 57
Poppin' Fresh, 129
Ring Mold 10.5", 144
Sculptured Mold (Coppertone), 134
1975
Blossom Pan, 69
Car (Mini Toy Cakes), 55
Fred Flintstone, 125
Holly Hobbie, 116
Insert for Ring Pan, Birthday, 64
Insert for Ring Pan, blue ribbon, 68
Insert for Ring Pan, horseshoe, 62
Insert for Ring Pan, Shower, 67
Pillsbury Poppin' Fresh Doughboy, 129
Rag Doll (Mini Toy Cakes), 44
Scooby-Doo, 125
Teddy (Mini Toy Cakes), 40
Train (Mini Toy Cakes), 56
Yogi Bear, 125
1976
Comical Car, 53
Heart Set, 75
Holly Hobbie, 116
Insert for Ring Pan, Pumpkin, 85
Insert for Ring Pan, heart, 77
Insert for Ring Pan, rabbit, 26
Insert for Ring Pan, Swirl, 132
Mini Disney Bambi, 103
Mini Disney Donald Duck, 102
Mini Disney Dumbo, 103
Mini Disney Goofy, 102
Mini Disney Jiminy Cricket, 103
Mini Disney Mickey, 103
Mini Disney Pinocchio, 103
Number Cake Pan 0, 143
Number Cake Pan 1, 143
Number Cake Pan 2, 143
Number Cake Pan 3, 143
Number Cake Pan 4, 143
Number Cake Pan 5, 143
Number Cake Pan 6, 143

Number Cake Pan 7, 143
Number Cake Pan 8, 143
Pooh with Honey Pot, small, golden, 103
Robby Hobbie, 116
Ziggy, 113
1977
Big Bird face, 106
Big Bird Full Figure, 107
Big Bird small pan, 106
Book Pan, 63
Cookie Monster, 108
Cookie Monster small pan, 108
Cuddly Bear, 40
Ernie and Bert, 108
Insert for Ring Pan, round, 144
Mini Disney Donald Duck, 102
Mini Disney Pluto, 102
Oscar the Grouch, 108
Pink Panther, 113
Super Heroes, 123
Superman, 123
The Count, 109
1978
Garfield the Cat, 1-2-3, 114
Mickey Mouse, 100
Mister Owl, 33
Playful Puppy, 22
SuperStar Shoe, 59
Tweety, 110
Van, 54
Wonder Woman, 122
1979
Blue Ribbon, 68
Bugs Bunny, 109, 110
Butterfly Fancifill, 34
Carousel Separator Set, 131
Double Bell, 99
Easter Bunny, 23
Football Helmet, 61
Frog, 36
Jolly Snowman, 130
Kitten, 21
Number One, 142
Petal Pan Fancifill, 69
Santa, 92
Spaceman Pan, 43
Spaceship, 57
Sports Car, 53
Toy Soldier, 44
T-Shirt, 50
Turkey, 33
Tweety Bird Mini, 111
1980
Darth Vader, 124
Double Heart Fancifill, 77
Easter Basket Pan, 80
Free-Wheelin' Truck, 54
Happy Birthday, 64
Popeye, 112
R2-D2, 124
Snowman, 88
Star, fancifill, 141
Wreath, 91
1981
Circus Clown, 47
Donald Duck, 102
Gentle Lamb, 29
High Flyin' Witch, 87
Li'l Cowboy, 43
Noel Candle, 89
Raggedy Ann, 126
Rudolph The Red Nosed
Reindeer, 126
Strawberry Shortcake, 118
Yosemite Sam, 112

1982
Cookie Monster, 108
Cupid's Delight, 76
Double Tier Heart, 75
Holiday House/Stand-Up House, 51
Huggable Teddy Bear, 40
Pink Panther, 113
Santa's List, 93
Scary Ghost, 86
Up 'N Away Balloon, 57
1983
Be Mine, 76
Big Bird, 107
Boba Fett, 124
Bugs Bunny, 110
C-3PO, 124
Care Bears, 119
Cathy, 113
Classic House Pan, 52
Donald Duck, 102
Ernie, 108
Good News Stork, 33
Happy Easter Egg, 81
He-Man Masters of the Universe, 123
Joyful Angel, 90
Little Locomotive, 56
Mickey Mouse, 100
Mini Pumpkin, 84
Mini Santa, 91
Mini Shamrock, 79
Porky Pig, 110
Rainbow Brite, 118
Rockin' Juke Box, 67
Smurf, 126
Smurfette, 126
1984
Big Fish, 36
Brave Heart Lion, 119
Cabbage Patch Kids, 117
Cabbage Patch Stand-up, 117
Care Bears Stand-up, 119
Computer, 63
Cupid's Heart, 76
Good Cheer Mug, 71
Holiday Bunny, 25
Mini Big Bird, 106
Mini Christmas Tree, 95
Mini Clown, 47
Mini Football Helmet, 61
Mini Smurf, 127
Mystical Dragon, 38
Rocking Horse, 30
Sailboat, 57
Santa's Sleigh, 93
Shortcakes 'N' Treats, 133
Shower Umbrella, 67
Snowman Stand-up, 90
Trail Rider, 54
Wizard, 45
1985
Angel Food, 144
Batman Emblem, 123
Bumblelion, 106
Cabbage Patch Preemie, 117
Charlotte Mold, 144
Chick-In-Egg, 30
Dotty Dog, 120
Eleroo, 106
Garfield, 114
Garfield Stand-up, 114
Gingerbread Boy, 48
Montgomery Good News Moose, 120
P. C. Popple, 119
Party Popple, 119
Patriotic Flag, 81
Popples, 1-2-3, 119
Ring mold 8", 144
Santa Stand Up, 92
Santa's Treasures, 93
Trophy, 68
1986
18-Wheeler Truck, 54
Barbie, 127
Charlie Brown, 112
Christmas Tree, 1-2-3/Step-by-Step, 97
Circus Clown, 1-2-3, 48
Classic Tube Pan, 133
Congratulations, 64
Cottontail Bunny, 24
Double Tier Round, 131
G. I. Joe, 116
Hamburger, 71

Holiday Tree, 96
Mini Loaf, 144
Precious Pony, 29
Puppy Dog, 22
Ribbed Loaf, 144
Snoopy, 112
Teddy Bear StandUp, 41
Teddy Bear, 1-2-3, 40
Two-Mix Book Pan, 64
Two-Mix Horseshoe, 62
1987
Baseball Glove, 58
Bird 'N Banner, 32
Butterfly, 34
Football Hero, 61
Golf Bag, 59
Gumball Machine, 71
I Love You, 78
Ice Cream Cone, 71
Jolly Santa, 92
Kitty Cat Pan, 21
Little Mouse, 36
Lovable Lamb, 29
Mini Ball, 58
Party Pumpkin, 1-2-3, 85
Petite Fancy Ring, 133
Puffed Heart, 76
Question Mark, 144
Star, 141
Sunny Bunny, 24
1988
Alf, 114
Big Bird, 1-2-3, 107
Big Bird Happy Birthday, 1-2-3, 107
Boo Ghost, 86
Cross, 2 mix, 99
Cuddles the Cow, 29
Friendly (?) Dinosaur, 1-2-3, 39
Goose /Country Goose, 32
Lone-Star State, 83
Round Tier Set, 130
Rudy Reindeer, 93
1989
Batman, 122
Big Bird Pan, 107
Bugs Bunny, 110
Cutie Cat, 1-2-3 (?), 21
Happy Clown, 46
Heart Quartet, 78
Heart Ring, 78
Little Ducky, 31
Mini Bell, 98
Oval pan set, 136
Quick as a Bunny, 1-2-3, 24
Scarecrow, 84
Shell, 142
Shooting Star, 141
Snowman, 88
Sporty Car, 53
Teenage Mutant Ninja Turtles, 115
USA, 82
Viennese Swirl, 69
1990
Bart Simpson, 114
Bowling a Strike, 60
Carousel Horse, 30
Christmas Tree Little Cakes, 95
First and Ten Football pan, 60
Gentle Lamb, 28
Little Train, 56
Mini Gingerbread Boy, 49
Race Car/Super Race Car, 55
Super Mario Brothers, 120
Wicked Witch, 88
1991
Darling Dolly, 1-2-3, 46
Fun Train, 1-2-3, 56
Good Time Clock, 65
Little Fire Truck/Firetruck, 54
Mini Bear, 41
Mini Ghost, 86
Mini Loaf Pan Set, 139
Playful Ghost, 1-2-3, 86
Precious Puppy, 1-2-3, 22
Santa Bear Pan, 41
Special Delivery Bunny, 24
Teenage Mutant Ninja Turtles, 115
1992
Ballerina Bear, 40
Barbie, 128
Big Bird with Banner, 107

Bugs Bunny, 109
Bunny Face, 1-2-3, 26
Circus Clown, 1-2-3, 46
Dinosaur, 1-2-3, 39
Handsome Guy, 42
Heart Angel Food, 99
Home Run Hitter, 58
Mini Balloon, 65
Mini Bunny, 27
Mini Snowman, 89
Peek-A-Boo Bunny, 23
Pretty Lady, 42
Race Car/Super Race Car, 55
Scary Cat, 21
Troll, 44
1993
Barney, 122
Classic Angel Food Pan, 132
Cute Clown, 48
Cute Witch, 87
Dalmatian Pup, 23
Embossed Heart, 77
Lamb Chop, 117
Lil' Pirate, 43
Merry Mermaid, 43
Mini Dinosaur, 39
Mini Garfield, 114
Mini Locomotive, 55
Petite Egg, 80
Precious Moments, 117
WWF Superstars, 124
1994
Barney and Baby Bop Mini, 121
Biker Mice from Mars, 115
Cute Baby, 42
Fred Flintstone, 125
Jungle Lion, 38
Mini Embossed Heart, 78
Mini Shell, 142
Numbers Set, 143
Petite Christmas Tree, 95
Petite Heart, 78
Petite Huggable Bear, 41
Petite Jack-O-Lantern, 84
Petite Loaf, 139
Power Rangers/Mighty Morphin Power
Rangers, 123
Sesame Street Mini Pan, 108
Swan Princess, 104
Sylvester and Tweety Mini, 111
Teenage Mutant Ninja Turtles Face, Mini, 115
1995
Barbie, Beautiful Day, 128
Bite-Size Gingerbread Boy, 49
Fancy Ring, 133
Graduate, 68
Heart Angel Food, 99
Jack-O-Lantern, 85
Jack-O-Lantern Stand-Up, 84
Mickey Mouse, 100
Mini Jungle Animals, 38
Mini Lamb, 27
Mini Mickey Mouse, 101
Mini Star, 141
Mini Umbrella, 67
Over the Hill Tombstone, 86
Pocahontas, 104
Santa Checking List, 93
Tasmanian Devil, 111
Teddy Bear with Block, 40
Thomas the Tank Engine, 126
Western Boot, 50
Winnie the Pooh, 104
1996
101 Dalmatians, 106
Bite-Size Bunny, 27
Bugs Bunny, 110
Elmo, 109
Esmeralda, 105
Mini Angel Food Pan, 132
1997
Computer, 63
Funny Bunny nonstick, 26
Mickey Mouse, 101
Oval Pans, 137
Poinsettia, 93
Race Car, 55
Smiling Santa, 91
Stand-up Tree Pan set, 96
Treats 4 You!, 97
1998
101 Dalmatians Singles!, 106

3 in. Round Singles!, 130
4 in. Ring Singles!, 134
Angel Food Singles!, 132
Angel Singles!, 90
Baby Bootie Singles!, 57
Barbie, 128
Barney, 122
Bat Singles!, 86
Bear-y Christmas, 41
Bell Singles!, 99
Bugs Bunny Singles!, 110
Bunny Singles!, 26
Bunny in a Basket, 24
Candy Cane Singles!, 94
Cat Singles!, 21
Cheerful Chick, 30
Chick Singles!, 30
Color Enamel #0 Singles!, 143
Color Enamel #1 Singles!, 143
Color Enamel #2 Singles!, 143
Color Enamel #3 Singles!, 143
Color Enamel #4 Singles!, 143
Color Enamel #5 Singles!, 143
Color Enamel #6/9 Singles!, 143
Color Enamel #7 Singles!, 143
Color Enamel #8 Singles!, 143
Color Enamel Exclamation Singles!, 144
Color Enamel Question Mark Singles!, 144
Egg Singles!, 81
Enchanted Castle, 51
Fanciful Heart Singles!, 76
Fancy Heart Singles!, 76
Fancy Ring Singles!, 133
Flag Singles!, 82
Flik Bug's Life, 105
Flower Pot, 70
Flower Power, 128
Flower Singles!, 69
Foot Singles!, 50
Ghost Singles!, 86
Gingerbread Boy, 48
Hand Singles!, 50
Haunted Pumpkin, 85
Heart Angel Food Singles!, 99
Hercules, 105
Hockey Player, 60
Hot Lips, 50
Jack-O-Lantern Singles!, 86
Loaf Singles!, 144
Marvin the Martian, 115
Minnie Mouse, 100
Paw Print Singles!, 40
Pooh #1, 104
Pooh Singles!, 104
Pooh Stand-up, 103
RugRats, 121
Scarecrow, 84
Shamrock Singles!, 80
Shell Singles!, 142
Shortcake Singles!, 133
Slot Machine, 62
Snowflake Singles!, 89
Snowman Singles!, 89
Sports Utility Vehicle, 54
Star Singles!, 141
Stocking Singles!, 90
Teddy Bear Singles!, 40
Tee It Up, 59
Tigger, 104
Tigger Singles!, 104
Tree Singles!, 95
Viennese Swirl Singles!, 69
1999
Aluminum #1 Singles!, 143
Baseball Singles!, 58
Basketball Singles!, 74
Blue's Clues, 121
Bowling Pin Singles!, 60
Cross Singles!, 79
Elmo Singles!, 109
Football Singles!, 60
Golf Ball Singles!, 59
Holiday Stocking, 90
Little Mermaid, 104
Maple Leaf Singles!, 70
Megasaurus, 38
Millennium Special 2000, 65
Monster Party Pan, 87
Motorcycle, 55
Noah's Ark, 39
Old World Santa, 93
Petal Angel Food, 144

Pumpkin Singles!, 71
Scooby-Doo, 125
Soccer Singles!, 59
Teletubbies, 121
Topping Off Success, 68
Tweety, 111

2000
Baby Doll, 46
Barbie, Dreamtime Princess, 127
Batman Beyond, 122
Bell with Bow, 98
Butterfly, 34
Carousel Separator Set, 131
Cat, 22
Christmas Stocking, 90
Christmas Tree, 97

Clown, 47
Contour Baking Pan Set, 131
Cruise Ship, 57
Cupid Pan, 76
Decorated Egg, 81
Double Heart with Embossing, 77
Funny Rabbit, 26
Gingerbread House, 52
Guitar, 66
Haunted House, 52
Juggling Clown, 48
Miniature Wedding Tiers, 130
Powerpuff Girls, 118
Sitting Dog with Bow, 22
Snowman Stand-up, 90
Special Delivery Baby, 129

Stars & Stripes, 82
2001
3-D Cruiser, 53
Bugs, 109
Candy Cane Pan, 94
Harry Potter, 111
Mickey Face, 101
Pokémon, 120
Pooh Face, 104
Sitting Rabbit, 26
Smiling Skull, 87
Snowman, 88
Soccer Ball, 59
Storybook Doll, 45
Sunflower, 70
Turks Head, 133

Veggie Tales, 120
2002
Ballet Slippers, 67
Barbie, 127
Bob the Builder, 127
Elmo, 109
Just Hatched Chick, 30
Playful Pup, 23
Rubber Ducky, 31
Snowflake, 89
Spider-Man, 123
Tractor, 54
Tweety, 111
Whimsical Witch, 88

Index of Pans by Size
(Excluding Full-Size Pans)

double
Cross, 2 mix, 99
Football, 60
Half Round, 130
Horseshoe, 2 mix, 62
Long Loaf, 139
Magic Mold Baking Pan, 136
Sculptured Mold (Coppertone), 134
Two-Mix Book Pan, 64

individual serving
101 Dalmatians Singles!, 106
3 in. Round Singles!, 130
4 in. Ring Singles!, 134
Aluminum #1 Singles!, 143
Angel Food Singles!, 132
Angel mold, 90
Angel Singles!, 90
Ani-Mold Set, 39
Baby Bootie Singles!, 57
Baseball Singles!, 58
Basketball Singles!, 74
Bat Singles!, 86
Bell Singles!, 99
Blossom Pans, 74
Bowling Pin Singles!, 60
Bugs Bunny Singles!, 110
Bunny Singles!, 26
Butterfly, 34
Butterfly Molds, 34
Candy Cane Singles!, 94
Cat Singles!, 21
Chick Singles!, 30
Christmas Tree Mold, 99
Color Enamel #0 Singles!, 143
Color Enamel #1 Singles!, 143
Color Enamel #2 Singles!, 143
Color Enamel #3 Singles!, 143
Color Enamel #4 Singles!, 143
Color Enamel #5 Singles!, 143
Color Enamel #6/9 Singles!, 143
Color Enamel #7 Singles!, 143
Color Enamel #8 Singles!, 143
Color Enamel Exclamation Singles!, 144
Color Enamel Question Mark Singles!, 144
Colored Snowflake Molds, 89
Coppertone Bell Mold, 99
Coppertone star mold, 141
Cross Singles!, 79
Dutch Boy Mold, 57
Easter Bunny Mold, 25
Egg Singles!, 81
Elmo Singles!, 109
Fanciful Heart Singles!, 76
Fancy Heart Singles!, 76
Fancy Ring Singles!, 133
Flag Singles!, 82
Flower Singles!, 69
Foot Singles!, 50
Football Singles!, 60
Ghost Singles!, 86

Golf Ball Singles!, 59
Hand Singles!, 50
Heart Angel Food Singles!, 99
Individual Fluted Molds, 135
Individual Fluted Ring Molds, coppertone, 134
Individual Fruit Mold Set, 72
Individual Heart Mold, 76
Individual Ring Molds, coppertone, 134
Individual Swirled Mold, 135
Individual Swirled Mold with Indent, 133
Jack-O-Lantern Singles!, 86
Jewel Mold, 140
Little Angels, 144
Little Boy Chick, 32
Little Dog Mold, 41
Little Girl Chick, 41
Little Loafers, 139
Loaf Singles!, 144
Maple Leaf Singles!, 70
Merry Monkey Mold, 57
Mickey Singles!, 101
Mini Molds, 74
Miniature Wedding Tiers, 130
Morning Glory, 70
Numbers Set, 143
Paw Print Singles!, 40
Pillsbury Poppin' Fresh Doughboy, 129
Policeman Mold, 57
Pooh Singles!, 104
Pumpkin Singles!, 71
Seashells, 142
Shamrock Singles!, 80
Shell Singles!, 142
Shortcake Singles!, 133
Silver Dollar Molds, 83
Small Animal Molds: Squirrel, Duck, Pony, Rabbit, 39
Snowflake Singles!, 89
Snowman Singles!, 89
Soccer Singles!, 59
Star Singles!, 141
Stocking Singles!, 90
Teddy Bear Singles!, 40
Tigger Singles!, 104
Treats 4 You!, 97
Tree Singles!, 95
Tweety Bird Mini, 111
Viennese Swirl Singles!, 69

mixed sizes in set
4-Tier Cake Pan Set, 131
Bevel Pan Set, 132
Contour Baking Pan Set, 131
Heart Set, 75
Tree Cake and Mold Set, 94

multiple cavity
Barney and Baby Bop Mini, 121
Bite-Size Bunny, 27
Bite-Size Gingerbread Boy, 49
Christmas Tree Little Cakes, 95
Easter Eggs, 81

Ghosts, 86
Ice Cream Cone, 71
Mini Angel Food Pan, 132
Mini Ball, 58
Mini Balloon, 65
Mini Bear, 41
Mini Bell, 98
Mini Big Bird, 106
Mini Bunny, 27
Mini Christmas Tree, 95
Mini Clown, 47
Mini Dinosaur, 39
Mini Egg, 80
Mini Embossed Heart, 78
Mini Football Helmet, 61
Mini Garfield, 114
Mini Ghost, 86
Mini Gingerbread Boy, 49
Mini Heart, 78
Mini Jungle Animals, 38
Mini Lamb, 27
Mini Loaf, 144
Mini Loaf Pan Set, 139
Mini Locomotive, 55
Mini Mickey Mouse, 101
Mini Pumpkin, 84
Mini Santa, 91
Mini Shamrock, 79
Mini Shell, 142
Mini Smurf, 127
Mini Snowman, 89
Mini Star, 140
Mini Umbrella, 67
Mini Wonder /Petite Doll Pan, 136
Petite Christmas Tree, 95
Petite Egg, 80
Petite Fancy Ring, 133
Petite Heart, 78
Petite Huggable Bear, 41
Petite Jack-O-Lantern, 84
Petite Loaf, 139
Santa Face, 91
Sesame Street Mini Pan, 108
Shamrock Minis, 79
Shortcakes 'N' Treats, 133
Sylvester and Tweety Mini, 111
Teenage Mutant Ninja Turtles Face, Mini, 115
Trees, 95

size not applicable
Carousel Separator Set, 131

small
Big Bird small pan, 106
Bugs Bunny, 109
Butterfly, 34
Car (Mini Toy Cakes), 55
Classic Angel Food Pan, 132
Clown, 47
Contessa, 138
Cookie Monster small pan, 108
Coppertone Fluted Mold, 135

Coppertone Oval Seasons Molds, 137
Coppertone Turkey Mold, 33
Cornucopia Mold, 72
Coronet, 134
Decorated Domed Mold, 135
Ear of Corn, 74
Elephant Chocolate Mold, 37
Fish, 35
Fluted Mold, 135
Flying Fish, 36
Fruit Basket Mold, 73
Gingerbread Man, 48
Grand Slam, 62
Grape Cluster, 74
Heart Angel Food, 99
Heart mold, small embossed coppertone, 78
Heart with Cherry, 79
Hen or Rooster Mold, 31
Holly Hobbie, 116
House, 52
Lobster, 35
Lovebirds, 32
Melon on Fluted Base, 73
Mickey Mouse, 101
Mini Disney Bambi, 103
Mini Disney Donald Duck, 102
Mini Disney Dumbo, 103
Mini Disney Goofy, 102
Mini Disney Jiminy Cricket, 103
Mini Disney Mickey, 101
Mini Disney Pinocchio, 103
Mini Disney Pluto, 102
Number Cake Pan 0, 143
Number Cake Pan 1, 143
Number Cake Pan 2, 143
Number Cake Pan 3, 143
Number Cake Pan 4, 143
Number Cake Pan 5, 143
Number Cake Pan 6, 143
Number Cake Pan 7, 143
Number Cake Pan 8, 143
Oval with Fleur-de-Lis, 137
Panda/Mini Stand-Up Bear, 41
Pineapple Mold, 73
Pooh with Honey Pot, small, golden, 103
Princess, 135
Proud Rooster, 31
Rag Doll (Mini Toy Cakes), 44
Ribbed loaf, staight ends, short, 139
Ring Twist, 134
Robby Hobbie, 116
Shamrock, 80
Shamrock, Coppertone, 80
Small house or barn, 52
Swirled Cone, 135
Swirled Fluted mold, 135
Teddy (Mini Toy Cakes), 40
Train (Mini Toy Cakes), 56
USA, 82

Bibliography

Aluminum Anodizers Council. "Anodizing, What Is It?" AAC Web Forum. http://www.anodizing.org/definitions.html (August 2002).

Aluminum Coil Anodizing Corp. "Coil Anodizing Defined." http://www.acacorp.com/defined/page1.html

"Cookware Guide." Fante's Kitchen Wares Shop. http://fantes.com/cookware.htm (August 2002).

General Foods Kitchen. *Joys of Jell-O®*. White Plains, NY: General Foods Corporation [5th Edition, late 1960s].

Marsh, Dorothy B., ed. *The Good Housekeeping Book of Cake Decorating*. New York: M. Barrows and Company, Inc., 1961.

Nordic-Ware. *Unusual Old World and American Recipes*. Minneapolis, MN: Nordic-Ware [1970?].

Tech, Marsha. *Wilton Collectors Guide to Character Cake and Cupcake Pans Book II*. Battle Creek MI. 1999. Photocopy.

Wilton Enterprises, Inc. *untitled product catalog*. Chicago IL: Wilton Enterprises, Inc. [1959].

Wilton Enterprises, Inc. *Cake and Food Decorating Ideas by Wilton*. Chicago IL: Wilton Enterprises, Inc., 1964.

Wilton Enterprises, Inc. *Cake and Food Decorating Ideas by Wilton*. Chicago IL: Wilton Enterprises, Inc., 1966.

Wilton Enterprises, Inc. *Your Personal Guide to Cake and Food Decorating Ideas by Wilton*. Chicago IL: Wilton Enterprises, Inc., 1969.

Wilton Enterprises, Inc. *Magic for Your Table…Cake and Food Decorating Ideas by Wilton*. Chicago IL: Wilton Enterprises, Inc., 1970.

Wilton Enterprises, Inc. *Cake & Food Decorating Yearbook by Wilton*. Chicago IL: Wilton Enterprises, Inc., 1972.

Wilton Enterprises, Inc. *The Wilton Yearbook of Cake Decorating*. Chicago IL: Wilton Enterprises, Inc., 1974.

Wilton Enterprises, Inc. *The Wilton Yearbook of Cake Decorating*. Chicago IL: Wilton Enterprises, Inc., 1975.

Wilton Enterprises, Inc. *The Wilton Yearbook of Cake Decorating*. Chicago IL: Wilton Enterprises, Inc., 1975.

Wilton Enterprises, Inc. *The Wilton Yearbook of Cake Decorating 1977 The American Art of Celebration*. Chicago IL: Wilton Enterprises, Inc., 1976.

Wilton Enterprises, Inc. *The Wilton Yearbook of Cake Decorating 1978*. Chicago IL: Wilton Enterprises, Inc., 1977.

Wilton Enterprises, Inc. *The Wilton Yearbook of Cake Decorating 1979*. Woodridge IL: Wilton Enterprises, Inc., 1978.

Wilton Enterprises, Inc. *The Wilton Yearbook of Cake Decorating 1980*. Woodridge IL: Wilton Enterprises, A division of The Pillsbury Company, 1979.

Wilton Enterprises, Inc. *The Wilton Yearbook of Cake Decorating 1981*. Woodridge IL: Wilton Enterprises, A division of The Pillsbury Company, 1980.

Wilton Enterprises, Inc. *The Wilton Yearbook of Cake Decorating 1982*. Woodridge IL: Wilton Enterprises, A division of The Pillsbury Company, 1981.

Wilton Enterprises, Inc. *The Wilton Yearbook Cake of Decorating 1983*. Woodridge IL: Wilton Enterprises, Inc., 1982.

Wilton Enterprises, Inc. *The Wilton Yearbook Cake of Decorating 1984*. Woodridge IL: Wilton Enterprises, Inc., 1983.

Wilton Enterprises, Inc. *The Wilton Yearbook of Cake Decorating 1985*. Woodridge IL: Wilton Enterprises, Inc., 1984.

Wilton Enterprises, Inc. *The Wilton Yearbook of Baking and Decorating 1986*. Woodridge IL: Wilton Enterprises, Inc., 1985.

Wilton Enterprises, Inc. *The Wilton Yearbook of Cake Decorating 1987*. Woodridge IL: Wilton Enterprises, Inc., 1986

Wilton Enterprises, Inc. *1988 Wilton Yearbook of Cake Decorating Let's Decorate!* Woodridge IL: Wilton Enterprises, Inc., 1987.

Wilton Enterprises, Inc. *1989 Wilton Yearbook of Cake Decorating*. Woodridge IL: Wilton Enterprises, Inc., 1988.

Wilton Enterprises, Inc. *Wilton 1990 Yearbook of Cake Decorating*. Woodridge IL: Wilton Enterprises, Inc., 1989.

Wilton Enterprises, Inc. *1991 Yearbook of Cake Decorating*. Woodridge IL: Wilton Enterprises, Inc., 1990.

Wilton Enterprises, Inc. *1992 Yearbook of Cake Decorating*. Woodridge IL: Wilton Enterprises, 1991.

Wilton Enterprises. *Wilton 1993 Yearbook*. Woodridge IL: Wilton Enterprises, 1992.

Wilton Enterprises. *Wilton 1994 Yearbook*. Woodridge IL: Wilton Enterprises, 1993.

Wilton Enterprises. *Wilton 1995 Yearbook Cake Decorating!* Woodridge IL: Wilton Enterprises, 1994.

Wilton Enterprises. *Wilton 1996 Yearbook*. Woodridge IL: Wilton Enterprises, 1995.

Wilton Enterprises. *Wilton 1997 Yearbook Cake Decorating!* Woodridge IL: Wilton Enterprises, 1996.

Wilton Enterprises. *Wilton 1998 Yearbook Cake Decorating!* Woodridge IL: Wilton Enterprises, 1997.

Wilton Enterprises. *Wilton 1999 Yearbook Cake Decorating!* Woodridge IL: Wilton Industries, Inc., 1998.

Wilton Enterprises. *Wilton 2000 Yearbook Cake Decorating*. Woodridge IL: Wilton Industries, Inc., 1999.

Wilton Industries. *2001 Wilton Yearbook Cake Decorating!* Woodridge IL: Wilton Industries, Inc., 2000.

Wilton Industries. *2002 Wilton Yearbook Cake Decorating!* Woodridge IL: Wilton Industries, Inc., 2001.

Wilton Industries. *2003 Wilton Yearbook Cake Decorating!* Woodridge IL: Wilton Industries, Inc., 2002.